Daniel Unsealed

Daniel Unsealed

*An exposition revealing what the Book of Daniel
says about the Jewish people and their God,
as understood and explained by*

Dan Bruce

The Prophecy Society

2011

Daniel Unsealed

Copyright © 2011 Dan Bruce
All rights reserved.

No content from pages 23-222, or from Plates 1 and 2 on unnumbered pages at the end of this book, may be reproduced, translated, stored in a retrieval system, displayed on the Internet, or transmitted in any form or by any means, electronic, mechanical, photocopying, recording, or otherwise, in whole or in part, without permission from the author.

The Prophecy Society
www.prophecysociety.org
770-679-0633
Monday-Friday, 10am-5pm
Eastern Time

First Edition

Printed in the United States of America

On the cover: The front cover features a photograph of the oil-on-canvas painting "Daniel in the Lions' Den" by Sir Peter Paul Rubens (*ca.* 1614-1616). The original painting is on permanent display at West Main Floor Gallery 45 in The National Gallery of Art, Washington D.C.

ISBN 978-0-9816912-1-3

Contents

Preface: The Scripture of Truth ix

Exposition of Prophecies

Introduction: I, Daniel, Understood 1
Chapter One: Then Shall the Sanctuary Be Restored (Daniel 8:1-27) 7
Chapter Two: What Shall Be The End of These Things? (Daniel 12:8-12) 23
Chapter Three: For a Season and Time (Daniel 12:5-7) 33
Chapter Four: That Which Shall Not Be Destroyed (Daniel 7:1-28) 41
Chapter Five: What Shall Befall Thy People (Daniel 10:1-12:4) 57
Chapter Six: Seventy Weeks Are Determined (Daniel 9:1-27) 79
Chapter Seven: He Shall Confirm the Covenant (Daniel 9:24-27) 95
Conclusion: The Wise Shall Understand 119

Appendices

Appendix One: Background Notes on the Book of Daniel 123
Appendix Two: The Hebrew Calendar in Ancient Times 127
Appendix Three: Calculating Sabbath and Jubilee Years (Daniel 4) 131
Appendix Four: Calendar of Sabbath and Jubilee Years 143
Appendix Five: Chronology in the Book of Ezekiel (Ezekiel 4) 151
Appendix Six: Biblical Chronology Synchronized with Daniel 155
    Part 1 - Abraham to the Exodus (2,202-1,482 BCE) 156
    Part 2 - The Exodus to the Divided Kingdom (1,482-961 BCE) 158
    Part 3 - The Divided Kingdom (961-586 BCE) 161
    Part 4 - The Reign of Hezekiah (726-697 BCE) 174
    Part 5 - Construction of Herod's Temple (20 BCE-28 CE) 177
    Part 6 - The Ministry of Jesus (28-30 CE) 179
Appendix Seven: The Modern Nation of Israel - Is it Biblical? 195
    Balfour Declaration - November 2, 1917 209
    Palestine Mandate - July 24, 1922 210

Contents (continued)

Declaration of the Establishment of the State of Israel - May 14, 1948	215
Law of Return, 5710/1950 - July 5, 1950	218
Liberation of the Temple Mount and Western Wall during the Six-Day War - June 7, 1967	219
HaTiqvah	222

Scripture

Book of Daniel, Chapter 4 and Chapters 7-12	
Chapter 4	223
Chapter 7	225
Chapter 8	227
Chapter 9	228
Chapter 10	230
Chapter 11	231
Chapter 12	234

Located at the end of this book for quick reference:

Plates

Prophecy Overview (chart)	PLATE 1
Places in Daniel (map)	PLATE 2

Abbreviations

AT	The Apocrypha: an American Translation
Au	Author's Paraphrase
b.	Born in *(with year), e.g., b.* 1922
BCE	Before the Common Era *(same as B.C.)*
BDB	Brown-Driver-Briggs Hebrew Lexicon
BHS	Denotes Hebrew (Masoretic) text reproduced verbatim from the *Biblia Hebraica Stuttgartensia (Leningrad Codex)* published by Deutsche Bibelgesellschaft (German Bible Society)
ca.	Latin *circa* - about *(with year), e.g., ca.* 1920
CE	In the Common Era *(same as A.D.)*
CJB	Complete Jewish Bible
d.	Died in *(with year), e.g., d.* 1951
ESV	English Standard Version
JPS	Jewish Publication Society
KJV	King James Version
MT	Masoretic Text
NASB	New American Standard Bible
NIV	New International Version
NJB	New Jerusalem Bible
NJV	New Jewish Version
NT	New Testament
NTG	Denotes Greek text reproduced verbatim from *Novum Testamentum Graece.* 26th ed., 1979; corrected, 1981; Erwin Nestle and Kurt Aland, eds., published by Deutsche Bibelgesellschaft (German Bible Society)
OT	Old Testament
p.	Page or pages *(with number or numbers), e.g., p.* 62 *or* p. 62-65
r.	Reigned *(with year or years), e.g., r.* 519-524
RSV	Revised Standard Version
Strong's	Biblesoft's New Exhaustive Strong's Numbers and Concordance with Expanded Greek-Hebrew Dictionary (© *1994, 2003, 2006 by Biblesoft, Inc., and International Bible Translators, Inc.*)
TWOT	Theological Workbook of the Old Testament
UBS	United Bible Societies
VED	Vine's Expository Dictionary

Preliminary Notes

Format for dates: Dates for events before October 4, 1582 CE on the Julian calendar are displayed as proleptic Gregorian dates, followed by a BCE or CE era notation. Dates for events after October 15, 1582 CE are displayed as standard Gregorian dates, usually without the CE era notation. Unless noted otherwise, proleptic Gregorian dates shown throughout this book were generated by using the *Jewish Calendar Conversions in One Step* calendar-conversion utility created by Stephen P. Morse and made available at: www.stevemorse.org.

Accuracy of dates: Dates obtained from ancient historical sources may not always reflect the exact moment when an event occurred. However, achieving 100% accuracy of interpretation of a chrono-specific biblical prophecy does not depend on knowing the exact moment any particular event occurred since the passage of time in ancient Israel was marked in a different manner, namely, by keeping track of the annual Jewish festivals, such as Passover, Pentecost, and the Day of Atonement. Thus, exact interpretation of a chrono-specific biblical prophecy can be accomplished as long as the occurrence of its prophetic events can be located with respect to the annual Hebrew religious festivals occurring during the same time period. For example, if the beginning event of a chrono-specific prophecy can be identified as having happened between Passover in one year and Passover in the following year, that location between the two Passovers, because the passage of time in the chrono-specific biblical prophecies is festival-related, provides the necessary degree of chronological precision that is needed to achieve absolute accuracy of interpretation.

Scripture quotations: The King James Version is the primary version used for Scripture quotations, chosen because of its familiarity to both Jewish and Christian readers, the consistency in the way it translates Hebrew, Aramaic, and Greek words into English, and because, as a document residing in the public domain, its use greatly simplifies copyright considerations and permissions. As a general rule, Scripture quotations embedded in the text are displayed in italics, followed by a version-used abbreviation in parenthesis.

PREFACE

The Scripture of Truth

The great 20th-century physicist Albert Einstein, acknowledged by many people, including me, as one of the truly brilliant thinkers of the modern age, when questioned in 1929 by Rabbi Herbert S. Goldstein זצ״ל about his belief in God, answered thus: "I believe in Spinoza's god, who reveals himself in the orderly harmony of what exists, not in a god who concerns himself with the fate and actions of human beings." Einstein was saying what many of the most learned people would probably say today, that, based on the evidence he could observe with his eyes and see with his mind's eye, his powers of reasoning would not allow him to believe in the living and faith-based personal God of the Bible. Instead, he preferred a god that exists only in the realm of cosmology, a god that always has been, is now, and will forever remain impersonal and abstract.

The concept of a cosmological god, understandable apart from the Bible, is not a new one. It was introduced during the early years of the Enlightenment by philosophers in Europe, such as Spinoza, and later advanced by Kant, who taught that the true nature of god could be discovered through reason alone. Predictably, reason alone produced a pantheon of philosopher-defined divinities that became fashionable in universities and among the educated class. At about the same time, biblical scholarship moved out of churches and into halls of learning, thereafter developing side by side with the arts and sciences, the latter of which depended on hypothesizing, testing, and drawing conclusions to advance knowledge. Man-made theories endorsed by peer review and approval became the standard of authority in academia, whereas the Bible was dethroned as the source of absolute truth about anything, including god. In such a milieu, it was inevitable that biblical studies would be overwhelmed by the emerging humanistic-scientific disciplines and their assumptions. Faith-based concepts were gradually consigned to the fringes by scholars in the secular disciplines, the end result being that biblical scholars wishing to maintain academic credibility among their secular peers also began to abandon the Bible as their ultimate source of authority.

The effects of the transition from faith-based Bible belief to belief based on human reasoning ratified by universal acceptance across academic disciplines is still being reflected in biblical scholarship today. In many contemporary Jewish and Christian seminaries, and in virtually all public and most private university schools of religion and biblical studies, belief in a transcendent, personal god who participates in the lives of individuals and controls the affairs of mankind is often no longer a requirement for students or professors. Biblical concepts, such as angels, visions, revelation, predictive prophecy, miracles, and divine providence are routinely discounted as being quaint. Extra-biblical scholarship often undermines biblical authority, as when the chronology for biblical times developed by archaeology says by implication that the Bible is not totally accurate about historical matters. And, absent the authority of Scripture, a Nietzschean anthropocentrism is usually the *de facto* rule, with man at the center and the concept of god just another clever human creation, allowing god to be anything one desires, even deceased. The latter actually happened here in Atlanta during the 1960s when a group of academics foolishly proclaimed that "God is dead!"

Now, before you get the impression that this preface amounts to nothing more than an exhortation to read yet another faith-based rant against the evils of science, reason, and academia, let me give you my assurances that just the opposite is true. As someone whose résumé includes years of scientific training, I place great value on rational thought, scholarly research, and use of scientific methodologies to validate existing and/or formulate new theorems. Thus, it is no accident that the basic scientific method—starting with an hypothesis, looking at the observable evidence, and then drawing logical conclusions from it—is the methodology used in this book to understand what the Bible's prophecies say about the Jewish people and their ongoing relationship with their God.

In the exposition of the Book of Daniel that follows, the seven chrono-specific predictive prophecies recorded in Daniel, by claiming to tell the history of God's people Israel well before that history occurred in time, collectively constitute an hypothesis that they are divine in origin, supernaturally revealed. The precise fulfillment of those prophesies by events documented in history provides sufficient evidence to prove the hypothesis true to all but the most hardened skeptics. The logical conclusion to be drawn from Daniel is that its multiple chrono-specific predictive prophecies, all having exact fulfillments in real time, establish that the Bible of the Jews is the Scripture of truth, and that the information about God and the Jewish people presented therein is trustworthy today. That same Bible also reveals why God provided his sure word of prophecy—to help us take heed and have faith in his eternal Word. That is the intent of this book, too.

Dan Bruce

October 18, 2010 • Atlanta, Georgia

Exposition of Prophecies

"The hearing ear and the seeing eye, the Lord has made them both." - Proverbs 20:12 (ESV)

Principles of Interpretation

"There are, indeed, difficulties in understanding the [*precise and complete*] meaning of the prophetic writings, but these are either owing to our ignorance of history and of the Scriptures, or because the prophecies are yet unfilled. The latter can only be understood when the events foretold in the prophecies have actually been accomplished. The former class of difficulties may be removed in many, if not in all, cases, and the knowledge, sense, and meaning of the prophets may, in a considerable degree, be attained by prayer, reading [*of both history and the Scriptures*], meditation, and [*as a way of knowing the mind of God on the matter directly from the divine source and final authority*] by comparing Scripture with Scripture" ... adapted from Thomas Hartwell Horne, *Introduction to the Critical Study and Knowledge of the Holy Scriptures* (London: Longman, Brown, Green, Longmans, and Roberts, 1856; Section II, p. 216).

"The prophecies concerning Israel [*meaning Jews as a people and, at times, as a nation living in the promised land*] are the key to all of the rest. True principles of interpretation, in regard to them, will aid us in disentangling and illustrating all prophecy together. False principles as to them will most thoroughly perplex and over cloud the whole Word of God" ... adapted from Horatius Bonar, *Prophetical Landmarks* (London: James Nisbet & Co., 1847, p. 273).

"Belief in divine providence is the foundation on which an understanding of biblical eschatology must be built. The reality of divine providence is demonstrated by the presence of chrono-specific predictive prophecy in the biblical text that has been exactly fulfilled at a time later than when it was revealed. The efficacy of divine providence is most evident when the history of God's chosen people Israel is examined in terms of its chrono-prophetic context, which Scripture extends from ancient times down to the present day" ... Dan Bruce (*ca.* 1982).

"A chrono-specific predictive prophecy will always have a starting point in time, an ending point in time, and a finite period of time in between, with at least two of those attributes defined by the biblical text. Its fulfillment will match both the biblical text and recorded history exactly. Since chrono-specific prophecies were revealed by God for mankind's edification, their fulfillments will never be arcane, approximate, incomplete, or unverifiable" ... Dan Bruce (*ca.* 2009).

INTRODUCTION

I, Daniel, Understood

The seven prophecies in chapter 4 and chapters 7-12 of the Book of Daniel[1] are unique, quite unlike any other prophecies found in the Bible. They are chrono-specific predictive prophecies that collectively tell the story of the Jewish people from the time of Solomon down to the present day. Despite their chronological and historical specificity, though, the seven chrono-specific prophecies recorded by the prophet Daniel while captive in Babylon[2] have proven to be an enigma, in that they have resisted conclusive interpretation by anyone for more than twenty-five-hundred years. Surprisingly, the one thing that should have been understood about the prophecies from the beginning—and the one thing that should not have been a mystery to any serious expositor—is why the prophecies have defied interpretation for so long. That reason why is plainly stated in Daniel itself, at the end of the twelfth chapter. There we are told that the prophecies were sealed up by commandment of God as soon as they were handed down to Daniel. We are also told how long they would remain sealed. The text clearly states that Daniel's prophetic words would stay closed up and sealed until the time of the end.[3]

Indeed, the very profusion of contradictory interpretations of the Danielic prophecies offered and rejected since their revelation in antiquity provides the best evidence that the end-time meanings of the prophecies have been divinely sequestered from the start. Heretofore, no expositor of Daniel has been able to interpret the prophecies with any degree of certainty, nor has any expositor been able to correlate all of the prophesied events with events in history. Acclaimed Torah sages and Talmudists, renowned Bible scholars and theologians, even one universally-recognized scientific genius—Sir Isaac Newton—all have strived to produce the definitive exposition of the Danielic prophecies, and all have come up short of achieving their goal. Their labors over the centuries have produced valuable insights and thought-provoking interpretations that have advanced our understanding of biblical prophecy in general, yet one undeniable fact remains: Every exposition of the chrono-specific predictive prophecies in Daniel published prior to modern times has now been shown by history to be inaccurate.

---

[1] See *Appendix One: Background Notes on the Book of Daniel* on page 123.
[2] Daniel was taken captive to Babylon in 605 BCE, after the Battle of Carchemish.
[3] Dan. 12:9: *"And he said, Go thy way, Daniel: for the words are closed up and sealed till the time of the end"* (KJV).

Expositions of the Danielic prophecies published in recent years have proven to be unsatisfactory in various ways as well. All too often, modern expositors have used what I call "approximate history" as substitutes for exact fulfillments of prophesied events. That method of interpretation is typical of the most popular interpretations of Daniel, chapter 8. Other expositors, in an attempt to achieve the precision expected of biblical prophecy, have gone to the opposite extreme, employing esoteric prophetic calendars and using complicated mathematical formulas to interpret the chrono-specific prophecies. The most popular of these manipulations are based on a postulated 360-day "prophetic year," support for which is found nowhere in the Bible, mainstream Jewish history, or astronomy. This latter method of interpretation is quite often associated with interpretations of Daniel, chapter 9. Additionally, many modern expositors, unable to find exact matches in history for events mentioned in the prophetic text, have simply consigned all such events to an indeterminate "end time" by default, with no justification for doing so other than the fact that the events do not fit anywhere else in their interpretive scheme. Still others have forgotten that the Danielic prophecies are focused almost exclusively on explaining the redemptive history of God's people and nation Israel, not the Christian church. These and similar interpretive errors have produced frequently well-received but nonetheless flawed interpretations of the Danielic prophecies.

Before continuing, however, let me emphasize that the above comments are not motivated by any desire for expository one-upmanship on my part, nor are they intended to disparage in any way the work of previous Daniel expositors by calling into question their biblical scholarship or spiritual integrity. Over the years, their efforts to expound Daniel have edified and sustained the faithful through good times and bad, and for that alone they deserve our gratitude and respect. Instead, my comments are simply pointing out the obvious—that God, after giving the chrono-specific prophecies to Daniel in Babylon, directed that they be sealed up until the time of the end. That act of divine sealing made it impossible for any expositor to expound them fully until the appointed time had arrived. No matter how clever the interpreter and diligent the effort, a definitive exposition of the Danielic prophecies simply could not be done until then. Even Daniel himself wrote that he did not understand everything that had been revealed to him.[1] The prophecies were sealed up, and that was that. Yet, the Bible clearly indicated that they would be unsealed for full understanding at the time of the end.

---

[1] Dan. 12:8: *"And I [Daniel] heard, but I understood not: ..."* (KJV).

Introduction: I, Daniel, Understood

So, is there any indication of when the "time of the end" foretold in Daniel will begin?[1] Yes, there is. Biblical prophecy and recent Jewish history indicate that we are already living in those prophesied days. The emergence of Zionism in the late 1800s, the Palestine Mandate approved by the League of Nations in 1922, the Holocaust and subsequent influx of Jews seeking refuge in Palestine after WWII, the partition of Palestine by the United Nations in 1947, the declaration of the nation of Israel as a Jewish state in 1948, and the passage of the Law of Return in 1950, all of these events taken together are an unmistakable end-time indicator to those who believe the prophecies that require a regathered Jewish people living in *Eretz-Israel*[2] at the end of days. Even without the hindsight we enjoy today, those events, once underway, indicated a clear eschatological progression that should not have been ignored by Bible scholars at the time, although most did so back then. Even the early Zionist leaders themselves did not embrace eschatology as the primary justification for seeking support for their movement. Nevertheless, the modern rebirth of Israel as a sovereign nation in Palestine was a prophetic turning point. That event, followed by the accelerated ingathering of Jews from around the world that began soon thereafter, signaled that the time of the end was at last underway.[3] This meant that it would henceforth be possible for the prophecies in Daniel to be unsealed at any time. The stage was set.

Meanwhile, as the momentous events of Jewish national rebirth were reaching their climax during the late 1940s, I was experiencing my earliest childhood years, far too young to realize that those events were setting the stage for unsealing the Danielic prophecies. Nor could I foresee that the process of understanding them would one day involve me. My spiritual awakening came many years later, when my curiosity about things sacred was overnight quickened by God. For days on end, I was filled with an around-the-clock desire to read the Bible, and given clarity of mind to understand what I was reading as I read. During this period of biblical immersion, I was especially drawn to the prophecies in Daniel, and my attention was repeatedly focused on the chrono-specific prophecy in the eighth chapter. Unfamiliarity with the historical details that provide context to the events described in Daniel soon compelled me to supplement my Bible study with a survey of ancient Jewish history, and that research ended up exposing me

---

[1] The phrase "time of the end" does not mean "end of the world" or "end of time"; the word "time" is used as a chronological unit in Daniel and denotes a time period, not a moment.
[2] Hebrew-to-English transliteration meaning "Land of Israel" (*i.e.,* the promised land).
[3] See *Appendix Seven: The Modern Nation of Israel - Is it Biblical?* on page 195.

to the details of modern Jewish history, and specifically Israeli history, as well. It was the latter exposure that would provide the key that unlocked everything.

The breakthrough moment—the instant of insight when I first considered the possibility that the chrono-specific prophecy in the eighth chapter of Daniel might have had a modern fulfillment—came in the spring of 1974, while I was reading a magazine article about the Six-Day War miraculously won by Israel seven years earlier. After finishing the paragraphs describing the liberation of the Temple Mount in Jerusalem by Israeli paratroopers on the morning of June 7, 1967, the third day of the war, I was struck by how closely the outcome of that event (return of the Temple Mount to Jewish sovereignty) matched the fulfillment event of the prophecy in Daniel, chapter 8, verse 14: "... [then] *the sanctuary will be restored to its rightful state*" (CJB). I wondered if it was possible that that event, which had been captured by the world's television cameras for anyone with eyes to see, was now begging to be recognized as a fulfillment of ancient Hebrew prophecy? I was unaware of any biblical scholar who had come forward to single out that event as being a prophetic fulfillment in the years since it had occurred, so I exercised caution, resisting the urge to embrace such a radical interpretation of events without solid biblical justification for doing so. And, not wanting to be a source of error, I was reluctant to share my discovery with anyone else. Consequently, years of Bible study would transpire before I overcame my doubt by finding confirmation that the 1967 event was an exact fulfillment of biblical prophecy.

More than three decades have now passed since I understood how to correctly interpret the chrono-specific prophecy in Daniel, chapter 8. That breakthrough in understanding, and the gradual strengthening of faith that resulted as I went through the decade-long process of questioning my interpretation against the Scriptures, gradually opened the door to more understanding. Knowledge gained from the eighth chapter provided the key for determining the starting point for working out the chronology of Daniel, chapter 12. The knowledge gained from the eighth and twelfth chapter then provided the key for understanding the meanings of the chronological terms "season" and "time" that are required for assembling the time lines of Jewish history that provide the chronological framework for understanding the remaining prophecies in Daniel. And so it went, year after year, as I continued to study and pray for understanding. I found that the more I understood about one prophecy, the more I was able to understand about another, with the result that over time, one by one, all of the chrono-specific prophecies in Daniel were understood, at last revealing their secrets.

Introduction: I, Daniel, Understood

This book will give you the keys for interpreting the seven chrono-specific predictive prophecies found in chapter 4 and chapters 7-12 of the Book of Daniel, and it will explain in detail how those prophecies have been fulfilled in history. More specifically, it will explain how they have been fulfilled in Jewish history. Beginning with the chrono-specific prophecy in the eighth chapter of Daniel, the prophecies are explained in the order in which they were understood. As you evaluate for yourself the exposition of the prophecies set forth in this book, it is important that you keep two principles of interpretation firmly in mind: First, a chrono-specific predictive prophecy will always have an exact fulfillment in real time. Second, that fulfillment will match both the biblical text and recorded history exactly. Those two principles are based on the assumption that the prophecies in Daniel were given for our end-time edification, and that they can be understood. Thus, as you will see, the interpretations offered in this book are clear and precise, not arcane, approximate, incomplete, or unverifiable.

You will also quickly discover that the interpretations of the chrono-specific Danielic prophecies set forth herein are anything but traditional. Giving them a fair reading may require that you set aside eschatological assumptions and familiar interpretations that you have read in other commentaries. If you will do so, however, following the explanations in the order presented and evaluating each prophecy with respect to the contribution it makes to the overall chronology of Jewish history, I can assure you that the interpretations will fit together to give undeniable evidence of God's sovereign presence in the affairs of mankind. And, as you begin to understand for yourself that the prophecies in Daniel were sealed in antiquity, preserved as a divine testimony for this appointed time, and unsealed as promised for understanding by this generation, my hope is that you will be inspired to join with me in giving praise to the living God of the Bible.

> *"O Lord, you are my God; I will exalt you; I will praise your name, for you have done wonderful things, plans formed of old, faithful and sure."* - Isaiah 25:1 (ESV)

Before reading the expository chapters ...

You should become familiar with the "Prophecy Overview" chart on Plate 1, which is conveniently located at the end of this book for quick reference.

Daniel Unsealed

PHOTO: COPYRIGHT © STATE OF ISRAEL, GOVERNMENT PRESS OFFICE, NATIONAL PHOTO COLLECTION. USED BY PERMISSION.

Prophecy being fulfilled for the whole world to see!

On the morning of June 7, 1967, an Israel Defense Forces half track carrying soldiers from the 55th Paratroopers Brigade sped toward the Dome of the Rock atop the Temple Mount during the Six-Day War, fulfilling ancient prophecies recorded in the Book of Daniel. To relive this event as it happened, read "Liberation of the Temple Mount and Western Wall" on page 219.

CHAPTER ONE

THEN SHALL THE SANCTUARY BE RESTORED

READ DANIEL 8:1-27 ON PAGE 227 | SEE TIME LINE ❶ ON PLATE 1

The interpretation of one particular chrono-specific prophecy in the Book of Daniel, the one found in chapter 8, verses 13-14, is key to understanding all of the chrono-specific prophecies in Daniel. The reason why the interpretation of that prophecy is so all-important is that it extends the efficacy of Bible prophecy from ancient into modern times. By so doing, it establishes the chronological context needed for accurately interpreting the remaining chrono-specific prophecies in Daniel, some of which also have post-biblical fulfillments, as will be shown in later chapters. In this chapter, though, the exposition of the prophecy in Daniel, chapter 8, will receive our full attention, since the correct interpretation of that prophecy is fundamental to understanding everything else.

The eighth chapter of Daniel can be divided into three parts. The first part is comprised of verses 1-12. Those verses set forth a prophetic vision predicting the history of the Jewish people for the immediate future—immediate, that is, from the standpoint of a Jewish person living in the Achaemenid Persian Empire during the reign of Darius III.[1] The vision describes a ram with two horns pushing westward, northward, and southward. The ram is next seen standing still before a river while a he-goat with a notable horn comes against the ram from the west with fury. The he-goat then proceeds to smite the ram and break his two horns. Thereafter, nothing the ram is able to do can stop the he-goat from waxing great and casting the ram to the ground. However, when the he-goat has achieved greatness, his horn is broken, and four notable ones take his place. Out of one of the four notable horns, a little horn comes forth to wax great toward the pleasant land, and this little horn takes away the daily sacrifice, casts down the sanctuary[2] and hosts to the ground, and prospers. So conclude the events described in the first part. The second part is a parenthesis comprised of verses 13-14, and it contains a cryptic chrono-specific prophecy predicting that the sanctuary will be restored (or "cleansed" in KJV) in the future. The third part is comprised of verses 15-27. These verses provide a partial interpretation of the prophetic vision recorded in the first part. The ram with two horns is identified in verse 20 as the

---

[1] Darius III Codomannus (r. 336-330 BCE), last king of the Achaemenid Persian Empire.
[2] The sacred Temple Mount area (Mount Moriah) in Old City Jerusalem.

kings of Media and Persia,[1] and the he-goat with the notable horn is identified in verse 21 as the first king of Greece.[2] The little horn that arises from the four notable horns is not identified by name, but is described as a king of fierce countenance who destroys the holy people. Most Bible expositors agree that the fierce-king imagery is referring to the Seleucid king Antiochus IV Epiphanes,[3] and most agree that the term "holy people" in verse 24 is a reference to the Jews living in Judea under his rule. A prediction of harsh oppression and persecution of the holy people closes part three, but that part closes with a reminder that the prophecy in part two, the one in verses 13-14 foretelling that the sanctuary will be restored to its rightful status after 2,300 "evening-morning"(s),[4] will most certainly come true. It is the eventual fulfillment of this two-verse prophecy that projects the context of Daniel from ancient to modern times.

Interpretive Schemes

Most modern expositors assign the fulfillment event of chapter 8, verse 14 (*i.e.*, the restoration of the sanctuary), to the time of Antiochus IV Epiphanes and the Maccabean revolt.[5] None of them allow for a modern-day fulfillment. In those expositions that assign fulfillment to the time of Antiochus, two main interpretive schemes are employed, one postulating that the 2,300 "evening-morning"(s) define a period of persecution of the Jews lasting 1,150 days (a calculation based on 2,300 twice-daily morning-and-evening sacrifices for 1.150 actual days) and another saying that the 2,300 "evening-morning"(s) are actual twenty-four-hour days. These two interpretive schemes are popular mainly among conservative expositors, those who interpret the Bible literally and believe in the reality of predictive prophecy.

One often-quoted conservative expositor, the late Dr. Leon Wood, professor of Old Testament at Grand Rapids Baptist Seminary for many years, correctly rejected the 1,150-day approach in his commentary on Daniel,[6] saying:

---

[1] General reference to all Achaemenid kings from Cyrus the Great to Darius III.
[2] Alexander the Great (*r.* 336-323 BCE), first king of unified Greece (all Greek city-states).
[3] Antiochus IV Epiphanes (*r.* 175-164 BCE), king of the Hellenistic Seleucid Empire.
[4] עֶרֶב בֹּקֶר (BHS) "evening-morning"(s), mistranslated as *"days"* in the KJV and other versions.
[5] The Maccabees were a priestly family that sparked and led a revolt by Jews in 167 BCE against Antiochus IV, who was attempting to replace Judaism with Hellenism.
[6] Leon J. Wood, *A Commentary on Daniel* (Eugene, Oregon: Wipf and Stock, 1998), p. 217-218.

Chapter One: *Then Shall the Sanctuary Be Restored (Daniel 8:1-27)*

"The angel's answer is a definite number of time units called 'evening-mornings' (*'ereb bôqer*), literally, 'evening-morning.' Some expositors take the expression to mean 2,300 evenings and mornings totaled together, equaling only 1,150 full days. They find supporting evidence in the mention in the immediate context of regular offerings and the fact that the regular burnt-offerings came every morning and evening, asserting that the true intent is to designate 2,300 occasions of burnt offerings. The commentary on verse eleven [previously discussed in Wood's book] has shown, however, that all ceremonial observances are in view in the context, not merely the regular offerings."

Wood further dismissed the two-a-day sacrifice approach as follows:

"Moreover, that two half-days are intended by the expression is not likely in view of the order of mention: evening-morning, rather than morning-evening.[1] The order of evening-morning suggests that part of the twenty-four-hour period at which a full day closes and a new one begins—a part which comes only once every twenty-four hours. Twenty-three hundred of these parts would mean the elapse of 2,300 full days."

On the other hand, Wood fails to point out the most serious flaw in that approach, namely, that counting 1,150 days from the desecration of the Temple by Antiochus IV Epiphanes on 25 Kislev in the 145th Seleucid year (or instead from the rededication of the Temple by Judah Maccabee on 25 Kislev in the 148th Seleucid year), the usual starting or ending points for those who espouse the 1,150-day approach, does not lead to any significant historical event at the other end of the count. Furthermore, since both the desecration and rededication dates are recorded in and verifiable from historical records,[2] a quick calculation shows that the time between them is only 1,093¾ days, not the required 1,150 days, so using those dates as the two end points cannot be accepted as a valid

---

[1] The twice-a-day burnt offerings are always referred to as "morning and evening" sacrifices (*cf.* 2 Ki. 16:15, 1 Chr. 16:40, 2 Chr. 2:4, 2 Chr. 13:11, 2 Chr. 31:3, Ezra 3:3), **never** as "evening and morning" sacrifices. The Hebrew construct in verse 14, translated literally as "evening-morning" (see footnote 4 on page 8), is found only this once in the entire Bible.

[2] According to Josephus, *Antiquities*, 12:5:4, the desecration of the Temple occurred on the 25th day of Kislev (*1 Maccabees* 1:54 gives the date as the 15th of Kislev) in the 145th year of the Seleucid Empire, which is equivalent to the modern Gregorian date December 13, 167 BCE, and according to Josephus, *Antiquities,* 12:7:6 and 1 *Maccabees* 4:52, the rededication of the Temple occurred on the 25th of Kislev in the 148th year of the Seleucid Empire, which is equivalent to December 10, 164 BCE; also, see footnote 1 on page 69.

interpretation. When using the 1,150-day interpretive scheme, the result always ends up depending on an approximation of history as the interpretation, which is unacceptable as fulfillment of chrono-specific predictive prophecy.

After reviewing the shortcomings of the 1,150-day approach, Wood then offers his exposition of verse 14 using the 2,300-actual-day approach, as follows:

> "How are 2,300 days to be fitted into the history concerned? The answer is that this amount of time was the duration of Antiochus' period of oppression of the Jews. Historical data available are insufficient for a precise reckoning to the very day, but an ***approximation*** [emphasis added] is definitely possible. The closing point of this period is indicated in the verse to have been the restoration of the Temple. The date when this was accomplished, under the leadership of Judas Maccabeus, was December 25, 165 B.C.,[1] according to Barnes, who refers to Prideaux. Figuring back from this date 2,300 days brings one to September 6, 171 B.C.; which should be, then, the day when an event occurred that was of sufficient significance to mark it as a beginning of these atrocities, and such an event could easily have occurred on that date."

Perhaps such an event could have occurred, but if indeed it had occurred and if it had been truly significant, it doubtless would have been recorded by some ancient scribe, yet there is nothing in the historical record to indicate that any such event ever happened. Wood himself does not seem to be bothered by the uncertainty at the core of his interpretation. However, it cannot be ignored, and it means that his 2,300-actual-day approach is just as inaccurate as the 1,150-day approach he rejected. Unfortunately, Wood is not alone in using an interpretive scheme that produces a result that is less than precise. Essentially all modern conservative expositors have based their interpretations on approximations.

Another example of an influential conservative expositor using approximation exegesis to interpret chapter 8 can be found in the commentary written by the late Dr. John F. Walvoord,[2] long-time president of Dallas Theological Seminary, who offered the following comments as his exposition of the 2,300-day prophecy:

> "Taking all of the evidence into consideration, the best conclusion is that the twenty-three hundred days of Daniel are fulfilled in the period from 171 B.C. and culminated

---

[1] See footnote 2 on page 9 showing that the December 25 date referenced here is incorrect.
[2] John F. Walvoord, *Daniel: The Key to Prophetic Revelation* (Chicago: Moody Press, 1971), p.190.

in the death of Antiochus Epiphanes in 164 B.C. The period when the sacrifices ceased was the latter part of this longer period. Although the evidence available today [this was published in 1971] does not offer fulfillment to the precise day, the twenty-three hundred days, obviously a round number, is ***relatively accurate*** [emphasis added] in defining the period when the Jewish religion began to erode under the persecution of Antiochus, and the period as a whole concluded with his death."

Curiously, Walvoord uses the death of Antiochus IV as his conclusion of the prophecy, an event which has nothing at all to do with the *terminus ad quem*, the restoration of the sanctuary stipulated by the biblical text in verse 14. Even more surprising coming from a biblical literalist, his comments seem to be saying that "relatively accurate" is good enough in this particular case.

More examples of this approximation method of interpreting the chrono-specific predictive prophecy in Daniel, chapter 8, could be provided, but the two examples of approximation exegesis by Wood and Walvoord mentioned above were chosen because they are typical of the many well-received and widely-referenced, but inaccurate, interpretive schemes offered in recent years by conservative expositors to explain chapter 8 in Daniel. So far, none of their various interpretive schemes have produced an interpretation that fits the constraints of the biblical text exactly and matches the historical record exactly, at least not in both ways at the same time. Either the time interval does not equal 2,300 units, or the starting date or ending date does not match any event specified in the biblical text that can be documented in history.

As for the interpretive schemes put forth in recent years by non-conservative expositors, most of whom are ensconced as biblical scholars at institutions of higher learning, their expositions usually deny the possibility of any predictive prophecy in Daniel, including those in the eighth chapter. Instead, they tend to focus on textual and literary aspects rather than the chrono-predictive elements. Consequently, the commentaries of these disbelieving scholars shy away from recognizing that the predictive prophecies recorded in the Bible text might have actual fulfillments in history, asserting that the prophecies in Daniel and elsewhere in the Scriptures are merely a telling of history recorded after the fact by some unknown scribe. Almost uniformly, these scholars ascribe all of the events of chapter 8, and the writing down of the Book of Daniel itself, to the time of Antiochus IV and the Maccabees, and they make a point of denying that anything supernatural was involved. Equally unsatisfying, but far less harmful to faith, more than a few expositors, unable to decipher the chronology revealed in chapter 8 and other chapters in Daniel, have simply chosen to remain silent about the chronological aspects of the prophecies altogether.

Exact Fulfillment

That brings us to the interpretive approach employed in this book, which uses a better principle of interpretation than the approximation of history, silence about chronology, or outright disbelief in predictive prophecy approaches used by most expositors to expound the Danielic prophecies, and it can be summed up as follows: The chrono-specific predictive prophecies in Daniel will always have exact and understandable fulfillments in real time. Thus, the interpretation of Daniel, chapter 8, offered in this chapter, as well as the interpretations of other prophecies set forth in later chapters, will fit the biblical text exactly and the historical record exactly. In fairness to past expositors, they had no choice but to settle for offering approximations or silence since the Bible stipulated that the prophecies in Daniel were sealed until the time of the end (but teaching disbelief in the meantime was unforgiveable). Fortunately, that was no longer the case for me. A modern event, the liberation of the Temple Mount by Israel on June 7, 1967, had unsealed the prophecy in chapter 8, verses 13-14, for full understanding by this generation. The restoration of the Temple Mount to Jewish sovereignty was the fulfillment event specified in verse 14, and it occurred while the whole world was watching during the Six-Day War.[1] Then, seven years after that event had occurred for all to see, my eyes were opened so that I could see its eschatological importance. Right away, I was thrilled at my discovery, but soon learned that my new interpretation incorporating a modern fulfillment of an ancient prophecy would not find easy acceptance in traditional circles, at least not until I could find Scriptural validation for such a radical interpretive approach. So, I began searching the Bible,[2] keeping in mind that my interpretation had to fit both Scripture and history exactly to be accepted as a true interpretation, and that is what I found. Now, I want to share with you the keys for interpreting the prophecy with exactitude.

---

[1] See photograph on page 6 showing the prophecy being fulfilled.
[2] While researching Daniel, chapter 8, in Bible commentaries, I came across Adam Clarke's *Commentary on the Bible* (1825) and found that he had offered the same interpretation of chapter 8. However, his calculations incorrectly yielded 1966 as the year for the restoration of the sanctuary. Still, it was brilliant exegesis, though generally ignored by later scholars.

Chapter One: Then Shall the Sanctuary Be Restored (Daniel 8:1-27)

Keys to Interpretation

The first key to interpretation of the chrono-specific prophecy found in Daniel, chapter 8, verses 13-14, is to understand the scope of the question being asked in verse 13, *"How long shall be the vision concerning the daily sacrifice, and the transgression of desolation, to give both the sanctuary and the host to be trodden under foot?"* (KJV). I quickly realized that past expositors had underestimated the question, assuming it to be asking only how long the interruption of the Temple sacrifices and other transgressions against the Temple would last. That was not the question being asked, however. The questioner was seeking to know the duration of the entire vision. A better translation of verse 13 reads, *"How long will the events of the vision last, this vision concerning the regular offering and the transgression which is so appalling, that allows the sanctuary and the army to be trampled underfoot?"* (CJB). This wording recognizes that the question about duration pertains to the all events in the vision, a time period that includes the events described in verses 1-12 as well as the trampling of the sanctuary underfoot that, we now know from history, continued in one form or another from the time of the exile in Babylon until June, 1967. When the full scope of the question is understood, it is easy to see that the first action event of the vision, the king of Greece going against the king of Persia described in verse 6, is the starting point for calculating the duration of the vision. Verse 14 then states that the final event of the vision will come after 2,300 "evening-morning"(s). Putting all of these pieces together, I understood that verse 14 was saying that the sanctuary would be restored after 2,300 "evening-morning"(s), with the count beginning from the time when Alexander the Great moved against Persia in 334 BCE.

The second key to interpretation of the prophecy is to understand the unit of time meant by the Hebrew phrase עֶרֶב בֹּקֶר (BHS, Strong's OT: 1242, 6153), literally "evening-morning," which is used in verse 14. I recalled that the King James Version renders it as "days," based on similar Hebrew wording in Genesis, chapter 1, verses 5-31, *"the evening and the morning were the* [first, second, third, *etc* ...] *day"* (KJV). Expositors adopting that translation have traditionally considered the phrase "evening-morning"(s) to mean literal twenty-four-hour days, as the late Leon Wood did, but I knew that none of them had been able to make that interpretation fit historical events. Other translations render the phrase in Daniel as "evening ***and*** mornings," adding the conjunction "and" which is not found in the best Hebrew manuscripts. This has led to expositions interpreting the phrase as a reference to 2,300 evening-and-morning sacrifices, which they usually postulate were interrupted for about 1,150 days between the desecration of the Temple by Antiochus in 167 BCE and its rededication by the Maccabees in 164 BCE. However, I also knew that none of the proponents of the 1,150-day approach had been able to make their exposition fit the historical record, either. Since both the 2,300 full-day approach and the 1,150 half-day approach had yielded only approximations as interpretations, I reasoned that a different interpretive approach was needed. Having had my eyes opened to the possibility that the ending event of the prophecy had occurred with the liberation of the Temple Mount during the Six-Day War in 1967, and now understanding that the starting event had occurred when Alexander the Great defeated the Persian army of Darius III for the first time in the year 334 BCE, I did a quick calculation that revealed the interval between the two events was essentially 2,300 years. Thus, an "evening-morning" somehow seemed to be equivalent to a year in actual time, but I could not see from the Hebrew wording how this could be. As was my custom, I turned to the Bible for clarification.

The insight came while reading the passage about the instructions given by God for instituting and observing Passover, as recorded in the Book of Exodus, chapter 12, verses 6-10, 14: *"And ye shall keep it* [the Paschal lamb] *up until the fourteenth day of the same month; and the whole assembly of the congregation of Israel shall kill it* **in the evening**. *And they shall take of the blood, and strike it on the two side posts and on the upper door post of the houses, wherein they shall eat it. And they shall eat the flesh in that night, roast with fire, and unleavened bread; and with bitter herbs they shall eat it. ... And ye shall let nothing of it remain until the morning; and that which remaineth of it* **until the morning** *ye shall burn with fire ... And this day shall be unto you* **for a memorial**; *and ye shall keep it a feast to the Lord throughout your generations; ye shall keep it a feast by an ordinance for ever"* (KJV). In those verses was the answer that I was seeking. The oldest memorial observance of the Jewish people, Passover, was an annual evening-until-morning event. I now realized that "evening-morning" did not represent a calendar unit, such as a day, a year, *etc.*, nor did it have anything to do with the morning and evening sacrifices, but instead it meant a night. More specifically, it meant the Passover night, the reminder of God's redemption of the people of Israel. Thus, 2,300 "evening-morning"(s) was understood to represent 2,300 Passovers.

The third key to interpretation of the prophecy is to understand how to count the 2,300 Passovers that determine the time span stipulated in verse 14, to

Chapter One: Then Shall the Sanctuary Be Restored (Daniel 8:1-27)

Diagram 1.1 - The 2,300 Passovers

know when to begin and when to end the count (see Diagram 1.1 above). I knew that the initial Passover in the count had to occur after the first action event of the prophecy, the Battle of Granicus stipulated in verse 6, had occurred. This battle was the first time that Alexander the Great met and defeated an army of Darius III of Persia. There is no direct historical reference to a specific date for the Battle of Granicus, but a mention by Plutarch of Chaeronea,[1] who recorded that the battle took place in the Macedonian month Daesius in the year 334 BCE, is sufficient to locate it chronologically. That reference shows that Alexander moved against the Persians in late May or early June. Passover was celebrated in March in 334 BCE, so it had already occurred before the battle began, and thus the next Passover, the one celebrated in 333 BCE, is the one that must be used to start the count that determines the duration of the 2,300-Passover time span

---

[1] *Life of Alexander* by Plutarch of Chaeronea (section 16, verses 1-3): "In the meantime, Darius' captains, having collected large forces, were encamped on the further bank of the river Granicus, and it was necessary to fight, as it were, in the gate of Asia for an entrance into it. The depth of the river, with the unevenness and difficult ascent of the opposite bank, which was to be gained by main force, was apprehended by most, and some pronounced it an improper time to engage, because it was unusual for the kings of Macedonia to march with their forces in the month called Daesius. But Alexander broke through these scruples, telling them they should call it a second Artemisius. And when Parmenion advised him not to attempt anything that day, because it was late, he told him that he should disgrace the Hellespont, should he fear the Granicus." ... translated by Mr. Evelyn for John Dryden's *Plutarch's Lives by Several Hands*, published in 1683.

specified in verse 14. I also knew that the count had to be concluded before the Temple Mount was liberated by Israeli army paratroopers on June 7, 1967. This meant that the last Passover in the count, the 2,300th Passover, had to be the Passover in 1967, which occurred on April 25th. Were there exactly 2,300 Passovers between the Battle of Granicus in 334 BCE and the liberation of the Temple Mount during the Six-Day War in 1967? There was only one way to find out, and that was to count the Passovers. So, I did, and you can, too.

Table 1.1 (on the opposite page) demonstrates how the 2,300 Passovers should be counted. Included in the count are all Passovers occurring after Alexander the Great led his army against Persia at the Battle of Granicus in 334 BCE, and before Israeli army paratroopers liberated the Temple Mount in 1967. The count is initiated with the Passover in 333 BCE, which is the first Passover that occurred after the Battle of Granicus. The count ends with the Passover that occurred in 1967. Each Passover in the table is denoted as "P#" (where "#" is its number in the count), followed by its corresponding Gregorian year. After the initial ten Passovers (P1 through P10), shown on the top line, Passovers are shown in ten-year increments, which allows you to count along on your fingers to verify the count. When you have completed verifying the count as demonstrated in the table, you will see that there are exactly 2,300 Passovers between the starting event of the vision, the Battle of Granicus specified in verse 6, and the concluding event of the vision, the restoration of the Temple Mount specified in verse 14, precisely the time span required for this interpretation to be an exact fulfillment of the chrono-specific prophecy set forth in verses 13-14. In addition, the dates for both the starting and ending events that are used for the count, namely, the Battle of Granicus and the liberation of the Temple Mount by Israel during the Six-Day War, between which

Table 1.1 continued from facing page (above)

P2010 - 1677 CE	P2020 - 1687 CE	P2030 - 1697 CE	P2040 - 1707 CE	P2050 - 1717 CE	P2060 - 1727 CE	P2070 - 1737 CE	P2080 - 1747 CE	P2090 - 1757 CE	P2100 - 1767 CE
P2110 - 1777 CE	P2120 - 1787 CE	P2130 - 1797 CE	P2140 - 1807 CE	P2150 - 1817 CE	P2160 - 1827 CE	P2170 - 1837 CE	P2180 - 1847 CE	P2190 - 1857 CE	P2200 - 1867 CE
P2210 - 1877 CE	P2220 - 1887 CE	P2230 - 1897 CE	P2240 - 1907 CE	P2250 - 1917 CE	P2260 - 1927 CE	P2270 - 1937 CE	P2280 - 1947 CE	P2290 - 1957 CE	P2300 - 1967 CE

Note that there was no year "0" (zero) when going from BCE to CE, so the count for the Passovers in the transition decade from 4 BCE to 7 CE is determined as follows: Passover number 330 in the count (P330 above) occurred in the year 4 BCE, P331 in 3 BCE, P332 in 2 BCE, P333 in 1 BCE, P334 in 1 CE, P335 in 2 CE, P336 in 3 CE, P337 in 4 CE, P338 in 5 CE, P339 in 6 CE, P340 in 7 CE.

Table 1.1 - How to Count the 2,300 Passovers

P1 - 333 BCE	P2 - 332 BCE	P3 - 331 BCE	P4 - 330 BCE	P5 - 329 BCE	P6 - 328 BCE	P7 - 327 BCE	P8 - 326 BCE	P9 - 325 BCE	P10 - 324 BCE
1-10 see above	P20 - 314 BCE	P30 - 304 BCE	P40 - 294 BCE	P50 - 284 BCE	P60 - 274 BCE	P70 - 264 BCE	P80 - 254 BCE	P90 - 244 BCE	P100 - 234 BCE
P110 - 224 BCE	P120 - 214 BCE	P130 - 204 BCE	P140 - 194 BCE	P150 - 184 BCE	P160 - 174 BCE	P170 - 164 BCE	P180 - 154 BCE	P190 - 144 BCE	P200 - 134 BCE
P210 - 124 BCE	P220 - 114 BCE	P230 - 104 BCE	P240 - 94 BCE	P250 - 84 BCE	P260 - 74 BCE	P270 - 64 BCE	P280 - 54 BCE	P290 - 44 BCE	P300 - 34 BCE
P310 - 24 BCE	P320 - 14 BCE	P330 - 4 BCE	P340 - 7 CE	P350 - 17 CE	P360 - 27 CE	P370 - 37 CE	P380 - 47 CE	P390 - 57 CE	P400 - 67 CE
P410 - 77 CE	P420 - 87 CE	P430 - 97 CE	P440 - 107 CE	P450 - 117 CE	P460 - 127 CE	P470 - 137 CE	P480 - 147 CE	P490 - 157 CE	P500 - 167 CE
P510 - 177 CE	P520 - 187 CE	P530 - 197 CE	P540 - 207 CE	P550 - 217 CE	P560 - 227 CE	P570 - 237 CE	P580 - 247 CE	P590 - 257 CE	P600 - 267 CE
P610 - 277 CE	P620 - 287 CE	P630 - 297 CE	P640 - 307 CE	P650 - 317 CE	P660 - 327 CE	P670 - 337 CE	P680 - 347 CE	P690 - 357 CE	P700 - 367 CE
P710 - 377 CE	P720 - 387 CE	P730 - 397 CE	P740 - 407 CE	P750 - 417 CE	P760 - 427 CE	P770 - 437 CE	P780 - 447 CE	P790 - 457 CE	P800 - 467 CE
P810 - 477 CE	P820 - 487 CE	P830 - 497 CE	P840 - 507 CE	P850 - 517 CE	P860 - 527 CE	P870 - 537 CE	P880 - 547 CE	P890 - 557 CE	P900 - 567 CE
P910 - 577 CE	P920 - 587 CE	P930 - 597 CE	P940 - 607 CE	P950 - 617 CE	P960 - 627 CE	P970 - 637 CE	P980 - 647 CE	P990 - 657 CE	P1000 - 667 CE
P1010 - 677 CE	P1020 - 687 CE	P1030 - 697 CE	P1040 - 707 CE	P1050 - 717 CE	P1060 - 727 CE	P1070 - 737 CE	P1080 - 747 CE	P1090 - 757 CE	P1100 - 767 CE
P1110 - 777 CE	P1120 - 787 CE	P1130 - 797 CE	P1140 - 807 CE	P1150 - 817 CE	P1160 - 827 CE	P1170 - 837 CE	P1180 - 847 CE	P1190 - 857 CE	P1200 - 867 CE
P1210 - 877 CE	P1220 - 887 CE	P1230 - 897 CE	P1240 - 907 CE	P1250 - 917 CE	P1260 - 927 CE	P1270 - 937 CE	P1280 - 947 CE	P1290 - 957 CE	P1300 - 967 CE
P1310 - 977 CE	P1320 - 987 CE	P1330 - 997 CE	P1340 - 1007 CE	P1350 - 1017 CE	P1360 - 1027 CE	P1370 - 1037 CE	P1380 - 1047 CE	P1390 - 1057 CE	P1400 - 1067 CE
P1410 - 1077 CE	P1420 - 1087 CE	P1430 - 1097 CE	P1440 - 1107 CE	P1450 - 1117 CE	P1460 - 1127 CE	P1470 - 1137 CE	P1480 - 1147 CE	P1490 - 1157 CE	P1500 - 1167 CE
P1510 - 1177 CE	P1520 - 1187 CE	P1530 - 1197 CE	P1540 - 1207 CE	P1550 - 1217 CE	P1560 - 1227 CE	P1570 - 1237 CE	P1580 - 1247 CE	P1590 - 1257 CE	P1600 - 1267 CE
P1610 - 1277 CE	P1620 - 1287 CE	P1630 - 1297 CE	P1640 - 1307 CE	P1650 - 1317 CE	P1660 - 1327 CE	P1670 - 1337 CE	P1680 - 1347 CE	P1690 - 1357 CE	P1700 - 1367 CE
P1710 - 1377 CE	P1720 - 1387 CE	P1730 - 1397 CE	P1740 - 1407 CE	P1750 - 1417 CE	P1760 - 1427 CE	P1770 - 1437 CE	P1780 - 1447 CE	P1790 - 1457 CE	P1800 - 1467 CE
P1810 - 1477 CE	P1820 - 1487 CE	P1830 - 1497 CE	P1840 - 1507 CE	P1850 - 1517 CE	P1860 - 1527 CE	P1870 - 1537 CE	P1880 - 1547 CE	P1890 - 1557 CE	P1900 - 1567 CE
P1910 - 1577 CE	P1920 - 1587 CE	P1930 - 1597 CE	P1940 - 1607 CE	P1950 - 1617 CE	P1960 - 1627 CE	P1970 - 1637 CE	P1980 - 1647 CE	P1990 - 1657 CE	P2000 - 1667 CE

Table 1.1 continued on facing page (below)

there must be a count of exactly 2,300 Passovers, can be verified in the historical record exactly as described in the Scriptures. This is a major improvement over the traditional interpretations mentioned earlier in this chapter, which always fail to identify either a starting event or an ending event that can be identified in recorded history and thus fail as legitimate interpretations of Daniel, chapter 8. The interpretation offered here, with a count of 2,300 Passovers occurring between the verified Battle of Granicus in late May-early June, 334 BCE, and the liberation of the Temple Mount on June 7, 1967, satisfies the textual constraints of Daniel, chapter 8, verses 13-14, exactly.

The exact correlation of Bible prophecy with recorded history (see insert of facing page) provides strong evidence for the reality of divine providence. However, most modern Bible scholars, including more than a few conservative scholars, have argued that the chrono-specific prophecies in the Book of Daniel claiming to foretell events that will happen in the future (from Daniel's viewpoint in the sixth century BCE) and later fulfilled exactly are nothing more than a record of events written down by anonymous scribes in the second century BCE, after those events had occurred. The reason for their attitude of skepticism is that they reject outright the concept of predictive prophecy, and, in many cases, they reject the concept of divine revelation of the Bible as well. The interpretation of Daniel, chapter 8, just explained shows the fallacy of that approach. The 1967 fulfillment of the predictive prophecy in verses 13-14, verses that even the most skeptical Bible scholar will have to agree were written down no later than the first or second century BCE (based on radiocarbon dating of the Dead Sea Scrolls), should settle the argument in favor of the reality of predictive prophecy once and for all, and that assumption underlies the remainder of this book.

Fulfillment in History

The chrono-specific predictive prophecy in Daniel, chapter 8, encompasses more than twenty-five-hundred years of Jewish history. Verse 6 starts things off by successfully predicting that the king of Greece (Alexander the Great) would defeat the king of Persia (Darius III) in battle. This prophecy was revealed more than two-hundred years before its fulfillment took place. In 334 BCE, after crossing the Hellespont from Greece to Asia, Alexander's disciplined foot soldiers and cavalry clashed with the forces of Darius III near the site of the ruins of Troy, in what history records as the Battle of Granicus because it took place

Historical events described in Daniel, chapter 8

559 BCE	— Achaemenid Empire begins with reign of Cyrus the Great.
551 BCE	— Daniel, chapter 8, is revealed to Daniel in the third year of the reign (coregency) of King Belshazzar. *(verse 1)*
539 BCE	— Cyrus the Great captures Babylon; Achaemenid Persian Empire expands for the next two-hundred years. *(verses 3, 4)*
336 BCE	— Darius III Codomannus becomes king of the Achaemenid Persian Empire *(verse 20)*, Alexander of Macedon becomes first king of a united Greece. *(verse 21)*
334 BCE	— (March 26) Passover is observed. (May/June) Battle of Granicus: Alexander the Great, king of united Greece, defeats the army of Darius III of Persia for the first time in battle at the Granicus River. *(verses 5, 6)*
333 BCE	— (April 14) Passover #1 in the count is observed. *(verse 14)* (November 5) Battle of Issus: Alexander the Great defeats the army of Darius III for the second time at the Issus River.
331 BCE	— (October 1) Battle of Gaugamela: Alexander the Great defeats the army of Darius III for the third and final time at Gaugamela.
175 BCE	— Antiochus IV Epiphanes becomes king of the Seleucid Empire, Hellenism made the official religion of Judea. *(verses 9, 23)*
167 BCE	— Antiochus IV Epiphanes bans Judaism, desecrates the Temple on December 13 by erecting altar to and statue of Zeus on the sacred altar, stops the daily sacrifices *(verses 10-12, 24, 25a)*; revolt led by the Maccabees begins as a result.
164 BCE	— (December 10) Judah Maccabee captures Jerusalem, rededicates the Temple and consecrates a new sacred altar, begins offering the daily sacrifices again.
163 BCE	— (January?) Antiochus IV Epiphanes dies. *(verse 25b)*
1967 CE	— (April 25) Passover #2,300 in the count is observed. *(verse 14)* (June 7) Israeli army paratroopers liberate the Temple Mount and restore it to Jewish sovereignty. *(verse 14)*

on the banks of the Granicus River. Alexander and his Greek army won a great victory over the numerically-superior Persian forces assembled by Darius III to oppose him, and they would go on to defeat the armies of Darius two more times, in the battle at the Issus River in 333 BCE and then in the climactic battle on the flat plains of Gaugamela in 331 BCE. The latter battle brought the Achaemenid Persian Empire to a close. From a biblical standpoint, though, the earlier Battle of Granicus in 334 BCE was the event in history that set into motion the conflict between Hellenism and Judaism that would profoundly shape the history of the Jewish people for many hundreds of years into the future.

The Battle of Granicus was the signal to begin the Passover count prescribed in Daniel, chapter 8, verse 14. As we now know, the count ended twenty-three hundred Passovers later, on April 25, 1967. The Six-Day War began soon after that 2,300th Passover was observed. In the morning hours of June 7, 1967, the third day of the war, soldiers from Israel Defense Forces (IDF) 55th Paratroopers Brigade were poised on the Mount of Olives, ready to fight their way through the Lion's Gate into the Old City of Jerusalem. Their commander was Colonel Mordechai "Motta" Gur, who exhorted his troops with these words: "Soon we will enter the city, the Old City of Jerusalem, about which countless generations of Jews have dreamed, to which all living Jews aspire. To our brigade has been granted the privilege of being the first to enter it ... Now, on, on to the gate!"[1] Within the hour, they had captured the walled Old City and liberated the sacred Temple Mount. Five days later, on June 12, the men of Brigade 55 assembled in parade formation atop the Temple Mount to commemorate their victory and remember their fallen comrades. They were again addressed by Colonel Gur, who told them, "You have been privileged to restore to the people of Israel their capital and their sanctuary."[2] As for Alexander the Great, there is no historical evidence that he understood the biblical importance of the Battle of Granicus or the role he played in Hebrew prophecy except Josephus' story of Alexander's visit to Jerusalem,[3] during which he was supposedly met as he entered the city by

---

[1] Mordechai Gur, *The Battle for Jerusalem* (New York, New York: Popular Library, 1974), p. 354.
[2] Amos Alon, *Jerusalem: City of Mirrors* (London, England: Flamingo, 1996), p. 91.
[3] From Josephus, *Antiquities*, 11:8:5 (Whiston): "When asked by one of his generals why he welcomed this group [the high priest and his entourage], Alexander replied: 'I did not adore him, but that God who hath honoured him with his high priesthood; for I saw this very person in a dream, in this very habit [garment], when I was at Dios in Macedonia, who, when I was considering with myself how I might obtain the dominion of Asia, exhorted me to make no delay, but boldly to pass over the sea thither, for that he would conduct my army, and would give me the dominion over the Persians; whence it is, that having seen no other in that habit, and now seeing this person in it, and remembering that vision, and the exhortation which I had in my dream, I believe that I bring this army under the divine conduct, and shall therewith conquer Darius [III], and destroy the power of the Persians, and that all things will succeed according to what is in my own mind.'"

the high priest and presented with the Book of Daniel, an account which most scholars believe to be based on a fable. Likewise, there is no historical evidence that Colonel "Motta" Gur and his troops recognized the exegetical significance of their heroic deeds during the Battle for Jerusalem in 1967. They obviously realized that what they had done was significant within the context of Jewish identity and Israeli history, but perhaps not that their actions were the literal fulfillment of a specific biblical prophecy. They were not alone, though, since no one else at the time recognized the prophetic significance of what had transpired by the return of Jerusalem's Old City and Temple Mount to Israeli sovereignty. Nevertheless, Gur and his men had carried out the fulfillment of the prophecy set forth in Daniel, chapter 8, verses 13-14, which foretold that the restoration of the Temple Mount to God's people Israel would take place as soon as the 2,300th Passover of the prophecy, the Passover of 1967, had occurred.

Restoration of the Sanctuary

So, now that the prophecy in Daniel, chapter 8, has been fulfilled exactly by the return of the Temple Mount to Jewish sovereignty in 1967, what are we to make of this restoration? In verse 14, the Hebrew word וְנִצְדַּק (BHS, Strong's OT: 6663), which I have been rendering as *"restored to its rightful state"* (ESV, CJB), has been translated in various ways. The King James translators rendered it as *"cleansed,"* whereas the JPS 1917 edition of the *Tanakh*[1] rendered it as *"shall be victorious."* Modern translations have been just as diverse: *"properly restored"* (NASB), *"restored to its rightful state"* (RSV), *"reconsecrated"* (NIV). The UBS Handbook says: "Then the sanctuary shall be restored to its rightful state, literally 'and the sanctuary will be justified.' ... Some take it to mean 'purified' or 'cleansed' (NJV). Others have the idea of rededication; NIV reads *'reconsecrated.'* Still others have a more general statement: *'then shall the wrongs of the sanctuary be righted'* (AT) or *' have its rights restored'* (NJB)." Taking all of these ideas into consideration, and viewing them in the context of the 1967 chronology dictated by the prophecy, it seems safe to assume that the word וְנִצְדַּק reflects a return of the Temple Mount to Jewish possession. Some have argued that the Temple Mount has, in reality, not been restored to Jewish ownership since, within days

---

[1] *Tanakh* (also Tanach) is the English name for the Jewish Bible, a name resulting from the acronym TNK formed by the initial letters of its three main sections, the Torah (Five Books of Moses), Neviim (Prophets), and Ketuvim (Writings).

Sovereignty over Jerusalem exercised by ...

Jebusites until 1,038 BCE	Latin Kingdom of Jerusalem: 1099-1187 CE
Kingdom of Israel: 1,038-961 BCE	Ayyubid Caliphate: 1187-1229 CE
Kingdom of Judah: 961-597 BCE	Sixth Crusaders-Moslems: 1229-1244 CE
Neo-Babylonian Empire: 597-539 BCE	Tatars-Egyptians-Ayyubids: 1244-1260 CE
Achaemenid Persian Empire: 539-333 BCE	Mongol Empire: April 1260 CE (disputed)
Empire of Alexander the Great: 333-312 BCE	Mamluk Sultinate: 1260-1517 CE
Ptolemaic Kingdom of Egypt: 312-198 BCE	Ottoman Empire: 1517-1625 CE
Seleucid Empire: 198-164 BCE	Mohammed ibn Faroukh: 1625-1627 CE
Hasmoneans-Kingdom of Israel: 164-63 BCE	Ottoman Empire: 1627-1703 CE
Roman Ethnarchy of Judea: 63-40 BCE	Naqib al-ashraf: 1703-1705 CE
Arsacid Parthian Empire: 40-37 BCE	Ottoman Empire: 1705-1825 CE
Roman Empire: 37 BCE-66 CE	Jerusalemite Moslems: 1825-1826 CE
Jewish rebels: 66-70 CE	Ottoman Empire: 1826-1831 CE
Roman-Byzantine Empire: 70 BCE-614 CE	Egyptians-Mohammed Ali: 1831-1840 CE
Sassanid Persian Empire: 614-628 CE	Ottoman Empire: 1840-1917 CE
Byzantine Empire: 628-638 CE	British Empire: 1917-1948 CE
Umayyard-Abbasid Caliphate: 638-973 CE	Hashemite Kingdom of Jordan: 1948-1967 CE
Fatimids-Seljuks-Arab Bedouins: 973-1099 CE	State of Israel: 1967 CE to present

Above list partially based on data from Jerusalem Besieged *by Eric H. Cline (U. of Mich. Press: Ann Arbor, 2004)*

after it was captured, the administration of the platform area by the Islamic Waqf was continued by Moshe Dayan, the Israeli Defense Minister at the time, and it remains so delegated today. The skeptics correctly point out that Jews (and Christians or persons of any faith other than Islam) still cannot pray openly there without risking rioting or worse by young Muslim hotheads. But, make no mistake about it, the Temple Mount is under the sole sovereignty of the State of Israel and has been since June 7, 1967. The government of Israel determines who has access, and when, and the Jewish people will determine its ultimate status. Judging from the turbulent history surrounding the Temple Mount since its liberation, it seems obvious to me that the restoration event that occurred on that June morning forty-plus years ago was but the beginning event in a progressive restoration that is unfolding daily before our eyes.

CHAPTER TWO

WHAT SHALL BE THE END OF THESE THINGS?

READ DANIEL 12:8-12 ON PAGE 234 | SEE TIME LINE ❷ ON PLATE 1

The liberation of the Temple Mount by Israel during the Six-Day War in 1967 was the fulfillment of the chrono-specific prophecy in Daniel, chapter 8. That event unsealed the prophecy and projected the efficacy of Bible prophecy into modern times. It also confirmed that the long-awaited "time of the end" had finally arrived in history. Understanding those developments was an important exegetical breakthrough for me, and a spiritual stimulus as well. Armed with my newfound understanding about the recent commencement of the time of the end, and infused with the knowledge gained by interpreting the chrono-specific prophecy in the eighth chapter, my attention turned to interpreting additional chrono-specific prophecies in the Book of Daniel. I was certain that they were all now unsealed and waiting to be fully interpreted. But, where to begin?

Without a clear answer to that question, I began a systematic study of the remaining chrono-specific prophecies in Daniel, looking for clues that would unlock more of them. Although I did not find the clues that I sought during this initial search,[1] over time I became intrigued by the chronological specificity and contextual ambiguity of the final chrono-specific prophecy in Daniel, the one at the end of the twelfth chapter, verses 8-12, that says: *"And I heard, but I understood not. Then said I, O my Lord, what shall be the end of these things? And he said, Go thy way, Daniel, for the words are closed up and sealed till the time of the end. Many shall be purified, and made white, and tried, but the wicked shall do wickedly, and none of the wicked shall understand, but the wise shall understand. And from the time that the daily sacrifice shall be taken away, and the abomination that maketh desolate set up, there shall be a thousand two hundred and ninety days. Blessed is he that waiteth, and cometh to the thousand three hundred and five and thirty days"* (KJV). Because this prophecy indicated that it was to be unsealed at the time of the end, and since I knew that the beginning of the time of the end had commenced, I decided to give it my full attention. I immersed

---

[1] This period of seeking through Bible study and prayer, though condensed in the narrative above, actually spanned more than a decade, and final understanding of the prophecy in Daniel, chapter 12, verses 8-12, came almost two decades after the initial breakthrough interpretation of Daniel, chapter 8, discussed in Chapter One of this book.

myself in the words of the prophecy, and in the text of the entire twelfth chapter for context, seeking insight through Bible study and prayer until I found the keys to its interpretation. Now, I am pleased to share those keys with you.

Keys to Interpretation

The first key to interpretation of the chrono-specific prophecy in Daniel, chapter 12, verses 8-12, is to identify a starting point for counting the time periods of 1,290 "days" and 1,335 "days" specified in verses 11-12. As I quickly discovered, identifying a starting point, an event mentioned in the biblical text and also associated with a date verifiable in history from which a count could begin, would not be as simple for this prophecy as it had been with the prophecy in the eighth chapter of Daniel. There the starting point (Alexander the Great of Greece moving against Darius III of Persia at Granicus) was obvious. From the text of the twelfth chapter, it was apparent that no such obvious starting point or ending point was anywhere mentioned. However, as I read and reread the text looking for clues, I realized that there were two chronological constraints provided in verses 8-9. The first time constraint was revealed by the question that was asked in verse 8, *"What shall be the end of these things?"* (KJV) or *"My lord, what will be the outcome of these events?"* (NASB). These verses made clear that the start of the time period specified in the prophecy had to occur after "these things," the events that had just been described in the preceding eleventh chapter, had occurred. The latest dated event that I could positively identify in the eleventh chapter was the desecration of the Temple by Antiochus IV described in verse 31, which took place in 167 BCE, so that gave me one end of a chronological bracket for determining the specified time span. The other chronological constraint was mentioned in verse 9, *"And he said, Go thy way, Daniel: for the words are closed up and sealed till the time of the end"* (KJV). This verse confirmed that the prophecy would not be understood until the time of the end, and this meant that the time period specified in the prophecy would not conclude until sometime during the time of the end. Otherwise, the prophecy would be understood ahead of time in history, and that was not possible. Together, these two chronological constraints meant that the 1,290 "days" and 1,335 "days" had to start after the time of the Temple desecration and end sometime during the time of the end, which I knew had recently commenced in history with the liberation of the Temple Mount. It was at this point that I had new insight. Since

Chapter Two: What Shall Be the End of These Things? (Daniel 12:8-12)

the time of the end was already underway, and since the time period specified in verses 11-12 had to conclude during the time of the end, the concluding event of the prophecy, if such an event could be identified and dated, could serve as the starting point for a backwards count. In other words, unlike the approach that I had used to interpret the prophecy in the eighth chapter of Daniel, where I found a starting event and then counted forward in time to reveal the meaning of the prophecy, interpreting this prophecy would instead be accomplished by counting backwards from its end point in time. Since the only end-time event in Daniel with which I could associate a specific date was the liberation of the Temple Mount by Israel on June 7, 1967—the concluding event that was key to the interpretation of the eighth chapter—I simply assumed that the Temple Mount liberation was the concluding event of the time period specified in verses 11-12 of the twelfth chapter as well, an assumption that proved to be correct. So, ironically, the starting point for doing a count turned out to be the end point of the prophecy in time, and the count of 1,290 "days" and 1,335 "days" would thus need to be done backwards to reveal the meaning of the prophecy.

The second key to interpretation of the prophecy is to understand the unit of time meant by the word "days" used in verses 11-12. The Hebrew word יָמִ֥ים (BHS, Strong's OT: 3117) is translated as "days" in the King James Version, and in most other versions of the Bible as well. It is almost always assumed to mean normal twenty-four-hour days by most expositors of Daniel, but that interpretation did not help to advance the interpretation as I tried to apply it to historical events. Since I had already assumed that the concluding event of the prophecy was the liberation of the Temple Mount by Israel on June 7, 1967, I quickly found that counting backwards either 1,290 or 1,335 literal days from that date yielded no significant event in the modern historical record as far as I could determine, so another interpretation of the word "days" was needed. Sensing that the term as used in this prophecy probably meant years in real time—an exegetically justifiable assumption since Daniel's contemporary in exile, the prophet Ezekiel, had established the day-for-a-year interpretive principle in Ezekiel, chapter 4, verses 5-6—I looked for a way in which "days" could be interpreted as marking the passage of years, and do so without such a substitution being specifically prescribed in Scripture as it was in Ezekiel. It was then that I recalled the substitution principle that I had discovered during the interpretation of chapter 8, in which the Passover night, cryptically denoted as an "evening-morning" in that prophecy, was used to mark the passage of years. However, the Hebrew words "evening-morning" עֶרֶב בֹּקֶר used as a substitute for the word Passover in that chapter were different from the Hebrew word יָמִים translated as "day" (literally from sunrise to sunset, or from one sunset to the next sunset) in verses 11-12, so I discounted the possibility that the word "days" in this prophecy was another way of saying Passovers. Still, the idea that the Passover had been referred to in such a cryptic manner in the eighth chapter made it reasonable to consider the possibility that this type of substitution, one using the time period associated with a festival of Israel instead of the name of the festival, was a pattern of encryption used by Daniel. As I studied the terminology used in the prophecies containing references to calendrical time periods, specifically those in the eighth, ninth, and twelfth chapters, I began to sense the pattern of encryption.[1] The terminology used in each of those chapters seemed to refer to a Jewish festival season, and each to one of the most important festivals, ones that were impossible for Israel to observe as specified in Scripture while in exile, separated from Jerusalem and without a Temple, as the prophet Daniel was. I already knew that the eighth chapter had used "evening-morning" to mean Passover. I suspected that the ninth chapter used "week" to mean Festival of Weeks (Pentecost). Carrying this association to its logical conclusion, the twelfth chapter would thus use "day" to refer to the Day of Atonement. In addition, the order of the encryption as arranged in Daniel reflected the order of those festivals in the Hebrew year: Passover in the first month; Pentecost (Festival of Weeks) in the third month; and the Day of Atonement in the seventh month. Chronologically, it all seemed to fit, so I felt confident in making the assumption that the 1,290 and 1,335 "days" in verses 11-12 actually meant 1,290 and 1,335 Day(s) of Atonement.

The third key to interpretation of the prophecy is to understand how to count the 1,290 and 1,335 Day(s) of Atonement that determine the time span stipulated in verses 11-12, specifically, to know when to begin and when to end the count. I had already decided that the starting point for doing the count had to be the concluding event of the prophecy, an end-time event which I assumed to be the liberation of the Temple Mount by Israel that happened on June 7, 1967. I also knew that it was generally agreed by most expositors that the 1,290 "days" time period was to be considered as part of the 1,335 "days." In other words, there were not two separate time periods, one of 1,290 "days" and a second of 1,335 "days," with no overlap, but only one time period extending forward in time for

---

[1] Previous military training in cryptography predisposed me to think in terms of encryption.

Chapter Two: *What Shall Be the End of These Things? (Daniel 12:8-12)*

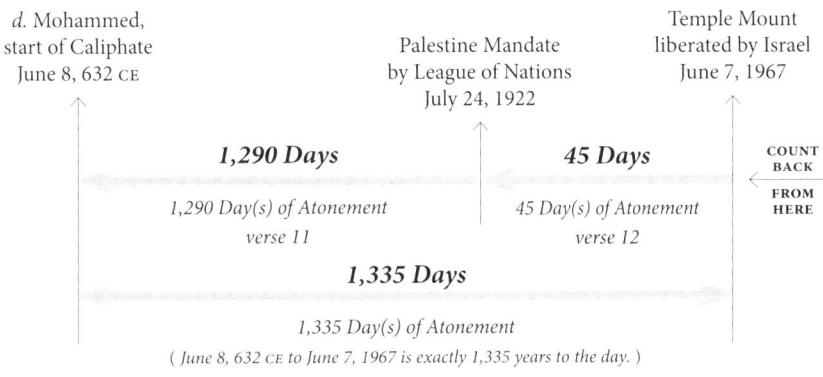

Diagram 2.1 - The 1,290 and 1,335 Days

1,290 "days," and then for forty-five additional "days," to make a total time period of 1,335 "days" in duration. So, taking all of these requirements into consideration, the count would need to be done in two stages, a first stage counting backwards for forty-five Day(s) of Atonement from the assumed concluding event of the prophecy—the 1967 liberation of the Temple Mount—to reveal an intermediate date somewhere back in history, and a second stage counting backwards from that revealed intermediate date an additional 1,290 Day(s) of Atonement to reveal a second date even further back in history. Since this backwards count had to begin with the last Day of Atonement observed before the liberation of the Temple Mount, the date for the Day of Atonement in the year 1967 had to be determined. By checking a Hebrew calendar, I easily determined that the Day of Atonement for that year was observed on October 14, four months after the Temple Mount liberation event, so the festival that year could not be the one used to initiate the count. Thus, the preceding Day of Atonement, the one observed on September 24, 1966, would be the initial Day of Atonement from which the backward count for the first stage would have to be initiated.

Table 2.1 (see page 29, top table) demonstrates how to count backwards for forty-five Day(s) of Atonement to reveal the intermediate time period that will help to unravel the meaning of the prophecy. The count is initiated with the Day of Atonement in the year 1966, which is the last Day of Atonement observed before the liberation of the Temple Mount on June 7, 1967. The backwards count of forty-five ends with the Day of Atonement that occurred in the year 1922. Each Day of Atonement in the table is denoted as "A#" (where "#" is its number in the count), followed by its corresponding Gregorian year. After the initial ten Day(s) of Atonement (A1 through A10), shown on the top line, Day(s) of Atonement are shown in ten-year increments, which allows you to count along on your fingers to verify the count. Table 2.2 (see page 29, bottom table) demonstrates how to continue the count backwards for another 1,290 Day(s) of Atonement to reach the total of 1,335 Day(s) of Atonement specified in the prophecy. It picks up the count with the Day of Atonement in the year 1921, and terminates it with the Day of Atonement in 632 CE. Elements in Table 2.2 are denoted in the same manner as those in Table 2.1. When you have completed verifying the counts for yourself, in both instances counting the specified number of Day(s) of Atonement backwards in time from the liberation of the Temple Mount by Israel on June 7, 1967, you will see that the forty-fifth Day of Atonement backwards from that date occurred in the year 1922, and the 1,335th Day of Atonement backwards from that date occurred in the year 632 CE. This means that three specific years in history are identifiable from the two counts and can be employed to interpret the prophecy in chapter 12, verses 8-12. The three years are the starting (earliest)year of the prophecy in history, 632 CE; an intermediate year, 1922; and the concluding year, 1967.

The significance of the most recent year in that sequence is already known, of course. 1967 is the year when modern Israel gained possession of the Temple Mount in Jerusalem, significant in Jewish history because it was the first time that a sovereign Jewish people living in *Eretz-Israel* had exercised control over that piece of real estate since the Bar Kochba revolt in 135 CE.[1] But, what is the significance of the other two years in Jewish history? And, some would ask, why look only at Jewish history? After all, many modern Bible scholars negate the eschatological importance of the Jews today, who they contend were once-chosen but are no longer the chosen people of God in post-biblical times. However, I do not hold such a view. It was obvious to me from the interpretation

---

[1] Historians debate whether Bar Kochba actually gained control of Jerusalem during the Second Jewish War. If not, then the last year of Jewish sovereignty over the Temple Mount occurred in 63 BCE, the year Pompey captured Jerusalem and placed it under Roman rule.

Table 2.1 - How to Count the 45 Days

A1 - 1966 CE	A2 - 1965 CE	A3 - 1964 CE	A4 - 1963 CE	A5 - 1962 CE	A6 - 1961 CE	A7 - 1960 CE	A8 - 1959 CE	A9 - 1958 CE	A10 - 1957 CE
A11 - 1956 CE	A12 - 1955 CE	A13 - 1954 CE	A14 - 1953 CE	A15 - 1952 CE	A16 - 1951 CE	A17 - 1950 CE	A18 - 1949 CE	A19 - 1948 CE	A20 - 1947 CE
A21 - 1946 CE	A22 - 1945 CE	A23 - 1944 CE	A24 - 1943 CE	A25 - 1942 CE	A26 - 1941 CE	A27 - 1940 CE	A28 - 1939 CE	A29 - 1938 CE	A30 - 1937 CE
A31 - 1936 CE	A32 - 1935 CE	A33 - 1934 CE	A34 - 1933 CE	A35 - 1932 CE	A36 - 1931 CE	A37 - 1930 CE	A38 - 1929 CE	A39 - 1928 CE	A40 - 1927 CE
A41 - 1926 CE	A42 - 1925 CE	A43 - 1924 CE	A44 - 1923 CE	A45 - 1922 CE	---	---	---	---	---

Table 2.2 - How to Count the 1,290 Days

A1 - 1921 CE	A2 - 1920 CE	A3 - 1919 CE	A4 - 1918 CE	A5 - 1917 CE	A6 - 1916 CE	A7 - 1915 CE	A8 - 1914 CE	A9 - 1913 CE	A10 - 1912 CE
1-10 see above	A20 - 1902 CE	A30 - 1892 CE	A40 - 1882 CE	A50 - 1872 CE	A60 - 1862 CE	A70 - 1852 CE	A80 - 1842 CE	A90 - 1833 CE	A100 - 1822 CE
A110 - 1812 CE	A120 - 1802 CE	A130 - 1792 CE	A140 - 1782 CE	A150 - 1772 CE	A160 - 1762 CE	A170 - 1752 CE	A180 - 1742 CE	A190 - 1732 CE	A200 - 1722 CE
A210 - 1712 CE	A220 - 1702 CE	A230 - 1692 CE	A240 - 1682 CE	A250 - 1672 CE	A260 - 1662 CE	A270 - 1652 CE	A280 - 1642 CE	A290 - 1632 CE	A300 - 1622 CE
A310 - 1612 CE	A320 - 1602 CE	A330 - 1592 CE	A340 - 1582 CE	A350 - 1572 CE	A360 - 1562 CE	A370 - 1552 CE	A380 - 1542 CE	A390 - 1532 CE	A400 - 1522 CE
A410 - 1512 CE	A420 - 1502 CE	A430 - 1492 CE	A440 - 1482 CE	A450 - 1472 CE	A460 - 1462 CE	A470 - 1452 CE	A480 - 1442 CE	A490 - 1432 CE	A500 - 1422 CE
A510 - 1412 CE	A520 - 1402 CE	A530 - 1392 CE	A540 - 1382 CE	A550 - 1372 CE	A560 - 1362 CE	A570 - 1352 CE	A580 - 1342 CE	A590 - 1332 CE	A600 - 1322 CE
A610 - 1312 CE	A620 - 1302 CE	A630 - 1292 CE	A640 - 1282 CE	A650 - 1272 CE	A660 - 1262 CE	A670 - 1252 CE	A680 - 1242 CE	A690 - 1232 CE	A700 - 1222 CE
A710 - 1212 CE	A720 - 1202 CE	A730 - 1192 CE	A740 - 1182 CE	A750 - 1172 CE	A760 - 1162 CE	A770 - 1152 CE	A780 - 1142 CE	A790 - 1132 CE	A800 - 1122 CE
A810 - 1112 CE	A820 - 1102 CE	A830 - 1092 CE	A840 - 1082 CE	A850 - 1072 CE	A860 - 1062 CE	A870 - 1052 CE	A880 - 1042 CE	A890 - 1032 CE	A900 - 1022 CE
A910 - 1012 CE	A920 - 1002 CE	A930 - 992 CE	A940 - 982 CE	A950 - 972 CE	A960 - 962 CE	A970 - 952 CE	A980 - 942 CE	A990 - 932 CE	A1000 - 922 CE
A1010 - 912 CE	A1020 - 902 CE	A1030 - 892 CE	A1040 - 882 CE	A1050 - 872 CE	A1060 - 862 CE	A1070 - 852 CE	A1080 - 842 CE	A1090 - 832 CE	A1100 - 822 CE
A1110 - 812 CE	A1120 - 802 CE	A1130 - 792 CE	A1140 - 782 CE	A1150 - 772 CE	A1160 - 762 CE	A1170 - 752 CE	A1180 - 742 CE	A1190 - 732 CE	A1200 - 722 CE
A1210 - 712 CE	A1220 - 702 CE	A1230 - 692 CE	A1240 - 682 CE	A1250 - 672 CE	A1260 - 662 CE	A1270 - 652 CE	A1280 - 642 CE	A1290 - 632 CE	---

of the chrono-specific prophecy in Daniel, chapter 8, after it had been unsealed by events that took place in Jerusalem in 1967, that the Book of Daniel is primarily concerned with the destiny of God's people Israel, and that its primary message concerns the status of the Jewish people with respect to *Eretz-Israel*, Jerusalem, and the Temple Mount (sanctuary) area. Thus, I focused exclusively on Jewish history to find the prophetic meaning for the years 632 CE and 1922.

Fulfillment in History

The events of Jewish history, those occurring both in the land and in the *Diaspora*, are fairly well-documented for the periods around the years 1922 and 632 CE, each revealed by the count as hosting a significant event in Jewish history. I knew that the end points of the time span that held the significant event of 1922 could be determined by calculating the dates for the last Day of Atonement in the backwards count of forty-five "days" and the first Day of Atonement in the resumed count of 1,290 "days." In other words, the event of major significance in Jewish history had to occur between October 12, 1921, and October 2, 1922. When I checked the historical records for that time frame, I found several events that were historically significant, and some were of major significance in Jewish history. All throughout 1921 and 1922, Adolf Hitler, after having become chairman of the National Socialist German Workers' (Nazi) Party on July 28, 1921, was having his first success at rallying the German people behind his message of virulent anti-Semitism, first publicly enunciated in a speech before a meeting of 50,000 Germans assembled at Königsplatz in Munich on the following August 16. In Italy, Hitler's ally in WWII, Benito Mussolini, became the youngest premier in the history of Italy on October 31. In Russia, Hitler's ally and later nemesis in WWII, Josef Stalin, was appointed General Secretary of the Communist Party on April 3. Of more pertinence to the destiny of the Jewish people, and to the prophecy under consideration in this chapter, the British White Paper of 1922, also known as the Churchill White Paper because Winston Churchill was the Colonial Secretary at the time, was published on June 3. It clarified how Britain viewed the idea of a Jewish homeland in Palestine, an idea that had been raised in world political circles for the first time by the Balfour Declaration of 1917. The White Paper separated the lands east of the Jordan River from Palestine and established the territory of Trans-Jordan, which later became the Hashemite Kingdom of Jordan from which Israel liberated Jerusalem and the Temple Mount in 1967. However, these important events paled in comparison to the momentous event that took place two months after the issuance of the White Paper.

On July 24, 1922, the League of Nations ratified the Palestine Mandate. That act, by which the nations of the world gave official status to "the establishment in Palestine of a national home for the Jewish people" (a quote from the preamble to "The Palestine Mandate" on page 210), was the intermediate event identified by the prophecy. Its importance cannot be overemphasized. For the first time since the Jews had been sent into exile among the nations by the Romans, a political process was set in motion that would eventually result in the rebirth of Israel as a sovereign nation in *Eretz-Israel* on May 14, 1948. Still, Jewish sovereignty over Jerusalem and the Temple Mount was not recognized in the Mandate of 1922. It would be another forty-five years before both the walled Old City and the Temple Mount would be back under Jewish sovereignty, something that was foreseen by the prophecy in chapter 12, verse 12, which says: *"Blessed is he that waiteth, and cometh to the thousand three hundred and five and thirty days"* (KJV).

The second time period specified by the prophecy, the one associated with the year 632 CE, was easy to determine. It could be identified by finding the dates for the Day of Atonement in the year 632 CE and the previous Day of Atonement in the year 631 CE. In other words, the significant event in Jewish history that marked the beginning of the prophecy would be found somewhere between September 11, 631 CE and September 30, 632 CE. A reading of historical records showed that the prior decades had been tumultuous ones in Jewish history. The Sassanid Persian Empire under Chosroes II was experiencing a period of rapid expansion, capturing Anatolia (now Turkey) and Syria from the Byzantine Empire. In 614 CE, as a prelude to their push into Egypt, the Sassanid Persians had wrested Judea and Jerusalem from Byzantine control. The Jews, who had been treated quite harshly under Byzantine rule for hundreds of years, had joined forces with the invading Sassanid Persian king, Chosroes, who they considered a "second Cyrus" after he appointed Nehemiah ben Hushiel, son of the Exilarch[1] in Babylon, to lead the Persian army into Palestine. After the conquest, Chosroes allowed the Jews living in Jerusalem to set up a semi-autonomous government with ben Hushiel as the governor. A council of Jewish elders was appointed to run daily civil and religious affairs, and preparations

---

[1] Exilarch ("Head of the Exile") was the title of the leader of the large Babylonian Jewish community living under the rule of the Sassanid Persian Empire.

were begun for rebuilding the Temple and consecrating a Levitical priesthood. However, before any serious rebuilding could begin, ben Hushiel was killed by a mob of Christian youths seeking retribution for perceived atrocities committed against Christian holy places by Jews. After ben Hushiel's murder, the Persians did an about-face and installed a Christian governor in Jerusalem as a way of placating the Byzantine majority in the city. Thereafter, Jewish access to the city of Jerusalem was seriously curtailed. In 628 CE, the Byzantine emperor Heraclius invaded Judea and recaptured Jerusalem from the Sassanids. As punishment for their siding with the Persians, Jews were banished from entering the city of Jerusalem on pain of death.

Gradually, all of this back-and-forth decades-long warfare between the Byzantine Empire and Sassanid Persia exhausted and permanently weakened both sides, setting the stage for an event in the year 632 CE that would thereafter be of major significance to the destiny of the Jewish people, and to the future status of Jerusalem and the Temple Mount as well. On June 8, 632 CE, the self-proclaimed prophet and founder of Islam Mohammed died in Arabia. His death was the event that marked the starting point of the prophecy about the 1,290 and 1,335 "days." It was important from a prophetic standpoint, not because of the man himself but because his death signaled the beginning of the Caliphate and the start of Muslim military and religious expansion out of Arabia that changed Jewish history forever. Six years after Mohammed's death, in the year 638 CE, Muslim forces conquered the city of Jerusalem from the Byzantine Empire. This event initiated a period of non-Jewish sovereignty over the city of Jerusalem and the Temple Mount that would endure for 1,329 years, until 1967 when Israeli troops restored Jewish sovereignty over *Eretz-Israel*, the walled Old City of Jerusalem, and the Temple Mount platform during the Six-Day War (see "Sovereignty over Jerusalem exercised by ..." on page 22). Especially interesting from the standpoint of prophetic specificity, the time span from the beginning of the Muslim Caliphate, which can date its beginning from the death of Mohammed on June 8, 632 CE, until the liberation of the Temple Mount by Israeli paratroopers on June 7, 1967, is precisely 1,335 years to the very day, an exact fulfillment of the chronological requirements specified by the prophecy recorded in Daniel, chapter 12, verses 8-12.

CHAPTER THREE

FOR A SEASON AND TIME

READ DANIEL 12:5-7 ON PAGE 234 | SEE TIME LINE ❸ ON PLATE 1

The exegetical knowledge gained from correctly interpreting the prophecy in Daniel, chapter 8, namely, understanding the eschatological importance of the liberation of the Temple Mount by Israel in 1967 and discovering the use of a Jewish festival (Passover) to mark the passage of years in ancient Israel, was the key needed for interpreting the chrono-specific prophecy in the twelfth chapter. In turn, the knowledge gained from the twelfth chapter, from which I learned that Day(s) of Atonement instead of Passovers were used to mark the passage of years, revealed even more clues about how to decipher the chronology embedded throughout the Book of Daniel. Equally important to me as an expositor, I now had confirmation that the process of progressive understanding was underway. This came as no surprise, though. From the start of my quest to interpret the prophecies in Daniel, I had accepted as fact that God would reward anyone who was diligently seeking to know the interpretations now that the prophecies were unsealed. So, counting on progressive understanding to help me, I reasoned that the next step would involve taking the knowledge gained from interpreting the prophecies in the eighth and twelfth chapters and using it as a key to unlock an additional prophecy, or possibly several additional prophecies.

It was at this point, realizing that I had two chronological pieces of a larger chronology, that I began using line drawings on a time-line chart to help me visualize how the prophecies related to one another.[1] This visual representation of chronological information was immediately helpful inasmuch as it showed me where to focus my next search for new interpretive insights. The eighth chapter had produced a time line that stretched from the Battle of Granicus in 334 BCE to the liberation of the Temple Mount in 1967. The time line for the twelfth chapter had started with the liberation of the Temple Mount in 1967 and then proceeded back to the start of the Muslim Caliphate after the death of Mohammed in 632 CE. In previous studies of related chronological references mentioned in the Book of Ezekiel, chapter 4, I had identified a 430-year-long time line that stretched from 597 BCE to 167 BCE, the latter being the year that Antiochus IV Epiphanes

---

[1] The end result was the "Prophecy Overview" chart on PLATE 1 at the end of this book.

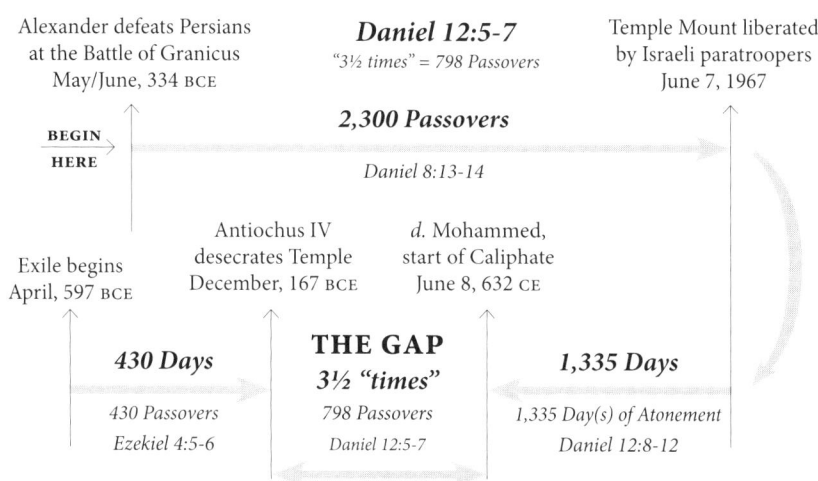

Diagram 3.1 - The Gap in the Chronology

desecrated the Temple in Jerusalem.[1] The importance of the Temple desecration event in Jewish history is emphasized by Daniel on two occasions, once in the eighth chapter, verse 11, *"Yea, he magnified himself even to the prince of the host, and by him the daily sacrifice was taken away, and the place of his sanctuary was cast down"* (KJV) and again in the eleventh chapter, verse 31, *"And arms shall stand on his part, and they shall pollute the sanctuary of strength, and shall take away the daily sacrifice, and they shall place the abomination that maketh desolate"* (KJV). Since the desecration plays such an important role in Daniel's eschatology, and knowing that Daniel and Ezekiel had complementary messages for their Jewish brethren in Babylon during the exile,[2] I felt comfortable adding the chronological information from Ezekiel to my diagram of time lines from Daniel. Once I had drawn parallel time lines for the chronologies given in the eighth and twelfth chapters, and added the time line from Ezekiel 4, I could see that there was a gap in the overall chronology (see Diagram 3.1 above). Thus, prophecy by prophecy, the chronology of Jewish history described in the prophecies of the Bible was beginning to take shape. Based on the chronological information gained from my interpretations of the chrono-specific prophecies

---

[1] See *Appendix Four: Chronology in the Book of Ezekiel* on p.143.
[2] Ezekiel possibly mentions Daniel by name (see Ezek. 14:14, 20), but whether they met or corresponded is open to speculation. Both were exiled to Babylon by Nebuchadnezzar.

Chapter Three: For A Season and Time (Daniel 12:5-7)

in Daniel, chapters 8 and 12, together with that from Ezekiel, chapter 4, I could trace a time line from 597 BCE to 167 BCE on my diagram, another from 334 BCE forward to 1967 in the modern era, and then another back from 1967 to the year 632 CE. However, that left an obvious gap in the chronology that stretched from 167 BCE to 632 CE, a time span of 798 years, and that intrigued me. I knew at once that the gap was where I needed to focus my attention. But, was the gap specified anywhere in the chrono-specific prophecies in Daniel?

Keys to Interpretation

The first key to interpretation of the prophecy about the gap is to realize that the gap itself is an interpretation, at least in chronological terms. The expository challenge thus becomes one of identifying the chrono-specific prophecy for which the gap is the exact interpretation. Obviously, it has to be a portion of Scripture that sets forth the 798-year (798-Passover) time period that is defined by the gap, but such a reference in Daniel was not obvious to me at first. As far as I could tell, there was no mention of such a time span in that book, so I expanded my search to include the text of the entire Bible, perusing it over and over again, seeking a clue that would point me in the right direction. After searching through every book of the Bible with not even a hint of success, my attention became focused once again on the place where I had most recently interpreted a chrono-specific prophecy, the twelfth chapter of Daniel.

As I resumed studying and meditating on the words of Daniel, chapter 12, I noticed that the gap on my line drawing (Diagram 3.1) was located immediately before the start of the 1,335 Day(s) of Atonement that were described in chapter 12, verses 8-12. It was at this point that I had a new insight that eventually led to the identification of the prophecy associated with the gap. I realized that the prophecy about *"a time, times, and an half"* (KJV) in verses 5-7, which comes in the text immediately before the prophecy in verses 8-12 specifying the 1,335 "days" time period, might be the prophecy that describes the gap located in the same position on my line drawing. Instead of running concurrently, I reasoned that the time periods described in verses 5-7 and verses 8-12 must run sequentially in real time, just as the gap and the 1,335 Day(s) of Atonement were depicted sequentially on my line drawing. This was a breakthrough. For the first time, I felt confident that the 798 years on my line drawing might be the same as the prophecy about *"a time, times, and an half"* in verses 5-7 of the twelfth

– 35 –

chapter of Daniel. Before exploring this reasoning further, I knew that I needed to verify that there were exactly 798 Passovers between the desecration of the Temple by Antiochus IV in 167 BCE, the starting point of the gap, and the death of Mohammed in 632 CE, the end point of the gap. I did so by counting the Passovers that occurred between those two events, and you can, too. Table 3.1 (on the opposite page) demonstrates how to count the 798 Passovers. The count is initiated with the Passover of 166 BCE, the first Passover after the desecration of the Temple as specified in verse 11a: *"And from the time that the daily sacrifice shall be taken away, and the abomination that maketh desolate set up ..."* (KJV). The count ends with the Passover of 632 CE, the last Passover that was observed before the death of Mohammed and beginning of the Caliphate on June 8, 632 CE, which occurred during the period when the Temple Mount was laying desolate under a layer of Byzantine garbage and excrement, an "abomination that maketh desolate" (see page 93 for a more complete discussion of the term "abomination" as used in Daniel). Each Passover in the table is denoted as "P#" (where "#" is its number in the count), followed by the corresponding Gregorian year. After the initial ten Passovers (P1 through P10), Passovers are shown in ten-year increments, which allows you to count along on your fingers to verify the count.

The second key to interpretation of the prophecy, now that the chrono-specific prophecy being interpreted has been identified as the one in chapter 12, verses 5-7, is to calculate the duration of the time period called a "time" by Daniel in his prophecy. Since most Bible expositors agree that the phrase translated as *"a time, times, and an half"* (KJV) means three and a half units of something called a "time," and since the time span denoted by the phrase *"a time, times, and an half"* is assumed for our purposes here to be the 798-year gap shown on the line drawing on page 34, a simple calculation reveals the following definition: A "time" is 798 years divided by 3½, which equals 228 years or, stated in the ancient Hebrew way of marking the passage of the years, a "time" is 228 Passovers. Of course, the definition in and of itself is nothing more than the result of a simple calculation. Some years ago, after I had initially calculated the definition for a "time," I knew then that a more Scripture-based explanation was needed, one showing that a "time" defined as 228 Passovers was a useful chronological marker employed by the Jewish people for religious purposes in accordance with Mosaic Law. So, I set about searching for such an explanation and found one that makes sense when considered in the context of the need for accurate time-keeping associated with ancient Jewish religious observances.

Chapter Three: For A Season and Time (Daniel 12:5-7)

Table 3.1 - How to Count the 798 Passovers

P1 - 166 BCE	P2 - 165 BCE	P3 - 164 BCE	P4 - 163 BCE	P5 - 162 BCE	P6 - 161 BCE	P7 - 160 BCE	P8 - 159 BCE	P9 - 158 BCE	P10 - 157 BCE
1-10 see above	P20 - 147 BCE	P30 - 137 BCE	P40 - 127 BCE	P50 - 117 BCE	P60 - 107 BCE	P70 - 97 BCE	P80 - 87 BCE	P90 - 77 BCE	P100 - 67 BCE
P110 - 57 BCE	P120 - 47 BCE	P130 - 37 BCE	P140 - 27 BCE	P150 - 17 BCE	P160 - 7 BCE	P170 - 4 CE	P180 - 14 CE	P190 - 24 CE	P200 - 34 CE
P210 - 44 CE	P220 - 54 CE	P230 - 64 CE	P240 - 74 CE	P250 - 84 CE	P260 - 94 CE	P270 - 104 CE	P280 - 114 CE	P290 - 124 CE	P300 - 134 CE
P310 - 144 CE	P320 - 154 CE	P330 - 164 CE	P340 - 174 CE	P350 - 184 CE	P360 - 194 CE	P370 - 204 CE	P380 - 214 CE	P390 - 224 CE	P400 - 234 CE
P410 - 244 CE	P420 - 254 CE	P430 - 264 CE	P440 - 274 CE	P450 - 284 CE	P460 - 294 CE	P470 - 304 CE	P480 - 314 CE	P490 - 324 CE	P500 - 334 CE
P510 - 344 CE	P520 - 354 CE	P530 - 364 CE	P540 - 374 CE	P550 - 384 CE	P560 - 394 CE	P570 - 404 CE	P580 - 414 CE	P590 - 424 CE	P600 - 434 CE
P610 - 444 CE	P620 - 454 CE	P630 - 464 CE	P640 - 474 CE	P650 - 484 CE	P660 - 494 CE	P670 - 504 CE	P680 - 514 CE	P690 - 524 CE	P700 - 534 CE
P710 - 544 CE	P720 - 554 CE	P730 - 564 CE	P740 - 574 CE	P750 - 584 CE	P760 - 594 CE	P770 - 604 CE	P780 - 614 CE	P790 - 624 CE	P791 see below
P791 - 625 CE	P792 - 626 CE	P793 - 627 CE	P794 - 628 CE	P795 - 629 CE	P796 - 630 CE	P797 - 631 CE	P798 - 632 CE	---	---

Note that there was no year "0" (zero) when going from BCE to CE, so the count for the Passovers in the transition decade from 7 BCE to 4 CE is determined as follows: Passover number 160 in the count (P160 above) occurred in the year 7 BCE, P161 in 6 BCE, P162 in 5 BCE, P163 in 4 BCE, P164 in 3 BCE, P165 in 2 BCE, P166 in 1 BCE, P167 in 1 CE, P168 in 2 CE, P169 in 3 CE, P170 in 4 CE.

Defining a Time and a Season

To understand the complete chronology recorded in Daniel, it is necessary to know the meaning of the word "time" מוֹעֵד (BHS, Strong's OT: 4150) as used by Daniel in his prophecies. To do so, it is necessary to consider the historical context in which he wrote. In the text of Daniel, we are told that he was living in exile in Babylon during the sixth century BCE, and for most of that time serving the king as chief of the governors, with authority over the wise men of Babylon, including the court astrologers and magicians who were the scientists of the day. As chief governor of the wise men, Daniel would have been well-versed in the sciences, especially mathematics and astronomy. The most important discipline in ancient times was astronomy, primarily because it was used to keep track of the reigns of kings and to predict the seasons, of which accurate knowledge was critical for the survival and well-being of the agriculture-based societies of that age. On a spiritual level, the times and seasons, which were directly related to the movement of the heavens, were considered by Daniel as expressions of the power of God in human affairs. Daniel himself stressed this connection when he said in Daniel, chapter 2, verses 20-21: *"Blessed be the name of God for ever and ever ... he changeth the times and the seasons: he removeth kings, and setteth up kings"* (KJV). So, considering the milieu in which Daniel lived, it is not surprising to find that Babylonian astronomy, which was fairly advanced even by the standards of today, plays an important role in the prophecies of Daniel.

In *Eretz-Israel* prior to the exile, the Jewish calendar had twelve months, with each month being 29 or 30 days in length, resulting in a Jewish year that was 354 days in length. The Bible established that a new month began when the crescent of the new moon was observed. No special instruments were needed. The appearance of the new moon could be determined visually by priests trained to do so. In addition, the Passover was designated to take place on the fourteenth day of the "first month" once the people had entered the promised land, although there is no mention of a special "new year" day in the Bible. Neither are there any instructions given about how to reconcile the 354-day lunar year with the longer 365¼-day solar year, although it can be assumed that some method of intercalation (adjustment to prevent calendar creep) was used since Passover had to coincide with the ripening of barley, which always happened in early spring in Israel. If no intercalation had been done, Passover would have come eleven days earlier each year, eventually cycling through summer, then fall, then

Chapter Three: For A Season and Time (Daniel 12:5-7)

winter, and then back again to spring as the eleven-day error added up over the centuries. Even with our limited knowledge of the pre-exilic Jewish calendar, we know for certain that did not happen. Passover was always observed in the spring in ancient Israel, proving that intercalation of some sort did take place.

During the exile, the Jews adopted the Babylonian lunisolar calendar. Like the Hebrew calendar, it had twelve months of either 29 or 30 days, but it also had a new feature, a leap month which was added to certain years on a fixed schedule to make sure that the seasons always occurred at the proper time in terms of climate, thus avoiding a drift through the seasons. Records show that "Babylonian astronomers, often called Chaldaeans, gradually developed rules to create the nearly perfect calendar. The key was the discovery, in the mid-eighth century BCE, that 235 lunar months are almost identical to 19 solar years. The difference is only about two hours. The Chaldaeans concluded that seven out of nineteen years ought to be leap years with an extra month. [After this discovery], intercalary months were still announced by the king, but he was advised by an astronomer. After Babylon had been captured by the Persian king Cyrus the Great in 539 [BCE], priestly officials took over. The Chaldaeans now started to look for a standard procedure for the intercalation of months. It was introduced in 503 BCE by Darius I the Great if not earlier."[1] The important thing to note in the excerpt just quoted is the reference to the 19-year cycle, in which 235 lunar months equal 228 solar months (19 solar years). There is ample evidence that the 19-year cycle was used in the Babylonian calendar at least as early as the time of Daniel's exile. It is also important to note that the 19-year cycle is not exact, since 235 lunar months are almost, but not quite, identical in length to 19 solar years, the difference being about two hours and 5 minutes for every 19-year cycle. So, in order to keep a calendar based on this system in near-perfect synchronization, one 24-hour day (2 hours x 12 cycles) has to be subtracted at the conclusion of each twelfth 19-year cycle, or, putting it in its most simple terms, one day must be subtracted at the end of every 228 years to ensure that the Passover occurs at the same time of the year over the centuries.[2] It is this 228-year span of time, an

---

[1] Jona Lendering, "The Babylonian Calendar" (from the *Livius* website: www.livius.org).
[2] More precise calendar adjustments can be calculated today (the next increment of correction would yield an accuracy of less than half an hour of error in 5,472 years), but making such adjustments would have been impossible for ancient astronomers without the precision of modern optical instrumentation and timepieces. The 228-year one-day adjustment is the last that could have been easily accomplished by using observations made only with the naked eye.

astronomical unit that Daniel most likely learned from the Babylonians (or possibly from the angel who delivered the prophecies, and then Daniel told the Babylonians), that defines the word "time" as used in chapter 12, verses 5-7. The 228-year time span fits exactly when applied to the prophecy about *"a time, times, and an half"* (KJV) specified by verses 5-7, and that is sufficient confirmation of the earlier calculation based on "the gap" in the chronology, which was derived from reasoning alone. Accordingly, for use in interpreting the chrono-specific prophecies in Daniel, a "time" can now be defined with confidence as 228 years, or, stated in the ancient Hebrew way of marking the passage of the years, 228 Passovers, a span of time that equals the twelve 19-year cycles required to keep the Jewish festivals aligned with their associated agricultural harvests.

Since the above definition of a "time" will be used in the next chapter to explain additional chrono-specific prophecies, it is appropriate at this point to explain the meaning of the word "season" זְמַן (BHS, Strong's OT: 2166, 2165), which is also used by Daniel as a chronological term together with the word "time," as in chapter 7, verse 12: *"a season and time"* (KJV). The Aramaic word translated as "season" in Daniel's seventh chapter is the same Hebrew word rendered as "appointed time" in the Book of Esther, where it is referring to Purim, a Jewish festival. The festival of Purim was instituted after the lifetime of Daniel, so the word "season" as used by Daniel must be referring to another festival. The most obvious alternative is Passover, the festival that Daniel uses chronologically as a marker in most of his other chrono-specific prophecies unless he specifies otherwise, as he does in the ninth and twelfth chapters. In addition, Passover is referred to as a "season" numerous times in the Bible, as in Numbers, chapter 9, verses 2-3: *"Let the children of Israel also keep the passover at his appointed season. In the fourteenth day of this month, at even, ye shall keep it in his appointed season: according to all the rites of it, and according to all the ceremonies thereof, shall ye keep it"* (KJV). So, the word "season," when used as a chronological marker by Daniel, means a single Passover.

Admittedly, the definitions for "time" and "season" developed above have no spiritual meaning in and of themselves, but they do have interpretive value insomuch as they can be used to understand chrono-specific prophecies and correlate the resulting interpretations with history, as has been demonstrated in this section with the interpretation of the prophecy in chapter 12, verses 5-7. The definitions will be used again in the next chapter of this book to interpret and understand the chronological references in Daniel, chapter 7.

CHAPTER FOUR

THAT WHICH SHALL NOT BE DESTROYED

READ DANIEL 7:1-28 ON PAGE 225 | SEE TIME LINES ❹ AND ❺ ON PLATE 1

The seventh chapter is the most chronologically complex chapter in the Book of Daniel, sweeping across eleven centuries with a three-pronged series of events relating to the status of God's people Israel as they lived in subjugation to the surrounding nations and empires. It begins with the Jews under the reign of Cyrus the Great, then progresses through the reigns of his successors in the Achaemenid Persian Empire, then through the empires and kingdoms of Alexander the Great, the Seleucid Greeks, the Hasmoneans, the Romans, the Byzantines (twice), and the Sassanid Persians, ending with the Muslim capture of Jerusalem. Over the years, many expositors have focused on the empires that populate the narrative of this chapter, and have thus interpreted its main purpose as revealing God's plan for the nations, but such an interpretation is missing the point. The non-Jewish empires are only incidentally important inasmuch as they provide context for understanding the travails of the Jews under their domination. The real focus is always on the relationship of the Jewish nation and people with Jerusalem and the Temple, and, ultimately, with God's divine plan for bringing redemption to mankind through Israel. It is this plan for universal redemption that underlies the exposition of Daniel, chapter 7, that is set forth in this chapter.

The seventh chapter of Daniel can be divided into three distinct parts. The first part is comprised of verses 1-12. Those verses record a prophetic vision of future events affecting the Jewish people as seen by Daniel in 553 BCE.[1] The vision starts with the four winds of heaven striving upon the great sea, with four beasts, each diverse from the other, rising out of the sea. The first beast appears as a lion with eagle's wings. Daniel watches as the wings are plucked off and the beast is lifted up and made to stand upon feet like a man, and a man's heart is given to it. The second beast is like a bear raised up on one side, with three ribs between its teeth, and it is told to arise and devour much flesh. The third beast is like a leopard with four wings on its back and four heads, and dominion is given to it. The fourth beast is

---

[1] Dates of Daniel's visions: chapter 7 corresponds to the first year of Belshazzar, *ca.* 553 BCE (Dan. 7:1); chapter 8 to the third year of Belshazzar, *ca.* 551 BCE (Dan. 8:1); chapter 9 to the first year of Darius the Mede, son of Ahasuerus, *ca.* 538 BCE (Dan. 9:1); chapters 10-12 to the third year of Cyrus the Great of Persia, *ca.* 536 BCE (Dan. 10:1).

perceived as dreadful and terrible and exceedingly strong, and it has great iron teeth with which it devours and breaks into pieces and stamps the residue with its feet. It is different from the other beasts, and it has ten horns. After this, a little horn arises and plucks up three horns by the roots, and this horn has the eyes of a man and a mouth speaking great things. Then thrones are cast down and the Ancient of Days sits, with multitudes ministering to him, and the court sits in judgement, and the books are opened. At the same time, the little horn is saying great words while the body of the beast is destroyed and burned. The other beasts have their dominion taken away, but their lives are prolonged for a season and time. The second part is a parenthesis comprised of verses 13-14, and involves a son of man coming with the clouds of heaven, to be brought before the Ancient of Days, where he is given an everlasting dominion, glory, and a kingdom, so that all nations and peoples should serve him. Daniel is told that this kingdom shall not be destroyed. The third part is comprised of verses 15-28, and it provides a partial interpretation of verses 1-12 in the first part.

In his vision, Daniel sees himself approach an angel standing nearby and, greatly grieved in his spirit and troubled in his thoughts, asks to know the truth of the things that he is seeing. He is told that the four beasts are four kings that will rise out of the earth, but that the kingdom will be taken by the saints of the Most High and they will possess it for ever and ever. Daniel asks for clarification about the fourth beast, and wants to know more about the actions of the fourth beast. He also wants to know more about the ten horns on the head of the beast and the horn that comes up after them by which three horns are broken, and he wants to know about the horn with a mouth. To Daniel, this horn speaking great things seemed greater than the others and waged war against and prevailed over the saints of the Most High until the Ancient of Days came and gave the judgement to the saints. Then, Daniel saw a future time when the saints possessed the kingdom forever. Daniel is then told that the fourth beast will be an earthly kingdom, different from all the other kingdoms, and that it shall devour the whole earth, and shall tread it down, and break it into pieces. Furthermore, ten kings will arise from this kingdom, and another king will arise after them, and he will be different from the ten kings, and he will subdue three kings, then speak great words against the Most High, wear out the saints, and think to change times and laws. After this, they will be given into his hand for a time, times, and the dividing of time. But, the judgement will sit, and his dominion will be taken away, to be consumed and destroyed to the end. Then

Chapter Four: That Which Shall Not Be Destroyed (Daniel 7:1-28)

the kingdom and dominion, and the greatness of the kingdom under the whole heaven, shall be given to the people of the saints of the Most High, whose kingdom is an everlasting kingdom, and all dominions shall serve and obey him. With this climactic promise, the events of the vision come to an end.

Keys to Interpretation

The first key to interpretation of the prophecy in Daniel, chapter 7, is to notice that it is composed of three time-defined parts, each with a story that is distinct from the other two parts. In verses 1-12, the first time-defined part tells a story that stretches in duration from the rise of the first kingdom to the conclusion of a time period defined by the phrase *"season and time"* in verse 12. In verses 13-14, the second time-defined part begins with the efficacy on earth of an everlasting kingdom but has no end point in time since it is everlasting. In verses 15-26, the third time-defined part tells a story that stretches in duration from the rise of the fourth kingdom to the conclusion of a time period defined by the phrase *"time, times, and the dividing of time"* in verse 25.

The second key to interpretation of the prophecy in the seventh chapter, which is composed of the three distinct but complementary prophetic time lines described above, is to remember that these prophecies are about Israel as the people and nation of God, and about God's plan of redemption for all mankind through Israel. Maintaining this Israel-centric viewpoint is critical if a proper interpretation is to be derived from the three prophetic time lines.

The third key to interpretation of the prophecy is to pick the correct period in history as the starting point for the events of the chrono-specific prophecy in the first part. These events, the rise of the four kings, are the first action events that can be identified as beginning in real time. The most obvious place to look for the time period in which the vision starts is in the historical period immediately following the time period when the vision was recorded. Daniel wrote down his vision in the first year of Belshazzar, king of Babylon,[1] which can be dated to sometime around the year 553 BCE. This year occurred in the closing years of the Neo-Babylonian Empire that had reached its apex under Nebuchadnezzar. As we know from history, Cyrus the Great conquered Babylon in 539 BCE, initiating a period of Persian rule over the region that had been predicted in the Book of Isaiah. Thus,

---

[1] Belshazzar ruled as coregent in Babylon while his father King Nabonidus lived in Arabia.

the Achaemenid Persian Empire, beginning with Cyrus, is the logical period in history for locating the action events in the seventh chapter.[1]

Fulfillment in History

The starting events of the prophecy in the seventh chapter are described in verses 3-7 and 17, which say that four kings will arise from the earth. Then, verses 7b and 24 clarify that the fourth king is really a composite representing ten kings. The most straightforward interpretation of these statements is to assume that there will be three kings of an empire, then a dynasty of ten kings in that empire. When the Achaemenid Persian Empire is examined—the portion when it became the empire that was sovereign over the Jews—that is exactly what we find in its history. The first king in the prophecy (the lion with eagle's wings that is made to stand like a man, and given the heart of a man) is Cyrus II the Great, who began his reign as King of Persia in 546 BCE. It is Cyrus who is referred to in Scripture as God's "anointed" (messiah) and who was called to kingship by God for the sake of the Jewish people.[2] He conquered and consolidated what is now most of the Middle East as his empire. His most famous action regarding the Jews was his decree *circa* 538 BCE that allowed them to end their exile in Babylon and return to rebuild Jerusalem and the Temple, both of which had been destroyed by Nebuchadnezzar in 586 BCE. After his death in 530 BCE, Cyrus was succeeded by his son Cambyses II, who is the second king in the prophecy (the bear with three ribs in its teeth). Cambyses extended the empire into Egypt, and pushed toward Cush (modern Sudan) and across the sand desert toward the Siwa Oasis (on the Libyan border). These ill-conceived desert expeditions seriously depleted his army, with the result that his brother Smerdis led a coup back in the capital and was recognized as king in most of the Asian part of the empire.[3] Cambyses was not able to re-establish his authority as king and either killed himself or was

---

[1] Expositors have often incorrectly identified the fourth kingdom in verses 1-12 as the Seleucid Empire or as the Roman Empire. In recent years, some expositors have incorrectly deferred the fourth kingdom to a future end-time scenario involving an Antichrist.

[2] See Isa. 45:1-4; note that Cyrus is mentioned by name 23 times in the Hebrew Scriptures, including three times in Daniel.

[3] In the Behistun Inscription, Darius I claims that Cambyses II executed Smerdis before leaving to conquer Egypt, and that, in his absence, an impostor named Gautama, a Magian priest, assumed the name Smerdis, led a coup to depose the absent Cambyses, and ruled as king. Darius I then claimed that he had killed Gautama to become king.

Chapter Four: That Which Shall Not Be Destroyed (Daniel 7:1-28)

> **Kings of the Achaemenid Persian Empire**
> *(showing only rulers exercising dominion over the Jews; all years BCE)*
>
> 1. First Beast - Cyrus II the Great (r. 546-530), begins rule over the Jews with defeat of Babylon in 539, Jews allowed to return to Jerusalem in 536.
> 2. Second Beast - Cambyses II (r. 530-522), adds Egypt to the Persian empire.
> 3. Third Beast - Gautama (*aka* Smerdis, r. 522-521), usurper killed by Darius I.
> 4. Fourth Beast with Ten Horns - Darian Dynasty with 10 kings as follows:
>   (1) Darius I Hystaspes (r. 521-486), "the Great," crosses the Bosporus in 512, expands the Persian empire into Europe, initiates two centuries of Greco-Persian hostilities, defeated at Battle of Marathon in the year 490; Second Temple dedicated in Jerusalem in 515.
>   (2) Xerxes I (r. 486-465), invades Greece, defeated Greek army at Battle of Thermopylae, burns the city of Athens and the Acropolis.
>   (3) Artaxerxes I Longimanus (r. 464-424), Egypt revolts, empire declines.
>   (4) Xerxes II (r. 424), killed by Sogdianus.
>   (5) Sogdianus (r. 424-423), killed by Darius II.
>   (6) Darius II Nothus (r. 423-404), troubles in Egypt, the Jewish Temple at Elephantine destroyed.
>   (7) Artaxerxes II Memnon (r. 404-358), further decline of empire.
>   (8) Artaxerxes III Ochus (r. 358-338), initiates minor resurgence of the Persian empire, Egypt reconquered.
>   (9) Artaxerxes IV Arses (r. 338-336), battles Phillip II of Macedonia.
>   (10) Darius III Codomannus (r. 336-330), deposes Artaxerxes IV, later defeated by Alexander the Great at Granicus River (331), Issus River, (333) and Gaugamela (331); last king of Achaemenid Persian Empire.

assassinated in 522 BCE. Smerdis, the third king in the prophecy (the leopard with four wings and four heads), reigned as king for only seven months until he was killed by a younger son of Cyrus, Darius I Hystaspes, the fourth king of the prophecy (the dreadful and terrible beast with ten horns) who began his reign in 521 BCE, the first king in a dynasty of ten kings (see list above), exactly the number of kings called for in the prophecy about the fourth beast. As can be seen from the list of kings, there was much turmoil in the region during the years of Persian domination, within the ruling families of the empire itself, between the empire and its rebellious satrapies of Egypt and Babylon, and between Persia and Greece. The Bible is silent about how all of this turmoil affected the Jews living in Jerusalem and the land of Israel at the time. The Books of Ezra and Nehemiah are generally thought to describe events that took place during the reign of Artaxerxes I, but determining which king is referenced in either book is difficult. Fortunately, the exact dates for the work of Ezra and Nehemiah, and whether they were contemporaries or served at separate times, are not germane to understanding the chrono-specific prophecies in Daniel, chapter 7.

Now that the fourth beast has been correctly identified as the Achaemenid dynasty of ten kings that began with the reign of Darius I the Great in 521 BCE, the little horn that arises and plucks up three horns (Persian kings) by the roots can be identified as Alexander the Great, the first king of Greece. Alexander moved against the Persian Empire in 334 BCE, defeated the Darian dynasty in the person of its last king, Darius III Codomannus, and brought the Achaemenid Persian Empire to a close. As to the identity of the three kings Alexander defeated, there are several possible answers. In one sense, Alexander defeated Darius I, Darius II, and Darius III, three kings who bore the name and spanned the duration of the dynasty that had initiated and maintained hostilities with Greece. In a more literal sense, Alexander, in his first battle against Persia on Asian soil at the Granicus River, defeated a Persian army which was being led by three Darian satraps, Arsites of Hellespontine Phrygia, Arsamenes of Cilicia, and Spithridates of Lydia and Ionia. Another possibility, and the one I prefer, is that Alexander defeated one king three times, which was perceived as defeating three separate kings from Daniel's viewpoint in the vision. This fits the historical record, which shows that Darius was defeated by Alexander in three battles, the Battles of Granicus in 334 BCE, Issus in 333 BCE, and Gaugamela in 331 BCE. After the final battle, Darius fled to Bactria, where he was killed. Alexander thereafter reigned supreme over the Persian Empire, which included Judea.

However, there is no credible evidence that Alexander ever visited Judea or Jerusalem. Most scholars consider that Josephus' story of Alexander visiting Jerusalem and bowing before the high priest to be based on a fable. Whether he did or did not visit, Alexander and his empire did bring Hellenism into the lives of the Jewish people, and the influence of Greek civilization was to create tension in the land of Israel for many years. After his death in 323 BCE, the empire of Alexander split into several smaller empires. Two of these dominions, one north of Judea ruled by the Seleucids in Coele-Syria and one south of Judea ruled by the Ptolemies in Egypt, were destined to wreak havoc on the inhabitants of the land of Israel, which was located geographically between the two contending military powers. The tenth, eleventh, and part of the twelfth chapters of Daniel describe the years of struggle between the Seleucids and Ptolemies in great detail, as will be shown in the next chapter of this book. However, in the seventh chapter, the focus is more limited, as indicated in verse 8b and verses 20b-21, where the horn represents only the Seleucid Empire in its latter days of dominion over the Jewish people. In verse 25a, the horn being given eyes and a mouth to speak great things against the Most High, to make war on and prevail against the saints of the Most High, and to think to change times and laws, is a description of the violently anti-Jewish Seleucid king, Antiochus IV Epiphanes.[1] It was Antiochus who, in an attempt to replace the practice of Judaism in his kingdom with the gods and games of Hellenism, built a fortress called "The Akra" in the City of David, stationed a garrison of troops there to enforce his decrees, appointed a Hellenistic high priest, forbade circumcision and sabbath observances on pain of death, confiscated and burned Torah scrolls, and desecrated the Temple by dedicating it to Olympian Zeus. The ultimate desecration was the erection of a secondary altar on top of the altar of burnt offerings, with the subsequent sacrifice of swine flesh on it. The latter sacrilege took place on the 25th day of Kislev in the 145th year of the Seleucid Empire, which is equivalent to December 13, 167 BCE in Gregorian reckoning. Verse 25b adds cryptically, *"and they shall be given into his hand until a time and times and the dividing of time"* (KJV).

"until a time, times, and the dividing of time"

Although I had previously learned from interpreting Daniel, chapter 12, verses 5-7, that a "time" is defined as being 228 Passovers in duration when used in a Danielic prophecy as a chronological marker, at first I could not figure out how to apply the definition to verse 25b. The logical approach was to assume that the *"time, times, and the dividing of time"* in this case covered the same time

---

[1] Antiochus IV Epiphanes is identified more clearly in Daniel, chapter 8, verse 23-25: *"And in the latter time of their kingdom, when the transgressors are come to the full, a king of fierce countenance, and understanding dark sentences, shall stand up. And his power shall be mighty, but not by his own power: and he shall destroy wonderfully, and shall prosper, and practise, and shall destroy the mighty and the holy people. And through his policy also he shall cause craft to prosper in his hand; and he shall magnify himself in his heart, and by peace shall destroy many: he shall also stand up against the Prince of princes; but he shall be broken without hand"* (KJV); also, see Dan. 11:31.

period as the similar *"time, times, and an half"* phrase that was used in the twelfth chapter of Daniel (see page 38). After all, verse 25a did describe Antiochus IV and the desecration of the Temple, which is the starting point for the 3½ "times" in chapter 12. However, I could not identify either the "they" or the "his" about whom it said *"and they shall be given into his hand until a time and times and the dividing of time"* (KJV). It was at this point that I had to go back to the history books to refresh my memory about events surrounding the persecution of the Jews and desecration of the Temple by Antiochus in 167 BCE, and about the revolt that followed. The desecration of the Temple was a major event in the life of the Jewish people. The revolt, led by the Maccabees, started that same year, 167 BCE, and the rebels soon gained the upper hand and began to defeat the forces of Antiochus. In late 164 BCE, they captured Jerusalem and rededicated the Temple, building a new altar of burnt offerings and reinstituting the daily sacrifices. The rededication took place on the 25th day of the month of Kislev in the 148th year of the Seleucid Empire, which is equivalent to the Gregorian date of December 10, 164 BCE. Soon thereafter, probably in January, 163 BCE, Antiochus IV died while fighting a war in Media and was succeeded by Antiochus V, against whom the Maccabees continued to fight for independence from Seleucid rule.

After the Battle of Nicanor in early spring of 161 BCE, in which Maccabean irregulars scored a decisive victory over a numerically-superior and far better-equipped Seleucid force led by Nicanor, one of their top generals, Judah Maccabee immediately sent emissaries to Rome seeking an alliance to strengthen the Jews in their fight against the Seleucids. He realized that, after such a humiliating defeat, the Seleucid king would be forced to put down the Judean rebellion at all costs, and Judah reasoned that his forces could not long hold out against the Syrian military might without outside help. In Rome, the Senate received the Maccabean delegation, heard their appeal for assistance, and ratified a treaty between Rome and the Jewish rebels. It was this act of reaching out to Rome by the Jewish leadership, an event that happened between the Battle of Nicanor on March 4 and Passover on April 4 in the year 161 BCE, that explains the meaning of verse 25b by identifying the "they" as the Jews and the "his hand" as symbolic language for the military protection of Rome.

So, summing up, the chrono-specific prophecy in Daniel's vision predicted that the Jewish people would be subject to the power of Rome (and later Byzantine Roman Empire) for *"a time, times, and the dividing of time,"* which equals 798 Passovers. Table 4.1 (see opposite page, top table) demonstrates how to count

Chapter Four: That Which Shall Not Be Destroyed (Daniel 7:1-28)

Table 4.1 - How to Count the 3½ "times" in Verse 25b

P1 - 161 BCE	P2 - 160 BCE	P3 - 159 BCE	P4 - 158 BCE	P5 - 157 BCE	P6 - 156 BCE	P7 - 155 BCE	P8 - 154 BCE	P9 - 153 BCE	P10 - 152 BCE
1-10 see above									
P110 - 52 BCE	P120 - 42 BCE	P130 - 32 BCE	P140 - 22 BCE	P150 - 12 BCE	P160 - 2 BCE	P170 - 9 CE	P180 - 19 CE	P190 - 29 CE	P200 - 39 CE
P210 - 49 CE	P220 - 59 CE	P230 - 69 CE	P240 - 79 CE	P250 - 89 CE	P260 - 99 CE	P270 - 109 CE	P280 - 119 CE	P290 - 129 CE	P300 - 139 CE
P310 - 149 CE	P320 - 159 CE	P330 - 169 CE	P340 - 179 CE	P350 - 189 CE	P360 - 199 CE	P370 - 209 CE	P380 - 219 CE	P390 - 229 CE	P400 - 239 CE
P410 - 249 CE	P420 - 259 CE	P430 - 269 CE	P440 - 279 CE	P450 - 289 CE	P460 - 299 CE	P470 - 309 CE	P480 - 319 CE	P490 - 329 CE	P500 - 339 CE
P510 - 349 CE	P520 - 359 CE	P530 - 369 CE	P540 - 379 CE	P550 - 389 CE	P560 - 399 CE	P570 - 409 CE	P580 - 419 CE	P590 - 429 CE	P600 - 439 CE
P610 - 449 CE	P620 - 459 CE	P630 - 469 CE	P640 - 479 CE	P650 - 489 CE	P660 - 499 CE	P670 - 509 CE	P680 - 519 CE	P690 - 529 CE	P700 - 539 CE
P710 - 549 CE	P720 - 559 CE	P730 - 569 CE	P740 - 579 CE	P750 - 589 CE	P760 - 599 CE	P770 - 609 CE	P780 - 619 CE	P790 - 629 CE	P791 see below
P791 - 630 CE	P792 - 631 CE	P793 - 632 CE	P794 - 633 CE	P795 - 634 CE	P796 - 635 CE	P797 - 636 CE	P798 - 637 CE	---	---

Note that there was no year "0" (zero) when going from BCE to CE, so the count for the Passovers in the transition decade from 2 BCE to 9 CE is determined as follows: Passover number 160 in the count (P160 above) occurred in the year 2 BCE, P161 in 1 BCE, P162 in 1 CE, P163 in 2 CE, P164 in 3 CE, P165 in 4 CE, P166 in 5 CE, P167 in 6 CE, P168 in 7 CE, P169 in 8 CE, P170 in 9 CE.

Table 4.2 - How to Count the "time" in Verse 12

P1 - 162 BCE	P2 - 161 BCE	P3 - 160 BCE	P4 - 159 BCE	P5 - 158 BCE	P6 - 157 BCE	P7 - 156 BCE	P8 - 155 BCE	P9 - 154 BCE	P10 - 153 BCE
1-10 see above									
P110 - 53 BCE	P120 - 43 BCE	P130 - 33 BCE	P140 - 23 BCE	P150 - 13 BCE	P160 - 3 BCE	P170 - 8 CE	P180 - 18 CE	P190 - 28 CE	P200 - 38 CE
P210 - 48 CE	P220 - 58 CE	P221 - 59 CE	P222 - 60 CE	P223 - 61 CE	P224 - 62 CE	P225 - 63 CE	P226 - 64 CE	P227 - 65 CE	P228 - 66 CE

Note that there was no year "0" (zero) when going from BCE to CE, so the count for the Passovers in the transition decade from 3 BCE to 8 CE is determined as follows: Passover number 160 in the count (P160 above) occurred in the year 3 BCE, P161 in 2 BCE, P162 in 1 BCE, P163 in 1 CE, P164 in 2 CE, P165 in 3 CE, P166 in 4 CE, P167 in 5 CE, P168 in 6 CE, P169 in 7 CE, P170 in 8 CE.

the 798 Passovers (3½ "times"). The count begins with the Passover of 161 BCE, which is the first Passover observed after the appeal to Rome by Judah Maccabee a few weeks earlier. The count ends with the Passover of 637 CE which is the last Passover before the capture of the Temple Mount by the Muslim Caliph Omar in February, 638 CE, the event which ended Roman-Byzantine dominion over the Jewish people for good and began centuries of Muslim sovereignty over the holiest site of the Jews. In the table, each Passover is denoted as "P#" (where "#" is its number in the count), followed by its corresponding Gregorian year. After the initial ten Passovers (P1 through P10), Passovers are shown in ten-year increments, which allows you to count along on your fingers to verify the count.

"for a season and time"

In addition to the prophecy about the 3½ "times" of Roman-Byzantine hegemony and dominion, the seventh chapter contains another chrono-specific prophecy that incorporates the chronological markers "season" and "time" to describe a second and concurrent period of Jewish history. This prophecy is found in verse 12, *"I beheld then because of the voice of the great words which the horn spake: I beheld even till the beast was slain, and his body destroyed, and given to the burning flame. As concerning the rest of the beasts, they had their dominion taken away: yet their lives were prolonged for a season and time"* (KJV).

The key to understanding this prophecy is found in the phrase "their lives were prolonged" found in verse 12. It is a reference to the last words spoken by Moses to the Israelites before they entered *Eretz-Israel*, recorded in Deuteronomy, chapter 32, verses 46-47, *"And he said unto them, Set your hearts unto all the words which I testify among you this day, which ye shall command your children to observe to do, all the words of this law. For it is not a vain thing for you; because it is your life: and through this thing ye shall **prolong your days in the land**, whither ye go over Jordan to possess it"* (KJV). This admonition was preceded by the Song of Moses, which foretold that the Israelites, once they had taken possession of the promised land, would go whoring after strange gods, causing God to render judgement by removing the people from the land. Moses, in his dying words, stressed that the only way Israel could prolong its days in the land was to be faithful to God's law, the observance of which was centered on the Tabernacle, and after the time of Solomon on the Temple in Jerusalem. As predicted, the people forsook the law of God, so he used the Babylonians to render judgement

Chapter Four: That Which Shall Not Be Destroyed (Daniel 7:1-28)

on Israel by destroying the Temple and removing them from the land, then brought them back after seventy years of exile. Within two decades after their return, the Temple had been rebuilt and the people were once again observing the Temple commandments and requirements of the law, but soon they drifted back to their old practices. When Antiochus IV banned the practice of Judaism, he had the cooperation of many Jews, especially those from the privileged priestly families that had adopted the Hellenism of their Seleucid overlords. However, Jews in the more rural areas resisted Hellenization, and it was a rural priest named Mattathias, together with his five sons (strengthened by the archangel Michael, the protector of God's people Israel; see Daniel, chapter 12, verse 1), who began the revolt against Antiochus in 167 BCE that led to the liberation of Jerusalem from Seleucid rule and the rededication of the Temple on December 10, 164 BCE. With the resumption of the Temple sacrifices and observance of the law that was centered on the Temple services and Levitical priesthood, the lives of the Jewish people were prolonged in the land for a "season" (a Passover) and a "time" (228 Passovers), as predicted in verse 12.

Table 4.2 (see page 49, bottom table) demonstrates how to count the "time" in verse 12. The count is initiated with the Passover of 162 BCE, which is the first Passover after the Passover that was observed on March 27, 163 BCE, which was the first Passover to be observed in the rededicated Temple and the "season" (single Passover) referred to in the vision. The count ends exactly 228 Passovers later, with the Passover of 66 CE. In the table for counting the "time" (228 Passovers) in the period of prolonged lives, each Passover is denoted as "P#" (where "#" is its number in the count), followed by its corresponding Gregorian year. Except for the initial ten Passovers (P1 through P10), and final eight (P221 through P228), Passovers are shown in ten-year increments, which allows you to count along on your fingers to verify the count.

The Passover of 66 CE, which was celebrated on March 27, marked the end of the period of prolonged lives for the Jewish people in the land exactly as it had been predicted to end in chapter 7, verse 12. Josephus records the unusual portents, omens, and other events leading up to and surrounding the Passover that year in his *The Wars of the Jews*, 6.5.2b-4:

2b. "A false prophet was the occasion of these people's destruction, who had made a public proclamation in the city that very day, that God commanded them to get upon the temple, and that there they should receive miraculous signs of their deliverance. Now

Daniel Unsealed

there was then a great number of false prophets suborned by the tyrants to impose on the people, who denounced this to them, that they should wait for deliverance from God; and this was in order to keep them from deserting, and that they might be buoyed up above fear and care by such hopes. Now a man that is in adversity does easily comply with such promises; for when such a seducer makes him believe that he shall be delivered from those miseries which oppress him, then it is that the patient is full of hopes of such his deliverance."

3. "Thus were the miserable people persuaded by these deceivers, and such as belied God himself; while they did not attend nor give credit to the signs that were so evident, and did so plainly foretell their future desolation, but, like men infatuated, without either eyes to see or minds to consider, did not regard the denunciations that God made to them. Thus there was a star resembling a sword, which stood over the city, and a comet,[1] that continued a whole year. Thus also before the Jews' rebellion, and before those commotions which preceded the war, when the people were come in great crowds to the feast of unleavened bread, on the eighth day of the month Xanthicus [Nisan, March/April], and at the ninth hour of the night, so great a light shone round the altar and the holy house, that it appeared to be bright day time; which lasted for half an hour. This light seemed to be a good sign to the unskillful, but was so interpreted by the sacred scribes, as to portend those events that followed immediately upon it. At the same festival also, a heifer, as she was led by the high priest to be sacrificed, brought forth a lamb in the midst of the temple. Moreover, the eastern gate of the inner court of the temple, which was of brass, and vastly heavy, and had been with difficulty shut by twenty men, and rested upon a basis armed with iron, and had bolts fastened very deep into the firm floor, which was there made of one entire stone, was seen to be opened of its own accord about the sixth hour of the night. Now those that kept watch in the temple came hereupon running to the captain of the temple, and told him of it; who then came up thither, and not without great difficulty was able to shut the gate again. This also appeared to the vulgar to be a very happy prodigy, as if God did thereby open them the gate of happiness. But the men of learning understood it, that the security of their holy house was dissolved of its own accord, and that the gate was opened for the advantage of their enemies. So these publicly declared that the signal foreshowed the desolation that was coming upon them. Besides these, a few days after that feast, on the one and twentieth day of the month Artemisius [Iyar, May/June], a certain prodigious and incredible phenomenon appeared: I suppose the account of it would seem to be

---

[1] This was a sighting of Halley's Comet, which made an appearance on January 23, 66 CE.

Chapter Four: That Which Shall Not Be Destroyed (Daniel 7:1-28)

a fable, were it not related by those that saw it, and were not the events that followed it of so considerable a nature as to deserve such signals; for, before sun setting, chariots and troops of soldiers in their armor were seen running about among the clouds, and surrounding of cities. Moreover, at that feast which we call Pentecost, as the priests were going by night into the inner court of the temple, as their custom was, to perform their sacred ministrations, they said that, in the first place, they felt a quaking, and heard a great noise, and after that they heard a sound as of a great multitude, saying, 'Let us remove hence.'[1] But, what is still more terrible, there was one Jesus, the son of Ananus, a plebeian and a husbandman, who, four years before the war began, and at a time when the city was in very great peace and prosperity, came to that feast whereon it is our custom for every one to make tabernacles to God in the temple, began on a sudden to cry aloud, 'A voice from the east, a voice from the west, a voice from the four winds,[2] a voice against Jerusalem and the holy house, a voice against the bridegrooms and the brides, and a voice against this whole people!' This was his cry, as he went about by day and by night, in all the lanes of the city. However, certain of the most eminent among the populace had great indignation at this dire cry of his, and took up the man, and gave him a great number of severe stripes; yet did not he either say any thing for himself, or any thing peculiar to those that chastised him, but still went on with the same words which he cried before. Hereupon our rulers, supposing, as the case proved to be, that this was a sort of divine fury in the man, brought him to the Roman procurator, where he was whipped till his bones were laid bare; yet he did not make any supplication for himself, nor shed any tears, but turning his voice to the most lamentable tone possible, at every stroke of the whip his answer was, 'Woe, woe to Jerusalem!' And when Albinus (for he was then procurator) asked him, Who he was? and whence he came? and why he uttered such words? he made no manner of reply to what he said, but still did not leave off his melancholy ditty, till Albinus took him to be a madman, and dismissed him. Now, during all the time that passed before the war began, this man did not go near any of the citizens, nor was seen by them while he said so; but he every day uttered these lamentable words, as if it were his premeditated vow, 'Woe, woe to Jerusalem!' Nor did he give ill words to any of those that beat him every day, nor good words to those that gave him food; but this was his reply to all men,

---

[1] This was apparently interpreted by the Temple priests as evidence of the departure of the Shekinah (the Divine Glory) from the Temple. Rabbi Jonathan, who was an eyewitness to the events surrounding the destruction of Jerusalem, testified of the departure of the Shekinah from the Temple as well.

[2] *cf.* Dan. 7:2b: *"... the four winds of the heaven strove upon the great sea"* (KJV).

and indeed no other than a melancholy presage of what was to come. This cry of his was the loudest at the festivals; and he continued this ditty for seven years and five months, without growing hoarse, or being tired therewith, until the very time that he saw his presage in earnest fulfilled in our siege, when it ceased; for as he was going round upon the wall, he cried out with his utmost force, 'Woe, woe to the city again, and to the people, and to the holy house!' And just as he added at the last, 'Woe, woe to myself also!' there came a stone out of one of the engines, and smote him, and killed him immediately; and as he was uttering the very same presages he gave up the ghost."

4. "Now if any one consider these things, he will find that God takes care of mankind, and by all ways possible foreshows to our race what is for their preservation; but that men perish by those miseries which they madly and voluntarily bring upon themselves; for the Jews, by demolishing the tower of Antonia, had made their temple four-square, while at the same time they had it written in their sacred oracles, 'That then should their city be taken, as well as their holy house, when once their temple should become four-square.' But now, what did the most elevate them in undertaking this war, was an ambiguous oracle that was also found in their sacred writings, how,' about that time, one from their country should become governor of the habitable earth.' The Jews took this prediction to belong to themselves in particular, and many of the wise men were thereby deceived in their determination. Now this oracle certainly denoted the government of Vespasian, who was appointed emperor in Judea. However, it is not possible for men to avoid fate, although they see it beforehand. But these men interpreted some of these signals according to their own pleasure, and some of them they utterly despised, until their madness was demonstrated, both by the taking of their city and their own destruction."

The First Jewish-Roman War began shortly after the Passover of 66 CE, marking the end of the period of prolonged life for the Jewish people in the land. Later that year, reacting to insults by Roman soldiers in Caesarea, Eleazar, son of Ananias the high priest, stopped the daily Temple sacrifices offered to honor Caesar, signaling the start of the revolt against Roman rule. Emboldened by this act of defiance, Zealots overran and killed the Roman garrison stationed in the Antonia Fortress in Jerusalem, and thereafter the revolt quickly spread throughout the city. The legate of Syria, Cestius Gallus in Damascus, sent troops to restore order, but his forces were defeated in the Battle of Beth Horon, further encouraging the uprising of Jews in Galilee and Judea. Late in 66 CE, the Roman emperor Nero summoned one of his best generals, Vespasian, and commanded

Chapter Four: That Which Shall Not Be Destroyed (Daniel 7:1-28)

		First Jewish-Roman War, 66-73 CE
Year	*Month*	*Important Events*
66 CE	July	Sacrifices for emperor stopped by Temple authorities, spirit of rebellion spreads throughout Jerusalem and Judea.
	September	King Agrippa sends troops to reinforce Jerusalem, Zealots led by Eleazar drive them out of the city; *Sicarii* led by Menahem seize Masada, capture large store of arms, head to Jerusalem; Jewish rebels burn the High Priest's house, Agrippa's palace, and kill the defending Roman cohort while seizing the Antonio fortress.
	October	Jews defeat Roman forces led by Cestius Gallus at Beth Horon.
	November	Emperor Nero selects Vespasian to quell the growing rebellion.
67 CE	Spring	Vespasian assembles his army, begins campaign in Galilee.
	Autumn	Vespasian subdues rebellion in Galilee, Josephus defects and becomes advisor to Vespasian; many Jews deported to Antioch and Rome to begin *Diaspora*; Jewish rebels retreat to Jerusalem.
68 CE	June	Emperor Nero commits suicide, beginning a year of turmoil back in Rome (known to historians as the "year of four emperors") and a year or so of relative calm on the battlefields of Judea.
69 CE	December	Vespasian returns to Rome to become emperor, leaves his son Titus in charge of prosecuting the war against the rebels in Judea.
70 CE	Spring	Titus prepares for final assault on Jerusalem, siege begins; Jewish factions led by Simon bar-Giora, John of Gischala, and Eleazar the Zealot fight among themselves more than against Romans.
	May	Romans break through outer defenses of Jerusalem.
	August	Roman forces capture Temple, destroy the Temple buildings and burn the city of Jerusalem, Tenth Legion plants its standard (featuring an image of the emperor/god) on the Temple Mount.
73 CE	April	Romans capture Masada to end the First Jewish-Roman War

him to put down the rebellion-prone Jews in Judea once and for all. Vespasian moved deliberately, assembling sufficient forces in the seaport town of Caesarea to ensure eventual victory over the lightly-armed Jewish irregulars in the north. Working from his headquarters in Caesarea, Vespasian first subdued the coastal plateau, then, in 67 CE, captured the Galilee and its surrounding territories. It was during this part of the campaign that the Jewish general who would later be known as the historian Flavius Josephus defected to the Romans. For the better part of three years, the Roman legions, first under Vespasian and then under his son Titus after Nero died and Vespasian was made emperor, methodically captured cities in the countryside, enslaving and deporting the Jews to other parts of the empire. Finally, in early 70 CE, Titus began the assault on Jerusalem itself, which ended with the destruction of the city and the Temple. This period of war ended the period of prolonged lives in *Eretz-Israel* and marked the beginning of the wholesale removal of Jews from their ancestral land for what would be an almost two-thousand-year *Diaspora* among the nations.

"an everlasting kingdom"

When God revealed the prophecies in the seventh chapter to Daniel, the things that the prophet saw in his dream-visions caused him much discomfort, or, as he put it in verse 28, *"my cogitations much troubled me, and my countenance changed in me"* (KJV). His reaction was appropriate for an exiled Jewish man who was looking forward to Israel's national redemption from exile in Babylon and its restoration to the promised land of Israel. Instead, God was telling him that Jerusalem and the Temple, after they had been rebuilt, would be destroyed yet again, and he was revealing that the Jewish people would once more be exiled from the land to dwell among the nations. Furthermore, Daniel was shown in his vision that the Gentile nations would have dominion over both the city of Jerusalem and the sanctuary (Temple Mount) for a very long time. This news made Daniel physically ill. However, in the midst of all of these dire predictions, hope was offered. It was revealed in verses 13-14, in verse 17, and in verse 27, verses which foretold that there would be an everlasting kingdom given to one like a Son of Man by the Ancient of Days, and to the saints of the Most High for ever and ever. So, as spectacular as were the prophecies predicting the 798-year-long Roman period that lasted from 161 BCE until the Muslim conquest of Jerusalem in 638 CE, and the 228-year-long period of prolonged lives that began with the Maccabean conquest of Jerusalem in 164 BCE and ended with the Roman expulsion of the Jews from *Eretz-Israel* and the start of the *Diaspora* among the nations in 66 CE, it seems that the ultimate purpose of the seventh chapter of Daniel is to introduce the promise of the coming kingdom, an everlasting messianic kingdom to be ruled by the Messiah of Israel, one like the Son of Man, and possessed forever by the saints of the Most High.

CHAPTER FIVE

WHAT SHALL BEFALL THY PEOPLE

READ DANIEL 10:1-12:4 ON PAGES 230-234 | SEE TIME LINE ❻ ON PLATE 1

The tenth, eleventh, and twelfth chapters of the Book of Daniel contain its longest continuous block of predictive prophecy. The narrative can be divided into three parts for interpretive purposes. Part one consists of the tenth chapter, plus the first verse of the eleventh chapter, and it serves as a preamble to all that follows. Since it contains no chrono-predictive prophecy, it will not be expounded except to note that it reveals in verse 14 the purpose of parts two and three, which is *"... to make thee understand what shall befall thy people in the latter days"* (KJV). Part two consists of chapter 11, verse 2, through chapter 12, verse 4. It provides a straightforward foretelling[1] of events that are predicted to happen to the Jewish people in the future—the future, that is, from the standpoint of the Jews who were returning from Babylon to *Eretz-Israel* in the year 536 BCE—and covers a period in history stretching from the early days of the Achaemenid Persian Empire down to time of Antiochus IV Epiphanes. Part three consists of verses 36-45 of the eleventh chapter. Many modern expositors have incorrectly interpreted those verses to have their fulfillment in the future, which has resulted in much misunderstanding about the Bible's teaching about the time of the end. That error in exegesis will be corrected at the end of this chapter.

Fulfillment in History (before 70 CE)

In this section, verses 2-35 of chapter eleven will be matched verse by verse with their fulfillment events in history, as documented in the works of Polybius, Livy, and Josephus, and in the books of 1 and 2 Maccabees, as follows:

536-334 BCE

verse 2: *"And now will I shew thee the truth. Behold, there shall stand up yet three kings in Persia; and the fourth shall be far richer than they all: and by his strength through his riches he shall stir up all against the realm of Grecia."* (KJV) ... This

---

[1] Some expositors claim that verses 2-35 are not prophecy at all but a later scribal record of events after they had happened in history, see comments on page 18, second paragraph; also note that the events of Daniel 12:1-4 overlap the time period covered by verses 20-35.

verse was written in 536 BCE, during the reign of Cyrus the Great, king of Persia, who had brought the Babylonian Empire to an end three years earlier. The "yet three kings" are thus easy to identify. They are the next three Achaemenid Persian kings that ruled after Cyrus the Great: Cambyses II (r. 530-522), the usurper Gautama (*aka* Smerdis, r. 522-521), and Darius I Hystaspes (r. 521-486) who was eventually known as Darius the Great. The reign of Darius the Great was a golden age for Persia. He established a new capital, Persepolis, which had walls sixty feet high. Roads were built to all parts of the empire, and a canal was built connecting the Red Sea to the Nile. Administration was greatly improved and slavery was forbidden. Darius is notable for his military incursions across the Bosporus, the first Persian king to expand his empire into Europe. In 490 BCE, Darius, seeking to punish Athens for encouraging the Ionian revolt among Greek cities along the coast of Asia Minor, invaded Greece, but was defeated in the Battle of Marathon. He was succeeded by his son Xerxes I (r. 486-465), who set out to remove the threat of Athenian influence on his western flank. Xerxes invaded Greece with an army estimated by Herodotus to number more than two million soldiers, including 10,000 elite Persian Immortals. After he won the Battle of Thermopylae, Xerxes burned Athens in 480 BCE, an act that created among the Greeks a lasting hatred for Persia and a hunger for revenge that was to result in Alexander the Great moving with fury against Persia two centuries later.

334-323 BCE

verse 3: *"And a mighty king shall stand up, that shall rule with great dominion, and do according to his will."* (KJV) ... Now the action moves forward to the time of Alexander the Great, who avenged the burning of Athens by conquering the Achaemenid Persian Empire under the rule of Darius III Codomannus, defeating him three times, first at the Granicus River in 334 BCE, then at the Issus River in 333 BCE, and finally on the plains at Gaugamela in 331 BCE. Alexander went on to extend his empire as far north as the Hindu Kush (modern Afghanistan) and as far east as India, before returning to Babylon to plan the conquest of Arabia.

323-301 BCE

verse 4: *"And when he shall stand up, his kingdom shall be broken, and shall be divided toward the four winds of heaven; and not to his posterity, nor according to his dominion which he ruled: for his kingdom shall be plucked up, even for others beside those."* (KJV) ... Alexander the Great died in Babylon in 323 BCE, at

Seleucid and Ptolemaic Kings, 311-163 BCE

(shown in the order each reign began; all years BCE)

<u>In Coele-Syria</u>	<u>In Egypt</u>
Seleucus I Nicator, r. 311-281	
	Ptolemy I Soter, r. 305-284
	Ptolemy II Philadelphus, r. 284-246
Antiochus I Soter, r. 281-261	
Antiochus II Theos, r. 261-246	
	Ptolemy III Euergetes, r. 246-222
Seleucus II Callinicus, r. 246-225	
Seleucus III Ceraunus, r. 225-223	
Antiochus III the Great, r. 223-187	
	Ptolemy IV Philopator, r. 222-204
	Ptolemy V Epiphanes, r. 204-180
Seleucus IV Philopator, r. 187-175	
	Ptolemy VI Philometor, r. 180-145
Antiochus IV Epiphanes, r. 175-163	

the height of his power. He did not designate an heir and his only legitimate son, Alexander IV, was not yet born when he died. Twenty-plus years of infighting among Alexander's generals followed his death, fracturing the empire. After the Battle of Ipsus in 301 BCE, Alexander's empire devolved into four main parts. Cassander ruled Greece, Lysimachus ruled Asia Minor, Seleucus I Nicator ruled Persia and Babylon, and Ptolemy I Soter ruled over Egypt and the land of Israel.

301-253 BCE, First Syrian War

verse 5: *"And the king of the south shall be strong, and one of his princes; and he shall be strong above him, and have dominion; his dominion shall be a great dominion."* (KJV) ... By 281 BCE, two major Greek dynasties remained from the four remnants of the empire of Alexander, the Seleucids in Coele-Syria and the Ptolemies in Egypt (see list of kings above). For the next century, these two dynasties would dominate the lives of the Jews living in the land of Israel, which was located between the two regional powers. The king of the south is a reference to Ptolemy I Soter, and the prince who was strong above him refers to his son and successor, Ptolemy II Philadelphus, who expanded the influence and power of Egypt throughout the eastern Mediterranean basin, including Judea. The First Syrian War was fought between Ptolemy II Philadelphus and Antiochus I Soter from 274-271 BCE, and the result was a victory for the Ptolemies.

253-246 BCE, Second Syrian War

verse 6: *"And in the end of years they shall join themselves together; for the king's daughter of the south shall come to the king of the north to make an agreement: but she shall not retain the power of the arm; neither shall he stand, nor his arm: but she shall be given up, and they that brought her, and he that begat her, and he that strengthened her in these times."* (KJV) ... The Second Syrian War, a fight between Ptolemy II and Antiochus II Theos, began in 260 BCE. Seven years later, the two armies had exhausted each other. The back-and-forth warfare with no apparent winner showed both sides the futility of more war, so they made peace. As a symbol of reconciliation, Berenice Syra, the daughter of Ptolemy II, the king of the south, was given in marriage to the king of the north, Antiochus II, who was forced to set aside his wife Laodice I so that the marriage could take place. In 246 BCE, both Ptolemy II and Antiochus II died. Tradition says that Antiochus was poisoned by Laodice, who wanted the throne for her son Seleucus, while Berenice, now an Egyptian outsider at the Seleucid court, persuaded her brother, the newly crowned Ptolemy III Euergetes of Egypt, to come to Antioch to help install her infant son as king. By the time Ptolemy arrived, however, Berenice and her son had been assassinated. Ptolemy III then declared war on the new Seleucid king, Seleucus II Callinicus.

246-223 BCE, Third Syrian War

verses 7-9: *"But out of a branch of her roots shall one stand up in his estate, which shall come with an army, and shall enter into the fortress of the king of the north, and shall deal against them, and shall prevail: And shall also carry captives into Egypt their gods, with their princes, and with their precious vessels of silver and of gold; and he shall continue more years than the king of the north. So the king of the south shall come into his kingdom, and shall return into his own land."* (KJV) ... Berenice was the daughter of Ptolemy II, so his son and her brother, Ptolemy III Euergetes, is the one being referred to as "a branch from her roots" in the prophecy. After his sister's assassination in 246 BCE, Ptolemy III declared war against Seleucus II, thus beginning the Third Syrian War from 246-241 BCE. At first, Ptolemy II won

Chapter Five: What Shall Befall Thy People (Daniel 10:1-12:4)

impressive victories in Syria and Anatolia, and his army was successful as far east as Babylon. Later, Seleucus II was betrayed by his younger brother, Antiochus Hierax, who declared his independence from Seleucus after the latter had been persuaded by his mother Laodice to grant Antiochus a coregency. Weakened by defection and defeats, Seleucus II sued for peace in 241 BCE, in exchange giving Ptolemy III extensive territory along the coast of Syria, including Antioch, and large quantities of gold and silver in tribute. Ptolemy III was succeeded by his son, Ptolemy IV Philopator.

223-218 BCE, Fourth Syrian War

verse 10: *"But his sons shall be stirred up, and shall assemble a multitude of great forces: and one shall certainly come, and overflow, and pass through: then shall he return, and be stirred up, even to his fortress."* (KJV) ... The narrative of the prophecy now switches back to the northern kingdom to focus on the Seleucids. After the death of Seleucus II, his eldest son, Seleucus III Ceraunus, became king and soon attacked Ptolemy III's provinces in Asia, initiating the Fourth Syrian War from 219-217 BCE. He was unsuccessful as a military leader and was assassinated by members of the Seleucid army. His ambitious 18-year-old brother, Antiochus III, later known to history as "the Great," was recognized as king in his place. Once established on the throne, Antiochus III set out to restore glory to the kingdom, his intention being to recover all territorial possessions lost since the days of Seleucus I Nicator. Antiochus first subdued the eastern provinces and Anatolia, then turned his attention toward Syria and Egypt. In 218 BCE, he marched his army through Judea to the border of Egypt, where he stayed for a year preparing for a major assault on Egypt. Meanwhile, the new king of Egypt, Ptolemy IV Philopator, presided over a kingdom in disarray after years of imperial intrigue and maneuvering, and, because he was very young, was but a pawn of his counselor, Sosibius, who began training an army to oppose the inevitable Seleucid attack. In addition to Greeks, Sosibius conscripted and trained Egyptians, the first time that native Egyptians had comprised part of a Ptolemaic army. By the summer of 217 BCE, the Battle of Raphia between the king of the north and king of the south was about to begin.

217-204 BCE, Battle of Raphia

verses 11-12: *"And the king of the south shall be moved with choler, and shall come forth and fight with him, even with the king of the north: and he shall set forth a great multitude; but the multitude shall be given into his hand. And when he hath taken away the multitude, his heart shall be lifted up; and he shall cast down many ten thousands: but he shall not be strengthened by it."* (KJV) ... The Battle of Raphia was fought on June 22, 217 BCE, between the armies of Antiochus III and Ptolemy IV. The battle took place on the sands of what is today called Gaza, near the modern town of Rafah. According to the historian Polybius, Antiochus III had superior forces, perhaps as many as 70,000 foot soldiers and 5,000 cavalry, with 73 war elephants of Indian stock. Ptolemy had fewer soldiers and calvary, and his war elephants from Africa were easily spooked by the Indian elephants. At first the battle went heavily in favor of Antiochus, but, thinking he had victory in hand, he made a strategic blunder that allowed Ptolemy's better-disciplined army to counter-attack and rout his forces. Antiochus was forced to withdraw to Lebanon while Ptolemy reconsolidated his dominion over Coele-Syria. The native Egyptians recruited and trained by Sosibius performed well and much of the victory was attributable to their effectiveness, but they would later rebel against the rule of Ptolemy and form a separate government in Upper Egypt that lasted from 207-186 BCE. Ptolemy IV lost about half of his kingdom in the process, which set the stage for the rise of the Seleucids as rulers of Judea.

204-194 BCE, Fifth Syrian War

verses 13-17: *"For the king of the north shall return, and shall set forth a multitude greater than the former, and shall certainly come after certain years with a great army and with much riches. And in those times there shall many stand up against the king of the south: also the robbers of thy people shall exalt themselves to establish the vision; but they shall fall. So the king of the north shall come, and cast up a mount, and take the most fenced cities: and the arms of the south shall not withstand, neither his chosen people, neither shall there be any strength to withstand. But he that cometh against him shall do according to his own will, and none shall stand before him: and he shall stand in the glorious land, which by his hand shall be consumed. He shall also set his face to enter with the strength of his whole kingdom, and upright ones with him; thus shall he do: and he shall give him the daughter of women, corrupting her: but she shall not stand on his side, neither be for him."* (KJV) ... Ptolemy IV died in 204 BCE, leaving the throne of Egypt to the child king, Ptolemy V. The power struggle that resulted among the Egyptian leaders soon led to anarchy. Antiochus III took advantage of the situation and invaded Coele-Syria in 202 BCE, after making a military alliance with Philip V

Chapter Five: What Shall Befall Thy People (Daniel 10:1-12:4)

of Macedon. The Seleucid forces first overran the coastal areas of Judea and then achieved a decisive victory over the army of Ptolemy in the Battle of Panium in 198 BCE. At this point, Rome, fearing disruption of vital grain supplies from Egypt, warned Antiochus and Philip not to invade Egypt, and they complied. Antiochus was content to consolidate his rule over Coele-Syria and the coastal areas. Since Ptolemy was facing a revolt at home, he sued for peace in 195 BCE, signing away Coele-Syria and agreeing to marry Cleopatra I, the daughter of Antiochus III. The marriage took place in 194 BCE, with Antiochus hoping to gain influence in the Egyptian court through his daughter, but she proved to be loyal to her husband. The most significant result of the peace treaty of 195 BCE was the permanent transfer of Judea and Jerusalem to Seleucid rule.

195-187 BCE

verses 18-19: *"After this shall he turn his face unto the isles, and shall take many: but a prince for his own behalf shall cause the reproach offered by him to cease; without his own reproach he shall cause it to turn upon him. Then he shall turn his face toward the fort of his own land: but he shall stumble and fall, and not be found."* (KJV) ... With peace secured on his southern flank, Antiochus III attacked Greece with 10,000 soldiers to aid the revolt against Greek rule by the Aetolians, who elected him their commander in chief. This westward thrust soon brought Antiochus into conflict with Rome, even causing him to give refuge to Rome's nemesis, Hannibal, at his court. The Romans responded by defeating Antiochus at Thermopylae, and he was forced to withdraw back into Asia. The Roman army then proceeded to wrest Anatolia away from Seleucid control by winning the Battle of Magnesia. This defeat, combined with the defeat of Hannibal at sea, gave Rome control of Asia Minor for good, a fact that was made official by the Treaty of Apamea in 188 BCE. The treaty saddled Antiochus with heavy debt to Rome, and he had to send his son Mithridates, who would later rename himself Antiochus IV Epiphanes, to Rome as a hostage. With Seleucid authority weakened, the eastern provinces gained independence. Antiochus III died in 187 BCE in Persia, trying to reassert his authority over his diminishing empire.

187-175 BCE

verse 20: *"Then shall stand up in his estate a raiser of taxes in the glory of the kingdom: but within few days he shall be destroyed, neither in anger, nor in battle. And in his estate shall stand up a vile person, to whom they shall not give the honour of the kingdom: but he shall come in peaceably, and obtain the kingdom by flatteries."* (KJV) ... Antiochus III was succeeded by Seleucus IV Philopater. Because of the heavy tribute now being demanded by Rome and the greatly reduced territory from which to generate revenue, Seleucus resorted to heavy taxation of his remaining subjects. The Jews in Judea suffered terribly under this burden. At one point, Seleucus ordered his treasurer, Heliodorus, to plunder the temples in his empire, including the treasury of the Temple in Jerusalem. The priests and people wailed and lamented and entreated God to prevent the sacrilege, but Heliodorus persisted. A vivid account of what happened next is given in the apocryphal book of 2 Maccabees 3:23-39 (KJV):

> "Nevertheless Heliodorus executed that which was decreed. Now as he was there present himself with his guard about the treasury, the Lord of spirits, and the Prince of all power, caused a great apparition, so that all that presumed to come in with him were astonished at the power of God, and fainted, and were sore afraid. For there appeared unto them an horse with a terrible rider upon him, and adorned with a very fair covering, and he ran fiercely, and smote at Heliodorus with his forefeet, and it seemed that he that sat upon the horse had complete harness of gold. Moreover two other young men appeared before him, notable in strength, excellent in beauty, and comely in apparel, who stood by him on either side; and scourged him continually, and gave him many sore stripes. And Heliodorus fell suddenly unto the ground, and was compassed with great darkness: but they that were with him took him up, and put him into a litter. Thus him, that lately came with a great train and with all his guard into the said treasury, they carried out, being unable to help himself with his weapons: and manifestly they acknowledged the power of God. For he by the hand of God was cast down, and lay speechless without all hope of life. But they praised the Lord, that had miraculously honoured his own place: for the temple; which a little afore was full of fear and trouble, when the Almighty Lord appeared, was filled with joy and gladness. Then straightways certain of Heliodorus' friends prayed Onias, that he would call upon the most High to grant him his life, who lay ready to give up the ghost. So the high priest, suspecting lest the king should misconceive that some treachery had been done to Heliodorus by the Jews, offered a sacrifice for the health of the man. Now as the high priest was making an atonement, the same young men in the same clothing appeared and stood beside Heliodorus, saying, Give Onias the high priest great thanks, insomuch as for his sake the Lord hath granted thee life: And seeing that thou hast been scourged from heaven, declare unto all men the mighty power of God.

And when they had spoken these words, they appeared no more. So Heliodorus, after he had offered sacrifice unto the Lord, and made great vows unto him that had saved his life, and saluted Onias, returned with his host to the king. Then testified he to all men the works of the great God, which he had seen with his eyes. ... For he that dwelleth in heaven hath his eye on that place, and defendeth it; ..."[1]

In the final years of Seleucus IV's rule, the Roman Senate, wanting a better guarantee of the king's fealty, demanded that he send his son and heir, Demetrius, to be held as a hostage, at the same time releasing Seleucus' brother Mithridates as a token of their good will. Seleucus IV died in 175 BCE, possibly poisoned by Heliodorus, but many attributed his demise to the machinations of his ambitious brother Mithridates. Whatever the case, this left the door open for Mithridates to work his mischief since the legitimate heir to the throne, Demetrius, was still being held in Rome. He moved quickly to secure the throne for himself when he heard of his brother's death, making his way to Pergamum, where he sought the help of King Eumenes II to establish his claim to the throne. Heliodorus had crowned another son of Seleucus named Antiochus, a five-year-old, but Mithridates quickly maneuvered himself into a coregency. The child-king Antiochus did not fair well under this arrangement, being murdered not long after it began. This left the throne in the sole possession of Mithridates.

175-168 BCE, Sixth Syrian War

verses 22-28: *"And with the arms of a flood shall they be overflown from before him, and shall be broken; yea, also the prince of the covenant. And after the league made with him he shall work deceitfully: for he shall come up, and shall become strong with a small people. He shall enter peaceably even upon the fattest places of the province; and he shall do that which his fathers have not done, nor his fathers fathers; he shall scatter among them the prey, and spoil, and riches: yea, and he shall forecast his devices against the strong holds, even for a time. And he shall stir up his power and his courage against the king of the south with a great army; and the king of the south shall be stirred up to battle with a very great and mighty*

---

[1] Daniel 12:1-4 describes the empowerment of the Jews by God that led to the Maccabean revolt provoked by the period of persecution beginning with Seleucus IV and Heliodorus in 187 BCE and culminating with the taking away of the daily sacrifices by Antiochus IV on 25 Kislev (December 13), 167 BCE. When Heliodorus was repelled from the Temple, that was the literal fulfillment of verse 1, *"And at that time shall Michael stand up ..."* (KJV).

army; but he shall not stand: for they shall forecast devices against him. Yea, they that feed of the portion of his meat shall destroy him, and his army shall overflow: and many shall fall down slain. And both these kings' hearts shall be to do mischief, and they shall speak lies at one table; but it shall not prosper: for yet the end shall be at the time appointed. Then shall he return into his land with great riches; and his heart shall be against the holy covenant; and he shall do exploits, and return to his own land." (KJV) ... After the death of the child-king Antiochus, Mithridates overpowered all further opposition, usurped the throne, and changed his name to Antiochus IV Epiphanes to bolster his authority. Immediately, Antiochus set about to Hellenize and unify his realm, including Judea, initiating a struggle for the hearts and minds of the Jewish people that would dominate the history of the Jews for several centuries. Onias III was the high priest in Jerusalem when Antiochus became king and was known for his faithfulness to the traditions of Judaism and resistance to Hellenization. He had a brother, Joshua, who had adopted the Hellenistic ways of the Seleucids, and had even changed his name to its Greek equivalent, Jason. Aware that Antiochus was in severe need of money, Jason offered him a bribe to set aside Onias and appoint himself as high priest in his brother's place. Antiochus was only too happy to do so, installing Jason as high priest in 174 BCE. Jason thus became the first high priest over the Jewish people to be appointed by a non-Jewish secular authority, much to the chagrin of the many faithful Jews still residing in the land. Two years later, Jason sent a Temple official named Menelaus to Antiochus bearing his tribute in gold and silver for that year. Instead of delivering the money, Menelaus added more gold to Jason's tribute and, representing the total as his own, bribed Antiochus to supplant Jason and install him as high priest in his place. Antiochus greedily did so.

While these priestly machinations were taking place in the inner circles of Temple leadership, Antiochus, eager to add the riches of the Nile to his imperial revenue, decided to tour Egypt, entering with a small army to act as bodyguard and posing as the protector of his nephew, the newly crowned 14-year-old king, Ptolemy VI Philometor, son of Antiochus' sister Cleopatra I. Once in Egypt as a benefactor of Ptolemy, Antiochus distributed money to gain the favor of the Egyptian people. At the same time, his generals reconnoitered the kingdom's defenses. In these deceitful ways, Antiochus laid the groundwork for his later attempt to conquer Egypt by force. By 170 BCE, Antiochus deemed everything in readiness, so he again set out for Egypt. He moved his army to the border, where he was met by a large Egyptian force, but the army of Ptolemy VI was

Chapter Five: What Shall Befall Thy People (Daniel 10:1-12:4)

unable to stop him. He captured Pelusium and Memphis, including his nephew Ptolemy VI, and set out to attack Alexandria. To curry favor with the Egyptians, Antiochus publicly supported Ptolemy VI as a puppet king, conducting many friendly meetings and war conferences with him in Memphis, and, to appease Rome, left Ptolemy on the throne when he withdrew from Egypt to return to Syria. As he passed through Judea in 169 BCE, Antiochus' soldiers killed anyone who opposed them and plundered the city of Jerusalem, a portent of even worse things to come on his next visit. Back in Egypt, the Alexandrians, once Antiochus and his army had gone home, renounced Ptolemy VI and declared their independence, crowning his younger brother, Ptolemy VII Euergetes, as their king. Still a puppet king in Memphis, Ptolemy VI initially praised his uncle Antiochus, but later formed a strategically wise but uneasy alliance with his brother, both agreeing to rule Egypt jointly and oppose Antiochus as one.

168 BCE-66 CE

verses 29-35: *"At the time appointed he shall return, and come toward the south; but it shall not be as the former, or as the latter. For the ships of Chittim shall come against him: therefore he shall be grieved, and return, and have indignation against the holy covenant: so shall he do; he shall even return, and have intelligence with them that forsake the holy covenant. And arms shall stand on his part, and they shall pollute the sanctuary of strength, and shall take away the daily sacrifice, and they shall place the abomination that maketh desolate. And such as do wickedly against the covenant shall he corrupt by flatteries: but the people that do know their God shall be strong, and do exploits. And they that understand among the people shall instruct many: yet they shall fall by the sword, and by flame, by captivity, and by spoil, many days. Now when they shall fall, they shall be holpen with a little help: but many shall cleave to them with flatteries. And some of them of understanding shall fall, to try them, and to purge, and to make them white, even to the time of the end: because it is yet for a time appointed."* (KJV) ... Angered by the alliance between the Ptolemy brothers, Antiochus invaded Egypt a second time in 168 BCE, and had his fleet capture Chittim (Cyprus). The Ptolemies appealed to Rome for help, and the Senate complied. As Antiochus approached Alexandria, he was met by three Roman senators. Popillius, speaking for the Senate, demanded that Antiochus withdraw from Egypt and Chittim (his ships were thus turned back against him). The Roman historian Livy described the meeting in his history of Rome, *Ab Urbe Condita*, xlv.12, as follows:

"After receiving the submission of the inhabitants of Memphis and of the rest of the Egyptian people, some submitting voluntarily, others under threats, [Antiochus] marched by easy stages towards Alexandria. After crossing the river at Eleusis, about four miles from Alexandria, he was met by the Roman commissioners, to whom he gave a friendly greeting and held out his hand to Popilius. Popilius, however, placed in his hand the tablets on which was written the decree of the senate and told him first of all to read that. After reading it through he said he would call his friends into council and consider what he ought to do. Popilius, stern and imperious as ever, drew a circle round the king with the stick he was carrying and said, 'Before you step out of that circle give me a reply to lay before the senate.' For a few moments he hesitated, astounded at such a peremptory order, and at last replied, 'I will do what the senate thinks right.' Not till then did Popilius extend his hand to the king as to a friend and ally. Antiochus evacuated Egypt at the appointed date, and the commissioners exerted their authority to establish a lasting concord between the brothers [Ptolemy VI and Ptolemy VII], as they had as yet hardly made peace with each other."

While Antiochus was preparing his army to retreat back to Syria after his humiliation by the Romans, erroneous news that he had been killed in Egypt arrived in Jerusalem. This report stimulated the former high priest Jason, who Antiochus had removed from that post in favor of the briber Menelaus, who gathered a thousand men and launched an attack on the city of Jerusalem and the Temple, hoping to regain his seat of authority. Menelaus was forced to take refuge inside the Akra fortress, where a garrison of Seleucid soldiers held out against the rebels. When Antiochus heard about the revolt, he hurried to Jerusalem[1]

---

[1] Scholars disagree about the number of times Antiochus IV passed through and plundered Jerusalem. One visit is indicated in each of the apocryphal books of 1 Maccabees 1:20-30 and 2 Maccabees 5:1-16, with plundering mentioned in both instances. A good case can be made that two separate instances are recorded, one in each book, thus providing evidence that there were indeed two visits. Two distinct visits are indicated in Josephus, *Antiquities*, 12.246-251, in the Dead Sea Scrolls (4Q248), and in Daniel, chapter 11, verses 28-32. Josephus mentions plundering on the second visit, as do the other two-visit sources. Since Antiochus invaded Egypt twice, it makes sense that he visited Jerusalem two times, once in 169 BCE and again in 168/7 BCE. It also makes sense that his army would have plundered and killed opponents on both occasions. However, it seems much more likely that the wholesale plundering of the Temple itself, and the widespread massacres described in several sources, both of which would have caused a severe reaction among the Jews in both Jerusalem and the countryside, is more logically associated with the period of unrest leading to the Maccabean revolt that began in 167 BCE.

to put down the insurrection, which he did with brutality, killing 40,000 Jewish men, women, and children, and enslaving even more. Antiochus also reinstated Menelaus to his post as high priest.

This was the beginning of a time of trouble for Jews that surpassed anything yet seen in Judea and in Jerusalem. During the next year, the practice of Judaism was forbidden by royal decree, as was the rite of circumcision and the observance of the sabbath. Torah scrolls were confiscated and burned. Anyone caught trying to observe Jewish rituals was summarily executed, usually by being burned alive. The Temple storehouses were looted with the help of Menelaus, its vessels removed and the treasury emptied. The daily morning and evening sacrifices were stopped for the first time since the return from Babylon when, to make a place for his soldiers to worship Zeus Olympius, Antiochus built an altar in the inner Temple, complete with a statue of the Greek god, building it atop the sacred altar of burnt offering. Then, on the 25th day of Kislev[1] in the 145th year of the Seleucid Empire, which is equivalent to the proleptic date December 13, 167 BCE in Gregorian reckoning, the flesh of swine was offered on the altar, the ultimate desecration of the place considered most holy by the Jewish people.

Scholars debate whether the desecration of the Temple was the spark that caused the Maccabean[2] revolt that began that year, but one thing is certain, the Jews had more than enough reason to rebel. The insurrection itself started in the rural town of Modin when a local priest named Mattathias refused to sacrifice to Greek gods on the town altar, publicly disobeying the decree by Antiochus that all of his subjects must worship the gods of the Hellenistic pantheon. Mattathias then proceeded to kill a Hellenized Jew who tried to comply in his place. He and his five sons immediately fled to the Judean wilderness to escape death and there began the fight for religious freedom,[3] but Mattathias died within the

---

[1] The 25th of Kislev (a day and month on the Jewish calendar) is not equivalent to December 25th (a day and month on the Gregorian calendar), as assumed by the authors of many commentaries and study Bibles. They incorrectly assume that the days in Kislev exactly align with the days in December. However, the alignment varies from year to year. This wrong assumption results in error when used to interpret chrono-specific prophecy.

[2] The term Maccabee is derived from the nickname of Judah, called "the Maccabee" ("the Hammer"), or it could be based on an acronym for the Torah verse "**Mi CH**amocha **BA**'elim YHWH", *"Who is like unto thee among the mighty, O Lord!"* from Exodus 15:11 (KJV).

[3] Dan. 12:1a: *"And at that time shall Michael stand up, the great prince which standeth for the children of thy people: and there shall be a time of trouble, such as never was since there was a nation ..."* (KJV).

year. His eldest son, Judah, gathered an army of irregulars and began the effort to gain independence from the rule of the Seleucids. The guerrilla tactics employed by the Maccabees were successful against the more-regimented Syrian troops, especially since the rebels knew the lay of the difficult Judean landscape infinitely better than their foreign adversaries. After three years of warfare, the Maccabean forces had captured Jerusalem. The priests immediately set about to rededicate the Temple and build a new altar of burnt offering. Daily sacrifices were resumed on the 25th day of the month of Kislev in the 148th year of the Seleucid Empire, which is equivalent December 10, 164 BCE in Gregorian reckoning, exactly 1,093¾ days after they had been stopped by Antiochus.

The prophecy in verses 2-32 of the eleventh chapter goes into great detail about the struggle between the Seleucids and the Ptolemies, and, more important theologically since it relates to the relationship of the Jewish people with God, between Hellenism and Judaism. After Antiochus profanes the Temple and stops the daily sacrifices, the prophecy reaches a turning point when Jerusalem was captured, the Temple altar was reconsecrated, and the daily sacrifices resumed, as described in verse 32b, *"but the people that do know their God shall be strong, and do exploits"* (KJV). The prophecy then jumps to the future in verses 33-35, *"And they that understand among the people shall instruct many: yet they shall fall by the sword, and by flame, by captivity, and by spoil, many days. Now when they shall fall, they shall be holpen with a little help: but many shall cleave to them with flatteries. And some of them of understanding shall fall, to try them, and to purge, and to make them white, even to the time of the end: because it is yet for a time appointed"* (KJV). The meaning of the last phrase in verse 35b, *"even to the time of the end: because it is yet for a time appointed"* (KJV), can be understood chronologically by recalling that the interpretation of Daniel, chapter 7, verse 12, in which the phrase *"their lives were prolonged for a season and time"* (KJV) is also referenced from that turning-point date, December 10, 164 BCE. Apparently this "time of the end" reference in verse 35 is looking ahead to and foretelling the beginning of the *Diaspora*, which can be dated from 66 CE (see page 56).

At this point, it is good to remember the stated purpose of the eleventh chapter, which is revealed in its introduction in the tenth chapter, in verse 14, *"Now I am come to make thee understand what shall befall thy people in the latter days"* (KJV). In pursuit of this goal of revealing what shall befall the Jewish people after the time of the prophet Daniel, the prophecy has so far described events that have taken the Jewish people through the Achaemenid Persian period that followed the exile in Babylon down to the evils of Hellenism, specifically mentioning the trauma of the profanation of the Temple altar by Antiochus and the subsequent temporary loss of the sacrificial system so central to observance of the Mosaic Law. The prophecy then proceeds to describe the restoration of the Temple and sacrificial system by the Maccabees, then continues on to the start of the First Jewish War in 66 CE, which marked the beginning of the dispersal of the Jewish people among the nations and saw the eventual destruction of the Temple itself in 70 CE. Not surprisingly, all of the events described in the prophecy so far have involved the Temple, the city of Jerusalem, and the covenant governing the Jewish people's possession of the land. Most will agree that it is logical to assume that the rest of the prophecy will also involve the fate of the city of Jerusalem, the Temple site, and the people's possession of the land, and so it does. After jumping forward in time to "the time of the end" in verse 35 which, in this case, means looking forward in time to the beginning of the *Diaspora* in 66 CE, the prophecy resumes its forward movement in time in verses 36-45.

Fulfillment in History (after 70 CE)

The placement in history of the events described in verses 36-45 has been the subject of much speculation by expositors over the years. Some expositors claim that the prophecy in those verses was fulfilled completely during the time of Antiochus IV. Others say that history has yet to see any fulfillment of those verses. A few expositors have proposed fulfillments that fall in between the two extremes chronologically. However, none have proposed fulfillments that are post-biblical, yet found in recorded history looking backwards from our viewpoint today. Nevertheless, that is where the fulfillments of the prophecies in these verses are to be found. Using clues in the verses themselves, the time frame for the events in these verses can be determined, and, once that time frame has been established, the various events mentioned in the verses can be identified as they correlate with history, and as they relate to the fate of the Jewish people.

The key to understanding the prophecy is found in verses 42-43: "*He shall enter also into the glorious land, and many countries shall be overthrown: but these shall escape out of his hand, even Edom, and Moab, and the chief of the children of Ammon. He shall stretch forth his hand also upon the countries: and the land of Egypt shall not escape. But he shall have power over the treasures of gold and of silver, and over all the precious things of Egypt: and the Libyans and the*

Ethiopians shall be at his steps" (KJV). These verses describe a king that will conquer Egypt after coming through the land of Israel, and will approach near to both Libya and Ethiopia (ancient Cush). Fortunately, from the standpoint of identifying this king, there have been only a few conquerors of Egypt since 66 CE, the year at which the prophecy in verse 35 left off. Another key to understanding the prophecy is to realize that the eleventh chapter of Daniel has a parallel chronology with respect to the seventh chapter of Daniel.[1] In the same way that the time period described in verse 35b of the eleventh chapter was related to the "season and time" in the seventh chapter, as explained on page 70, verses 36-45 that follow that verse have a parallel structure in the seventh chapter as well, in verse 25b: *"and they shall be given into his hand until a time and times and the dividing of time"* (KJV). This parallel time period is the 798 years of Roman-Byzantine hegemony over the Jewish people and the city of Jerusalem that began in 161 BCE, when Judah Maccabee appealed to Rome for help against the Seleucid army, and it ended when Caliph Omar captured Jerusalem and the Temple Mount for Islam in the year 638 CE. The period from 161 BCE through 638 CE gives the time frame in which the conqueror of Egypt described in the prophecy in verses 42-43 will be found in history.

Since Antiochus IV never captured all of Egypt, and there is no record in history that he ever threatened Libya or Ethiopia militarily, he cannot be the conqueror of Egypt described in verses 42-43 of the eleventh chapter. Looking at the history of Egypt during the specified time frame, there is only one king who came down through the land of Israel and conquered all of Egypt, then made military excursions into both Libya and Ethiopia that are documented in the historical record. That king is Chosroes II Parvez, the twenty-second king of the Sassanid Persian Empire, who reigned from 590-628 CE. Skipping over verses 36-39 for the moment,[2] the narrative in verses 40-44 describes the struggle between the Byzantine and Sassanid Persian empires from 602-628 CE, and it specifically describes the conquests of Chosroes II during that period. So, let us take verses 40-45 and examine them verse by verse as follows:

---

[1] See the "Prophecy Overview" chart (located on PLATE 1 at the end of this book) for a comparison of the time lines for the seventh and the eleventh chapters. Note that the seventh chapter divides into three time lines, one for a "season and time" ending in 66 CE, another for "time and times and the dividing of time" (3½ "times") ending in 638 CE, and a third that is everlasting, without end.

[2] Verses 36-39 describe an earlier king, not Chosroes II, as will be shown later in this chapter.

624-638 CE

verse 40a: *"And at the time of the end shall the king of the south push at him: and the king of the north shall come against him like a whirlwind, with chariots, and with horsemen, and with many ships ..."* (KJV) ... In this case, the phrase "time of the end" refers to the conclusion of the time period defined in Daniel, chapter 7, verse 25b, the 3½ "times." A description of the events that will happen at the very end of this time period is being given in verse 40a, and three political entities are described: 1) the king of the south, who shall push at **him**, 2) the king of the north who will come against **him**, and then 3) the entity described as **him**. Since the "him" can be identified as the king of the Sassanid Empire (Chosroes II and his successors), the identities of the other two personalities can be easily determined from history. The king of the south can be identified as Mohammed and the nascent army of Islam, which, after 622 CE, was pushing northward toward Persian lands after consolidating its rule over Arabia, even making a few tentative excursions into the Persian lands east of the Jordan River just before Mohammed's death in 632 CE. The king of the north is the emperor of the Byzantine Empire, Heraclius, who reigned as emperor from 610-641 CE. Using his large navy, he sailed his army across the Black Sea in 624 CE, landed in Armenia, then marched overland and attacked the Sassanid Empire through its northern back door while Chosroes was preoccupied with solidifying his gains in Anatolia and Egypt, and was thus unprepared to defend his heartland. The events described in verse 40a are a climax, and bring to a close the events described in verses 40b-44, which detail the rapid expansion of the Sassanid Persian Empire. Verse 40a foretells the decline and final defeat of the Sassanid Persians by Byzantium in 628 CE, and gives the first hint at the rise of Islam, which would go on to supplant both powers in the region, conquering Judea and Jerusalem in 638 CE.

602-616 CE

verses 40b-43a: *"... and he shall enter into the countries, and shall overflow and pass over. He shall enter also into the glorious land, and many countries shall be overthrown: but these shall escape out of his hand, even Edom, and Moab, and the chief of the children of Ammon. He shall stretch forth his hand also upon the countries: and the land of Egypt shall not escape. But he shall have power over the treasures of gold and of silver, and over all the precious things of Egypt: ..."* (KJV) ... Verses 40b-44 are a description of the rapid expansion of the Sassanid Persian Empire from 605-628 CE. As pointed out in the preceding section, this period of expansion of the empire comes immediately before the events describing the final demise of the empire in real time as described in verse 40a.[1] The empire's expansion began in 602 CE. That year, the Byzantine emperor Maurice, who had helped establish Chosroes II on the Sassanid throne, was killed in a palace coup in Constantinople. The young Sassanid king, using the murder of Maurice as a pretext to break the peace treaty that had been signed before the death of Maurice, attacked the Byzantine provinces in Asia Minor, the area known today as central and western Turkey. From 605-613 CE, the Sassanid armies of Chosroes captured the important cities of Dara, Amida, Edesa, Hierapolis, Aleppo, Apamea, Caesarea, and Damascus, plus all of the surrounding provincial territories. Emboldened by his relatively easy victories, Chosroes declared a holy war against the Byzantine Christians, and boasted that he would extend the empire and its Zoroastrian religion even beyond the far-flung boundaries that had existed under Darius III a thousand years earlier.

Pausing in Damascus, Chosroes made a strategic political decision that was designed to weaken the Byzantine defenses in Judea, through which he had to pass to invade Egypt. He appointed the son of the Jewish Exilarch in Babylon, a mystic named Nehemiah ben Hushiel, as nominal head of his armies, although his general Shahrbaraz, known as "the king's boar," actually led the invasion. The Jews in the land of Israel rallied behind the invading army of Chosroes, who was considered by many Jews to be a "second Cyrus" who would return them back to self-governance and restore their Temple in Jerusalem. They had been treated harshly by the Byzantine Christians for more than three-hundred years and were eager for a change of regimes. With the help of thousands of Jewish citizens inside its walls, Jerusalem was captured by the Persians in 614 CE, and a massacre began. Centuries of hatred and resentment were unleashed against the Christian populace, holy sites, and clerics.[2] The bishop of Jerusalem, Zechariah, and the "true cross" were carried captive back to the Persian capital.

As for the lands of Moab, Edom, and the chief of Ammon mentioned in verse 41 of the prophecy, that is referring to the Arabs living in the lands formerly occupied by those kingdoms, since all three kingdoms had long since ceased to

---

[1] Apparently Daniel saw and thus chose to describe the demise of the empire first, followed by the description of its rise given out of chronological order.

[2] The sack of Jerusalem by the Sassanids and their Jewish allies was undoubtedly a bloody affair, but the best-preserved account, that of the monk Antiochus Strategos, is probably an exaggeration skewed toward a Byzantine perspective.

exist as recognizable political entities by the time of Chosroes II. The former territories of the Moabites, Edomites, and Ammonites were occupied by the Bani Ghassanids, a tribe of Monophysite Christians who had been allied with Byzantium for many years, essentially acting as buffers against Sassanid Persia. When Chosroes captured Syria and Judea in 614 CE, he only partially overran the territory of the Ghassanids. When Heraclius began his final push against Persia in 624 CE, the Ghassanids came against Chosroes and reclaimed their lost lands east of the Jordan River. This guerilla warfare against the Sassanids in what is today eastern Syria and western Jordan greatly aided the Byzantine cause. In appreciation, Heraclius appointed the chief of the Ghassanids, Jabala ibn al-Ayham, as King of the Arabs. The part of the prophecy about Egypt was fulfilled in 616 CE, two years after the capture of Jerusalem, when Egypt was captured by the army of Chosroes II under the command of Shahrbaraz.

616-624 CE

verses 43b-44: *"... and the Libyans and the Ethiopians shall be at his steps. But tidings out of the east and out of the north shall trouble him: therefore he shall go forth with great fury to destroy, and utterly to make away many."* (KJV) ... After capturing Egypt, the army of Chosroes II apparently made incursions into Libya as far as Tripoli, and pushed up the Nile toward Ethiopia. There is no evidence that the Sassanids captured these territories during this period, but historical documents, and some archeological evidence, indicate that the Sassanids plundered in Cyrenaica on the coast of Libya and perhaps inland to the Siwa oasis in the west and beyond the first Nile cataract in the south.[1] Whether or not the Sassanids actually entered Libya and Ethiopia in force is not the point of the prophecy, however. It merely says that these regions "shall be at his steps," and this was certainly the case. Chosroes II had expanded his empire to its greatest extent by 624 CE, being almost unstoppable for more than two decades, but his fortunes began to turn that year when Heraclius felt strong enough to begin a counteroffensive. With Chosroes' resources devoted to consolidating his gains in Egypt and Anatolia, the eastern provinces began to revolt. Heraclius then sailed his Byzantine army across the Black Sea and attacked the Sassanid rear through Armenia. This required Chosroes to leave Egypt and rush his army to met the challenges in the north and east, as the prophecy had foretold.

---

[1] Comparetti, Matteo "The Sassanians in Africa," *Transoxiana*, vol. 4 (July, 2002).

614-617 CE, Second attempt to rebuild the Temple

verse 45: *"And he shall plant the tabernacles of his palace between the seas in the glorious holy mountain; yet he shall come to his end, and none shall help him."* (KJV) ... Verse 45 now drops back in time to the capture of Jerusalem in 614 CE. After taking the city, Chosroes II established Nehemiah ben Hushiel, son of the Exilarch in Babylon and figurehead commander of the Persian army during the invasion, as governor in Jerusalem, thus planting the tabernacles of his palace on the holy mountain (Temple Mount). Ben Hushiel governed the city with a twelve-man "council of the righteous," exercising political and religious authority. Soon after being installed as governor of Judea, he began making preparations for rebuilding the Temple, and he also began sorting out genealogies in anticipation of resuming the priesthood. However, ben Hushiel was killed by a mob of rioting Christian youths only a few months after being appointed governor. Chosroes, then needing to placate the city's anti-Jewish Christian majority, appointed a Christian governor to replace ben Hushiel and banned Jews from approaching within three miles of the city gates, dashing all hopes for a rebuilt Temple or even a Jew-friendly Jerusalem. In 628 CE, Jerusalem was recaptured by Heraclius, with thousands of Persians and Jews killed in the process, and the city reverted to Byzantine rule. A decade later, after the Muslims captured Jerusalem from the Byzantines, Sebeos recorded that a small group of Jewish rebels succeeded in building an altar on the Mount, but "Ishmaelites" forced its removal.

Returning to verses 36-39

Now that the king (the "him") who is opposed by the king of the north and the king of the south in verses 40-45, and who would overrun Egypt after passing through the land of Israel, has been identified as Chosroes II of the Sassanid Persian Empire, this leaves the identity of the king described in verses 36-39 still to be determined, since those verses were skipped over several paragraphs ago to examine verses 40-45. The explanation of verses 40-45 established that the last time period specified by the prophecy in the eleventh chapter of Daniel is the one from 602-638 CE, so now the interpretation of verses 36-39 can be done. Remember, the king must be a person who ruled after 66 CE and before 602 CE, who was important with respect to the fate of the Jewish people, and whose actions fit the description given in the prophecy. Looking at history, we find an emperor of Rome who meets all of the requirements, as follows:

Chapter Five: What Shall Befall Thy People (Daniel 10:1-12:4)

Attempts to Build a Jewish Temple in Jerusalem		
Year	*Attempted by*	*Result*
ca. 1,008 BCE	David, King of Israel	Prevented by God
1,002-995 BCE	Solomon, King of Israel	Built
ca. 535-515 BCE	Zerubbabel, Governor of Judah	Rebuilt
ca. 19 BCE	Herod, King of the Jews, *etc.*	Enlarged (rebuilt?)
132 CE	Hadrian, Emperor of Rome	Promised
132-135 CE	Simon bar Kochba, *Nasi* of Israel	Disputed
363 CE	Julian the Apostate, Emperor of Rome	Prevented by fire
614 CE	Nehemiah ben Hushiel, Gov. of Judea	Aborted
638 CE	Small group of Jewish rebels	Built only an altar

363 CE, First attempt to rebuild the Temple

verse 36-39: *"And the king shall do according to his will; and he shall exalt himself, and magnify himself above every god, and shall speak marvellous things against the God of gods, and shall prosper till the indignation be accomplished: for that that is determined shall be done. Neither shall he regard the God of his fathers, nor the desire of women, nor regard any god: for he shall magnify himself above all. But in his estate shall he honour the God of forces: and a god whom his fathers knew not shall he honour with gold, and silver, and with precious stones, and pleasant things. Thus shall he do in the most strong holds with a strange god, whom he shall acknowledge and increase with glory: and he shall cause them to rule over many, and shall divide the land for gain."* (KJV) ... Twenty-three years after the death of Constantine I, who opened the Roman Empire to Christianity by issuing the Edict of Milan that proclaimed religious toleration throughout the empire in 313 CE, his nephew Julian, known to history as Julian "the Apostate," was installed as the last non-Christian ruler of the Roman Empire. He was sustained as emperor mainly by the power of the western Roman army. During his reign from 360-363 CE, Julian actively encouraged the return of the Roman people to pagan Hellenism and forcefully rejected the teachings of both Judaism and Christianity. He wrote a number of blasphemous treatises whose sole purpose was to convince his subjects that both religions were nothing but hoaxes. He was considered a Neo-Platonist, but, judging from his existing writings, he seems to have had no real religious convictions. However, Julian is important in Jewish history because of his attempt to rebuild the Temple in Jerusalem in 363 CE, the first serious attempt to rebuild it after its destruction by the Romans in 70 CE. The fourth-century historian Ammianus Marcellinus, in his *Roman History* 23.1.1-3, offered the following account of Julian's attempt to rebuild the Temple:

> "To pass over minute details, these were the principal events of the year. But Julian, who in his third consulship had taken as his colleague Sallustius, the prefect of Gaul, now entered on his fourth year [363 CE], and by a novel arrangement took as his colleague a private individual; an act of which no one recollected an instance since that of Diocletian and Aristobulus. And although, foreseeing in his anxious mind the various accidents that might happen, he urged on with great diligence all the endless preparations necessary for his expedition, yet distributing his diligence everywhere; and being eager to extend the recollection of his reign by the greatness of his exploits, he proposed to rebuild at a vast expense the once magnificent temple of Jerusalem, which after many deadly contests was with difficulty taken by Vespasian and Titus, who succeeded his father in the conduct of the siege. And he assigned the task to Alypius of Antioch, who had formerly been proprefect of Britain. But though Alypius [as manager of construction on site in Jerusalem] applied himself vigorously to the work, and though the governor of the province co-operated with him, fearful balls of fire burst forth with continual eruptions close to the foundations, burning several of the workmen and making the spot altogether inaccessible. And thus the very elements, as if by some fate, repelling the attempt, it was laid aside."

A month after the first attempt to rebuild the Temple was halted by the mysterious fire erupting from excavations on the Temple Mount, Julian the Apostate died in battle against the Sassanid Persians. After the failed attempt by Julian, only one more serious attempt to rebuild the Temple would be made, that being the aborted attempt made by Nehemiah ben Hushiel in 614 CE, during his brief governorship under the rule of the Sassanid Persians. That second and final attempt to rebuild the Temple building itself was foretold in verse 45 (previously explained on page 76), the verse that brings the vision recorded by Daniel in the tenth and eleventh chapters of his book to a close.

CHAPTER SIX

SEVENTY WEEKS ARE DETERMINED

READ DANIEL 9:1-27 ON PAGE 228 | SEE TIME LINE ❼ ON PLATE 1

The ninth chapter of Daniel says that it was revealed in *"the first year of Darius the son of Ahasuerus, of the seed of the Medes, which was made king over the realm of the Chaldeans"* (KJV). This is possibly a reference to Cyrus the Great, but more likely to his general Gubaru who accepted the surrender of the city of Babylon and was appointed governor after its capture on October 29, 539 BCE. The chrono-specific prophecy in the ninth chapter is thus dated to the first year after the conclusion of the seventy years of subjugation to Babylon that had been prophesied by Jeremiah. Besides Daniel's prayer of confession, which takes up most of the text, the ninth chapter features the much-debated prophecy of the seventy weeks, found in verses 24-27 at its end. Those four verses are certainly the most misinterpreted and perhaps most controversial verses in the entire Bible. Christian scholars and theologians have long disagreed with one another, and with Jewish rabbis and sages, about their meaning. Much of the disagreement between Christianity and Judaism comes from the theological biases inherent in each faith. In modern times, neither faith has been able to approach the ninth chapter without preconceived ideas and beliefs, in the case of Christian expositors the certainty that the seventy weeks must speak about the death of Jesus and, in the case of Jewish expositors, the certainty that the Hebrew Scriptures cannot say anything at all about him. This exposition makes neither assumption.

The ninth chapter of Daniel can be divided into three distinct parts. The first part is comprised of verses 1-2. Those verses confirm that Daniel was familiar with the prophecies that had been made before he was born by his contemporary, Jeremiah, specifically those foretelling the seventy-year duration of Babylon's hegemony over the people of Judea. The Jewish subjugation to Babylon ended in 539 BCE when the Achaemenid Persians under their king, Cyrus the Great, captured Babylon. Daniel may also have been familiar with the prophecies of Isaiah that foretold the appearance of Cyrus on the stage of Jewish history, even though the prophet Isaiah is not mentioned by name in Daniel. The second part is comprised of verses 3-23. Those verses contain Daniel's prayer of confession and repentance for the nation of Israel in exile. Such repentance was proscribed by Moses in Leviticus, chapter 26, verses 39-45. Daniel acknowledges the reason for the destruction of the Temple, exile from *Eretz-Israel*, and subjugation to surrounding nations that have befallen the people of God, and follows that confession by asking for forgiveness and redemption, as recorded in verses 11-14: *"Yea, all Israel have transgressed thy law, even by departing, that they might not obey thy voice; therefore the curse is poured upon us, and the oath that is written in the law of Moses the servant of God, because we have sinned against him. And he hath confirmed his words, which he spake against us, and against our judges that judged us, by bringing upon us a great evil: for under the whole heaven hath not been done as hath been done upon Jerusalem. As it is written in the law of Moses, all this evil is come upon us: yet made we not our prayer before the Lord our God, that we might turn from our iniquities, and understand thy truth. Therefore hath the Lord watched upon the evil, and brought it upon us: for the Lord our God is righteous in all his works which he doeth: for we obeyed not his voice"* (KJV).[1] The third part of the ninth chapter, comprised of verses 24-27, sets forth the prophecy of the seventy weeks. That prophecy will be the focus of the remainder of this chapter, mainly because it is the single most important prophecy in the Book of Daniel from the standpoint of soteriology.[2] It will also be the focus of the next chapter as well. But, before delving into the expository details of the enigmatic prophecy of the seventy weeks, a few words about the themes running through the prophecy in verses 24-27 are in order.

Two Major Themes

The chrono-specific prophecy in Daniel, chapter 9, verses 24-27, has two major themes, a chronological theme that involves the time period identified as "seventy weeks" and a soteriological theme that involves a covenant and its confirmation by someone identified as the "anointed one." The chronological theme, which locates the seventy weeks in history, will be examined in this chapter, where the focus will be on identifying the commandment that initiates the seventy weeks and then on relating the various divisions of the seventy weeks to specific events in Jewish history. The soteriological theme will be examined in the next chapter of this book, where the focus will be on identifying the covenant and the anointed one who is prophesied to confirm the covenant. By examining

---

[1] *cf.* Leviticus, chapter 26.
[2] Soteriology is the study of religious doctrines of salvation.

the two themes in two separate chapters, it will be easier to understand both the chronology and the soteriology contained in the prophecy. Of course, the ultimate purpose of the chronological discussion in this chapter is to provide a historical framework for understanding the soteriology in the next, and the soteriological discussion in the next chapter will involve the history in this one, so the two themes will frequently intertwine. However, the primary focus of each chapter's discussion will be developed separately by theme as described above, beginning below with the examination of the chronology associated with the prophecy of the seventy weeks as specified in verse 25.

Keys to Interpretation

The first key to interpretation of the prophecy of the seventy weeks is to focus on the action events and time periods specified in the text of verse 25, which reads as follows in the King James Version: *"Know therefore and understand, that from the going forth of the commandment to restore and to build Jerusalem unto the Messiah the Prince shall be seven weeks, and threescore and two weeks: the street shall be built again, and the wall, even in troublous times."* The King James translation is improved somewhat in the JPS translation of verse 25 from the Masoretic text,[1] which removes a Christological bias that is not justified by the text, as follows: *"Know therefore and discern, that from the going forth of the word to restore and to build Jerusalem unto one anointed, a prince, shall be seven weeks; and for threescore and two weeks, it shall be built again, with broad place and moat, but in troublous times."* In verse 25 itself, there are essentially three action events: 1) the going forth of a commandment to build Jerusalem, 2) the restoring of an anointed one-prince to Jerusalem (which happens twice, as a later examination of history in this chapter will show), and 3) the rebuilding of Jerusalem's street and wall. Associated with the three action events are two time periods, one of seven weeks in duration followed by another of sixty-two weeks. The seven-week time period seems to be framed by the commandment to rebuild Jerusalem on one end and restoration of the anointed one-prince to Jerusalem on the other. The prophecy also seems to clarify that the timing of the "seventy weeks" is dependant in some way on the completion of the building of the street and wall.

---

[1] וְתֵדַע וְתַשְׂכֵּל מִן־מֹצָא דָבָר לְהָשִׁיב וְלִבְנוֹת יְרוּשָׁלִַם עַד־מָשִׁיחַ נָגִיד שָׁבֻעִים שִׁבְעָה וְשָׁבֻעִים שִׁשִּׁים וּשְׁנַיִם תָּשׁוּב וְנִבְנְתָה רְחוֹב וְחָרוּץ וּבְצוֹק הָעִתִּים ... Masoretic Text of Dan. 9:25 (BHS)

The second key to interpretation of the prophecy of the seventy weeks in verse 25 is to understand which decree to restore and rebuild Jerusalem is being referred to in that verse. Most expositors focus on the decrees issued to the Jews by various Persian rulers who lived around the time of Daniel, starting with the decree by Cyrus II the Great that was issued *circa* 539-538 BCE. That decree specifically directed the Jews to return to Jerusalem and rebuild the Temple, but there is no exact record of the year it was issued. Darius I the Great issued another decree *circa* 520 BCE, ratifying and extending the earlier decree of Cyrus. Almost a century after the decree issued by Cyrus, Artaxerxes I Longimanus issued two decrees to the Jews, the first to Ezra *circa* 458/457 BCE and the second to Nehemiah *circa* 445/444 BCE. The first decree gave Ezra permission to collect money for supporting the Temple, then instructed him to go to Jerusalem, there making sacrifices to God and setting up a system for teaching the Law of God to the people of Israel. The second decree was given to Nehemiah thirteen years later in the form of letters to governors of the lands surrounding Judea, authorizing him to rebuild the walls of Jerusalem with the cooperation of the surrounding governors. Expositors who pick the year of one of the above Persian decrees as the starting year of the prophecy of the seventy weeks usually go on to develop their interpretive scheme by assuming that a "week" means a "week of years" (*i.e.,* seven years) and that "seventy weeks" thus means 490 years. They then count forward in time to end their interpretation of the prophecy sometime around the assumed date for a significant event in the life of Jesus.

One very popular exposition in conservative circles is based on the *circa* 445 BCE decree. It was developed and set forth by Sir Robert Anderson in his book, *The Coming Prince* (1895). The late Dr. John Walvoord, in his commentary on Daniel,[1] had this to say about Anderson's interpretive scheme:

> "Sir Robert Anderson has made a detailed study of the possible chronology for this period beginning with the well-established date of 445 B.C. when Nehemiah's decree was issued and culminating in A.D. 32 on the very day of Christ's triumphal entry into Jerusalem shortly before his crucifixion. Sir Robert Anderson specifies that the seventy sevens began on the first of Nisan, March 14, 445 B.C. and ended on April 6, A.D. 32, the tenth of Nisan. The complicated computation is based upon a prophetic year of 360 days ..."

---

[1] John F. Walvoord, *Daniel: The Key to Prophetic Revelation* (Chicago: Moody Press, 1971), p. 228.

Chapter Six: Seventy Weeks Are Determined (Daniel 9:1-27)

Walvoord then adds this interesting observation:

"That Sir Robert Anderson is right in building upon a 360-day year seems to be attested by the Scriptures. It is customary for the Jews to have twelve months of 360 days and then to insert a thirteenth month occasionally when necessary to correct the calendar. ... The conclusions reached by Anderson, however, are quite complicated in their argument and impossible to restate simply. While the details of Anderson's arguments may be debated, the plausibility of a literal interpretation ... makes this view very attractive."[1]

Although incorrect about the 360-day Jewish calendar, Walvoord is correct about one thing. Anderson's mathematical exposition is quite complicated. But, contrary to its basic assumption, use of a 360-day calendar is documented nowhere in the Bible or official Judaism. The lack of Scriptural or historical support for Anderson's basic premise invalidates his approach, and, without the benefit of his calendar manipulation, using the 445 BCE decree as the *terminus a quo*, as he does, yields an ending date in the year 38 CE, long after its *terminus ad quem* (the triumphal entry of Jesus) could have occurred in real time.

Another popular conservative interpretation of the prophecy of the seventy weeks uses the year of the second decree of Artaxerxes in 458 BCE as the starting point. This is the preferred interpretation of the late Dr. Leon Wood, who offers the following comments on Daniel, chapter 9, in his commentary:

"... the third possible *terminus a quo* may provide the best solution. This terminus is the earlier decree of Artaxerxes, given to Ezra in 458 B.C. Figuring on the basis of solar years, the 483-year period [69 weeks] ends now at A.D. 26, and this is the accepted date for Jesus' baptism. To this answer, the objection is sometimes made that actually the decree relative to Ezra's return was, of the three possible, the furthest removed from the idea of rebuilding Jerusalem. In reply, however, it may be stated that both the decree and Ezra's resultant work did concern rebuilding Jerusalem **in a moral and spiritual way** [emphasis added]; and there is reason to believe that considerable building operations, of a physical nature, occurred as well (*cf.* Ezra 9:9)."[1]

Wood then questions his own interpretation by adding the following:

---

[1] Leon J. Wood, *A Commentary on Daniel* (Eugene, Oregon: Wipf and Stock, 1998), p. 253-254.

"One question yet remains. What of the division of the 483 years into groups of 49 (seven weeks) and 434 (sixty-two weeks)? What occurred 49 years after the edict of Artaxerxes in 458 B.C., *i.e.,* in 409 B.C., which was of sufficient importance to call for this grouping? The context suggests that it must have concerned the building of Jerusalem, because the next phrase of the verse speaks of 'street' and 'moat' being constructed. Can the completion of rebuilding activity in Jerusalem be placed at 409 B.C.?"

Wood then goes on to suggest other possibilities for explaining the seven-week division, but admits that all of his speculations provide no real answer by concluding that, "**Details are lacking for certainty** ..." [emphasis added]. Thus, he ends up with no cogent explanation for the seven-week division specified in verse 25, offering only unverifiable assumptions as a possible interpretation.

The two interpretive schemes used for illustration above are typical of the dozens of interpretive schemes for the seventy weeks that use a starting date based on a decree by a Persian monarch. And, like those two examples, all of the other expositions using a Persian decree have failed to produce an ironclad interpretation that incorporates every element specified in verse 25 and also cites fulfillment events that can be verified from the historical record. In view of the fact that the interpretive approach of so many previous expositors had failed to achieve a satisfactory interpretation using the aforementioned Persian-period decrees, I reasoned that there must be an overlooked decree buried somewhere else in the historical record, one that would yield a correct interpretation. So, I began searching through works of history, looking for mention of decrees that involved the Jews. I soon found that Julius Caesar, between 47 BCE and 44 BCE, had issued at least two major decrees specifically pertaining to Jews in Judea. One decree in particular seemed to have all of the elements mentioned in verse 25. It was issued by Caesar just before his assassination on the Ides of March in the year 44 BCE, ratified by the Roman Senate soon after his death, and recorded in Josephus, *Antiquities of the Jews* 14.10.5 (Whiston translation), as follows:

"Gaius Caesar, consul the fifth time [*in 44 BCE*], hath decreed, That the Jews shall possess Jerusalem, and may encompass that city with walls; and that Hyrcanus, the son of Alexander, the high priest and ethnarch of the Jews, retain it in the manner he himself pleases; and that the Jews be allowed to deduct out of their tribute, every second year the land is let [*in the Sabbatic period*], a corus of that tribute; and that the tribute they pay be not let to farm, nor that they pay always the same tribute."

Chapter Six: Seventy Weeks Are Determined (Daniel 9:1-27)

When the details are examined closely, the 44 BCE decree by Julius Caesar can be seen to fit the description in the text of verse 25 exactly. In it, he decreed that Hyrcanus II, who served as the high priest and also as ethnarch (secular ruler) of the Jews from 63-40 BCE, was granted the city and people of Jerusalem to rule as he saw fit, and the decree gave him permission to rebuild the walls of Jerusalem that had been destroyed by Pompey twenty years earlier, in 63 BCE, when Rome first established its sovereignty over Judea. The lack of walls, which had included large tower gates (with broad places behind them for assembling troops) and a moat (trench) at the base of the wall to increase its height prior to their destruction by Pompey, had left the city vulnerable to its enemies, especially the hated Parthians to the east. Caesar wanted a refortified Judea to serve as a defensive buffer between the Parthians and Egypt, Rome's breadbasket, so he was eager for his figurehead ruler in Judea, Hyrcanus II, and the procurator Antipater, Rome's appointed power behind the throne, to begin rebuilding the city's walls as quickly as possible. History records that the defenses were rebuilt by Antipater sometime in the year spanning 44/43 BCE, immediately after the decree issued by Caesar in 44 BCE and obviously before Antipater's death in 43 BCE. Thus, the decree issued by Julius Caesar just before his death is identified as the decree that begins the events described in the prophecy of the seventy weeks.

The third key to interpretation of the prophecy is to understand the time period meant by the Hebrew word "weeks" שָׁבֻעִי (BHS, Strong's OT: 7620) in verse 25. As already mentioned, most traditional expositors have interpreted the word "weeks" in that verse to mean a "week of years." In other words, a week in Daniel is interpreted as meaning a period of seven years. In such a scenario, the seven weeks then become forty-nine years, and the sixty-two weeks become 434 years. However, "week of years" is not the meaning of the word "weeks" used to specify the seven weeks and sixty-two weeks in verse 25. In that verse, the word "weeks" is used in the same way that, elsewhere in the Book of Daniel, Jewish calendar units were used as cryptic references to Jewish festivals. In the eighth chapter of Daniel, the phrase "evening-morning"(s) was used to indicate Passovers. In the twelfth chapter, the word "days" was used to indicate Day(s) of Atonement. Here in the ninth chapter, the word "weeks" means Feast of Weeks, or, focusing on the main festival day as shorthand, it means the Day of Pentecost. Thus, the time periods being designated in verse 25 are seven Pentecosts and sixty-two Pentecosts. Accordingly, it can be seen that the time period covered by the prophecy of the seventy weeks is seventy years, not 490 years. For the purpose of brevity, the word "week" in this chapter will hereafter represent the Day of Pentecost, although using the full fifty-day time period of the Feast of Weeks will work equally well in the interpretation offered in this chapter.

The fourth key to interpretation of the prophecy is to understand that the starting point for counting the seven Day(s) of Pentecost is specified at the end of verse 25, which reveals that *"... the street shall be built again* [more accurate: shall have been built again]*, and the wall, even in troublous times"* (KJV). The word "street" רְחוֹב (BHS, Strong's OT: 7339) is a reference to the wide space inside the wall of the city, directly behind a tower gate where troops were assembled to defend the city, as revealed by its usage in 2 Chronicles, chapter 32, verse 6: *"And he* [Hezekiah] *set captains of war over the people, and gathered them together to him in the street of the gate of the city ..."* (KJV). In addition, the word translated as "wall" וְחָרוּץ (BHS, Strong's OT: 2742) in the King James Version is better translated as "trench" according to the UBS Old Testament Handbook, which says, "The second word, rendered 'moat' by RSV, is literally the word for 'cut' and refers to a trench cut into the rock on the exterior walls of a city in order to make the wall a more difficult obstacle for those who would attempt to attack from the outside." According to Josephus in his *Wars of the Jews* 1.7.3, Pompey had destroyed the northern wall of Jerusalem and its tower gates, and his troops had filled in the trench in front of the wall to make a platform for his siege engines. Caesar's decree to Hyrcanus II gave permission to rebuild the defenses of Jerusalem which Pompey had destroyed twenty years earlier. The street and trench were the major part of the fortifications covered by the permission to rebuild. Thus, their completion serves as a time marker that had to occur before the count of the seventy weeks could begin. Antipater finished the rebuilding of the fortifications before his death in 43 BCE.

The fifth key to interpretation of the prophecy is to understand that the seven weeks in verse 25 are seven Pentecosts that coincide with a seven-year sabbath cycle. To begin the interpretation of the prophecy, the seven Pentecosts specified in the prophecy must be matched with the seven-year sabbath cycle that occurred immediately following the completion of the rebuilt fortifications of Jerusalem in early 43 BCE. However, that presents a challenge since there are no surviving records of the sabbath and jubilee years as observed in ancient Israel. Those records were lost during the destruction of the Temple in 70 CE. Instead, several competing sabbath-jubilee calendars have been suggested by Jewish scholars over the years. The calendar put forth by Benedict Zuckermann, a 19th-century professor of mathematics and calendric science at the Jewish Theological Seminary of Breslau, is perhaps the system most widely accepted today. In modern times, an alternative calendar has been proposed by Dr. Ben Zion Wacholder, professor of Talmud and Rabbinics at Hebrew Union College's Jewish Institute of Religion, and his system has found favor in academic circles. Both systems rely heavily on Josephus and rabbinical writings for determining sabbath years. However, the calendar of sabbath and jubilee cycles in *Appendix Four: Calendar of Sabbath and Jubilee Years* on page 143, which has been calculated solely from biblical data, is preferred and is the one used in this exposition.

Fulfillment in History

Using the calendar of sabbath and jubilee years listed in *Appendix Four* (see table on page 147), the decree issued by Julius Caesar to Hyrcanus II in the year 44 BCE can be examined in relationship to the seven-year sabbath cycle. By referring to the calendar in *Appendix Four*, it can be seen that the Jewish year that occurred in 43/42 BCE was a sabbath year. That means that the next sabbath cycle began in the following year, 42/41 BCE, so the first Pentecost in the count of the seven weeks (Pentecosts) in verse 25 was the one that occurred in 42 BCE, and the count ended with the Pentecost that occurred in 36 BCE. The sixty-two Pentecosts followed the seven Pentecosts, which means that the first Pentecost in the count of sixty-two was the one that occurred in the year 35 BCE, and the sixty-second Pentecost in the count of the sixty-two occurred in the year 27 CE. Table 6.1 (see page 89) shows the seven Pentecosts and the sixty-two Pentecosts and how they are to be counted. As specified in verse 25, the prophecy of the seventy weeks began with the decree of Caesar that confirmed Hyrcanus II as ruler in Jerusalem. Based on the authority given to him by Caesar, Hyrcanus returned to Jerusalem as the high priest and ethnarch (the anointed one-prince of the prophecy), along with the procurator Antipater. By early 43 BCE, they had rebuilt the street behind the tower gate and cleared the moat below the wall that had been destroyed by Pompey in 63 BCE. Antipater was poisoned in 43 BCE, and replaced by his son, Herod. Then, in the year 40 BCE, Antigonus, brother of Hyrcanus II, lead a rebellion, capturing Jerusalem with the aid of the Parthians and setting himself up as high priest in place of Hyrcanus. Herod fled to Rome, appealed for help, was declared King of the Jews by the Senate, and sent back to Judea with several legions to put down the rebellion. In early January of 36 BCE,

Herod recaptured the walled city of Jerusalem. Fearing that Hyrcanus II would convince his Parthian captors to attack and set him up as ruler in Jerusalem, Herod invited him to return to Jerusalem as part of his court, and Hyrcanus accepted the invitation. The anointed one and prince returned in the summer of 36 CE, bringing to a close the seven-week (seven-Pentecost) time period.

Taking all of the above textual and historical evidence into account, a good paraphrase of verse 25, substituting real events and real names from history for the prophetic language, would read something like this: *"Observe with your eyes and calculate with your mind, that after the issuance of the decree by Julius Caesar to Hyrcanus II, high priest and ethnarch (the anointed one-prince) of the Jews, restoring him to rule in Jerusalem (the first restoration) and granting him permission to rebuild its fortifications, until his repatriation to Jerusalem by Herod (the second restoration), there will be seven weeks, followed by sixty-two weeks. Before the seven weeks begin, the tower gate with its broad place and the wall and trench in front of the wall that were destroyed by Pompey will have been rebuilt"* (Au).

Now that the chronology of the first sixty-nine weeks of the seventy weeks has been established as having already occurred during Roman times, between 42 BCE and 27 CE, what about the seventieth week? When does it occur? Since the completion of the broad place behind the gate and wall and moat of Jerusalem signaled the start of the seven weeks, as the events of history confirm, it seems logical to assume that the completion of the gate and moat signaled the start of the seventy weeks as well, ruling out adding the Pentecost of 43 BCE to the count. Thus, the Pentecost of 28 CE, the Pentecost that follows immediately after the seven Pentecosts and sixty-two Pentecosts, is the one week that must be added to bring the total to seventy weeks (see Diagram 6.1 on page 91). The events of that seventieth week will be examined in detail in the next chapter of this book. Before moving on to do so, however, some additional chronological items in verses 24-27 need to be correlated with Jewish history, as follows:

Verse 24

Verse 24: *"Seventy weeks are determined upon thy people and upon thy holy city, to finish the transgression, and to make an end of sins, and to make reconciliation for iniquity, and to bring in everlasting righteousness, and to seal up the vision and prophecy, and to anoint the most Holy"* (KJV). This verse sets forth six things that must be accomplished during the seventy weeks. The first item, *"to finish the*

Chapter Six: Seventy Weeks Are Determined (Daniel 9:1-27)

Table 6.1 - How to Count the Seventy Weeks (Pentecosts)

Each Pentecost (week) in the count is shown under its equivalent Gregorian year. Sabbath and jubilee years begin in the Gregorian year shown and end in the following year. Jubilee years begin on the 10th day of Tishri (usually corresponding to September-October) in the 49th sabbath year in a seven-sabbath cycle. For a listing of all sabbath and jubilee years, see page 145-147.					**44 BCE** Year of Julius Caesar's Decree to Hyrcanus II	**43 BCE** Sabbath Year, Jerusalem's street and wall rebuilt

The 7 weeks

Year 1	Year 2	Year 3	Year 4	Year 5	Year 6	Sabbath Year
42 BCE 1st of 7 Pentecosts	**41 BCE** 2nd of 7 Pentecosts	**40 BCE** 3rd of 7 Pentecosts	**39 BCE** 4th of 7 Pentecosts	**38 BCE** 5th of 7 Pentecosts	**37 BCE** 6th of 7 Pentecosts	**36 BCE** 7th of 7 Pentecosts

The 62 weeks

35 BCE 1st of 62 Pentecosts	**34 BCE** 2nd of 62 Pentecosts	**33 BCE** 3rd of 62 Pentecosts	**32 BCE** 4th of 62 Pentecosts	**31 BCE** 5th of 62 Pentecosts	**30 BCE** 6th of 62 Pentecosts	**29 BCE** 7th of 62 Pentecosts
28 BCE 8th of 62 Pentecosts	**27 BCE** 9th of 62 Pentecosts	**26 BCE** 10th of 62 Pentecosts	**25 BCE** 11th of 62 Pentecosts	**24 BCE** 12th of 62 Pentecosts	**23 BCE** 13th of 62 Pentecosts	**22 BCE** 14th of 62 Pent. JUBILEE YEAR
21 BCE 15th of 62 Pentecosts	**20 BCE** 16th of 62 Pentecosts	**19 BCE** 17th of 62 Pentecosts	**18 BCE** 18th of 62 Pentecosts	**17 BCE** 19th of 62 Pentecosts	**16 BCE** 20th of 62 Pentecosts	**15 BCE** 21st of 62 Pentecosts
14 BCE 22nd of 62 Pentecosts	**13 BCE** 23rd of 62 Pentecosts	**12 BCE** 24th of 62 Pentecosts	**11 BCE** 25th of 62 Pentecosts	**10 BCE** 26th of 62 Pentecosts	**9 BCE** 27th of 62 Pentecosts	**8 BCE** 28th of 62 Pentecosts
7 BCE 29th of 62 Pentecosts	**6 BCE** 30th of 62 Pentecosts	**5 BCE** 31st of 62 Pentecosts	**4 BCE** 32nd of 62 Pentecosts	**3 BCE** 33rd of 62 Pentecosts	**2 BCE** 34th of 62 Pentecosts	**1 BCE** 35th of 62 Pentecosts
1 CE 36th of 62 Pentecosts	**2 CE** 37th of 62 Pentecosts	**3 CE** 38th of 62 Pentecosts	**4 CE** 39th of 62 Pentecosts	**5 CE** 40th of 62 Pentecosts	**6 CE** 41st of 62 Pentecosts	**7 CE** 42nd of 62 Pentecosts
8 CE 43rd of 62 Pentecosts	**9 CE** 44th of 62 Pentecosts	**10 CE** 45th of 62 Pentecosts	**11 CE** 46th of 62 Pentecosts	**12 CE** 47th of 62 Pentecosts	**13 CE** 48th of 62 Pentecosts	**14 CE** 49th of 62 Pentecosts
15 CE 50th of 62 Pentecosts	**16 CE** 51st of 62 Pentecosts	**17 CE** 52nd of 62 Pentecosts	**18 CE** 53rd of 62 Pentecosts	**19 CE** 54th of 62 Pentecosts	**20 CE** 55th of 62 Pentecosts	**21 CE** 56th of 62 Pentecosts
22 CE 57th of 62 Pentecosts	**23 CE** 58th of 62 Pentecosts	**24 CE** 59th of 62 Pentecosts	**25 CE** 60th of 62 Pentecosts	**26 CE** 61st of 62 Pentecosts	**27 CE** 62nd of 62 Pentecosts	**28 CE** (see below) ↓

The 70th week

Between Pentecost of 27 CE and Pentecost of 28 CE, John the Baptist began his ministry of introducing the new covenant to the Jewish people; Jesus was baptized in the Jordan River by John, tempted for forty days and forty nights in the wilderness, and began his public ministry in Judea. The prophecy of the 70 Weeks ended on Pentecost of 28 CE.	**28 CE** 70th Pentecost JUBILEE YEAR

– 89 –

transgression," can be more accurately translated by the phrase "to shut up the national religious revolt" by using alternate translations offered by BDB, TWOT, and VED for the words rendered in the King James Version as "to finish" לְכַלֵּא (BHS, Strong's OT: 3607) and "the transgression" הַפֶּשַׁע (BHS, Strong's OT: 6588). The alternate translation precisely describes the history of the year 36 BCE that was foretold by the prophecy. As previously mentioned, after the decree issued by Caesar in 44 BCE, Jewish history records that a major revolt by Antigonus, brother of Hyrcanus II, the Hasmonean high priest and ethnarch, began in 40 BCE. That year, Antigonus, in alliance with Rome's archenemy Parthia, overran Judea and captured Jerusalem and the Temple from Hyrcanus. Antigonus installed himself as high priest after biting off the ear of Hyrcanus to make him ritually ineligible to serve as high priest in the future, then sent him to Parthia in chains. Herod fled to Rome where he was proclaimed King of the Jews by the Senate and sent back to Judea with several Roman legions to put down the insurrection. Herod finished the transgression (*i.e.,* quelled the insurrection by Antigonus) by besieging Jerusalem until the city fell, whereupon he brought the former high priest and ethnarch Hyrcanus II back from Parthia to Jerusalem in 36 BCE. It is these two latter events that fulfill the first item in the list of six things in verse 24 that had to be accomplished during the seventy "weeks." The fulfillment of the remaining five items in verse 24, *"to make an end of sins, to make reconciliation for iniquity, to bring in everlasting righteousness, to seal up the vision and prophecy, and to anoint the most Holy"* (KJV), will be discussed at length in the next chapter.

Verse 25

Verse 25: *"Know therefore and understand, that from the going forth of the commandment to restore and to build Jerusalem unto the Messiah the Prince shall be seven weeks, and threescore and two weeks: the street shall be built again, and the wall, even in troublous times"* (KJV). As previously discussed, the phrase "Messiah the Prince" in the King James Version has been discredited as a Christological reference. The anointed one and prince being referred to is Hyrcanus II, high priest and ethnarch from 66-40 BCE. Caesar's decree in 44 BCE restored Hyrcanus to Jerusalem, and the broad place and wall-moat were rebuilt in 43 BCE. After seven Pentecosts that coincided with a sabbath cycle, Herod recaptured Jerusalem from Antigonus and brought Hyrcanus back to the city in 36 BCE. The seven-Pentecost period was followed by a period of sixty-two Pentecosts from 35 BCE to 27 CE.

Chapter Six: Seventy Weeks Are Determined (Daniel 9:1-27)

Diagram 6.1 - Time Line for the Seventy Weeks (Pentecosts)

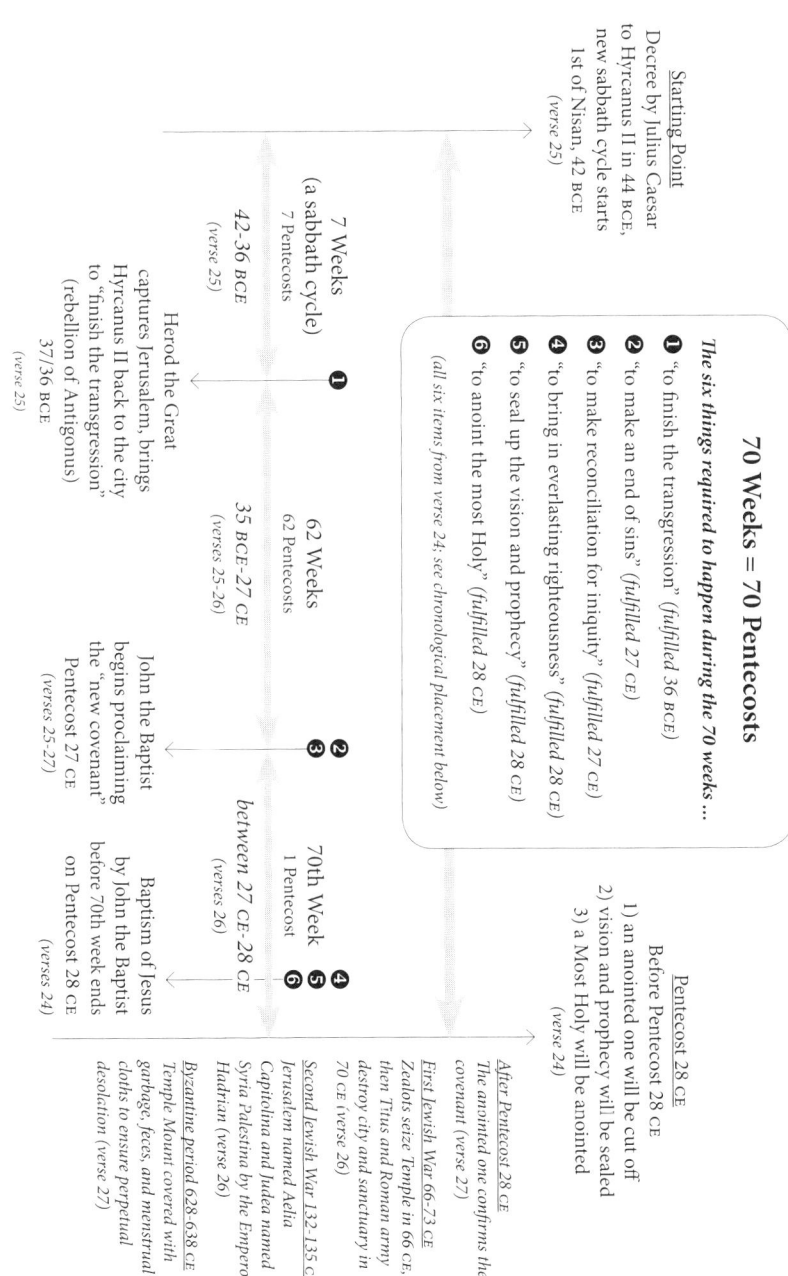

Verses 26-27

Verses 26-27: *"And after threescore and two weeks shall Messiah be cut off, but not for himself: and the people of the prince that shall come shall destroy the city and the sanctuary; and the end thereof shall be with a flood, and unto the end of the war desolations are determined. And he shall confirm the covenant with many for one week: and in the midst of the week he shall cause the sacrifice and oblation to cease. And the people of the prince that shall come shall destroy the city and the sanctuary, and the end thereof shall be with a flood, and unto the end of the war desolations are determined, and for the overspreading of abominations he shall make it desolate, even until the consummation, and that determined shall be poured upon the desolate"* (KJV). In history, the sixty-two weeks ended on the Day of Pentecost in the year 27 CE, after which date it was predicted that an anointed one [1] would be cut off. The Hebrew word "cut off" יִכָּרֵת (BHS, Strong's OT: 3772) is better translated as "will cut a covenant" based on the explanation in TWOT, which observes: "The most important use of the root *bᵉrit* is 'to cut' a covenant." The precedent for this usage is found in Genesis, chapter 15, verse 18, where the same word translated as "cut off" in Daniel, chapter 9, verse 26, is translated as *"made a covenant."* By using the identical word "cut off" in verse 26 as that used in Genesis, chapter 15, when God gave the promise of an heir and made the land covenant with Abraham, the idea being conveyed is that the anointed one in verse 26 is to make a covenant in fulfillment of that earlier promise and covenant. In other words, Abraham's promised heir is to be the anointed one who will mediate a new covenant with the people of Israel. The phrase *"but not for himself"* that follows can be better paraphrased as *"and he shall choose to have nothing"* (Au), a reference to the servant's status voluntarily assumed by the anointed one.[2] The first part of verse 27 continues the covenant narrative, revealing that the anointed one will confirm the covenant for one week, causing the sacrifice and oblation to cease in the midst of the week (events that will be covered in greater detail in the next chapter). The last half of verse 26 goes on to state that after the above sequence of events *"the people of the prince that shall come shall destroy the city and the sanctuary;*

---

[1] This anointed one in verse 26 cannot be Hyrcanus II again, since Herod had persuaded the Romans to execute him for treason several decades earlier, in the year 30 BCE.

[2] Philippians 2:5-7: *"... Christ Jesus, who, though he was in the form of God, did not count equality with God a thing to be grasped, but made himself nothing, taking the form of a servant, being born in the likeness of men"* (ESV); also, see Isaiah, chapters 42 and 53.

and the end thereof shall be with a flood, and unto the end of the war desolations are determined" (KJV), thus foretelling the destruction of Jerusalem and the Temple by the Romans in 70 CE. After the Temple was destroyed, Roman soldiers then offered sacrifices to their standards, which featured the image of their emperor-god, on the Temple Mount ruins, as recorded in Josephus, *Wars of the Jews* 6.6.1. Followers of Jesus at the time saw this as the "abomination of desolation" foretold in the Gospel of Matthew, chapter 24, verse 15. The final words of verse 27 look even further forward in time to the total destruction of Jerusalem and Judea by Hadrian during the Second Jewish War (132-135 CE), which ended with the Temple Mount area being plowed under, a new city named Aelia Capitolina being built on the ruins of Jerusalem, and the name of the province of Judea being changed to Syria Palestina. The phrase translated as "overspreading of abominations" in the final part of verse 27 is an interpretation of the Hebrew words כְּנַף שִׁקּוּצִים (BHS, Strong's OT: 3671, 8251) meaning literally "wing of abominable filth." By using this imagery of being covered over with a protective wing (as a mother hen covers her chicks with her wing), but instead covered with a covering of impurity and filth, the prophecy comes to its end by again looking forward in time to the final days of Byzantine rule over Jerusalem, just before the fall of the city to Caliph Omar. This event was predicted in the seventh chapter of Daniel, which foretold that the end of the Roman-Byzantine rule of Jerusalem would occur in 638 CE (see page 50). During this final period of Byzantine rule, Christians had intentionally covered the Temple Mount with their garbage, feces, and soiled menstrual cloths, some items of filth even being sent to Jerusalem from Rome and Constantinople, in a misguided effort to ensure that the Temple area remained ritually impure for use by Jews, and thus desolate as had been prophesied.

In the year 638 CE, Omar, leading the armies of Islam, accepted the surrender of the city of Jerusalem. Ironically, at that time, it was the Muslim Caliph Omar, and not Sophronius, the Catholic Bishop of Jerusalem, who revered the Temple Mount area as a most holy place, as indicated by this account of Omar's first visit to Jerusalem and the Temple Mount recorded in the writings of the Muslim scholar and historian Mujīr al-Dīn al-'Ulaymī (*b.* 1456):

> "When 'Umar reached the old ruined gates of the Temple he was horrified to see the filth, 'which was then all about the holy sanctuary, had settled on the steps of the gates so that it even came out into the streets in which the gate opened, and it had accumulated so greatly as almost to reach up to the ceiling of the gateway.' The only

way to get up to the platform was to crawl on hands and knees. Sophronius went first and the Muslims struggled up behind. When they arrived at the top, the Muslims gazed appalled at the vast and desolate expanse of Herod's platform, still covered with piles of fallen masonry and garbage. The shock of this sad encounter with the holy place whose fame had reached them in far-off Arabia was never forgotten: Muslims claimed that they called Anastasis al-qumamah, 'the Dungheap,' in retaliation for the impious behavior of the Christians on the Temple Mount. 'Umar does not seem to have spent any time on this occasion examining the [Sakhrah] rock, which would later play such an important part in Islamic piety. Once he had taken stock of the situation, he threw handfuls of dung and rubble into his cloak and then hurled it over the city wall into the Valley of Hinnom. Immediately his followers did the same." [1]

A few decades after the conquest of Jerusalem by Omar and his Muslim army, his successors built the Al-Aqsa Mosque, recognizable today by its dark silver gray dome on the southern end of the Temple Mount platform, and, to the north, they built a shrine, the (now golden) Dome of the Rock. The latter was purposefully erected over the rock presumed to be the exact spot where the Jewish Temple's Holy of Holies was once located, and the dome's inner surface was purposefully adorned with an anti-Christian Arabic inscription.[2] These acts were meant to proclaim to the world that Islam had superseded both Judaism and Christianity as the one true monotheistic religion. After more than thirteen centuries, the Dome of the Rock, with its blasphemous inscriptions,[3] continues to desecrate the sacred Temple Mount site day by day.

---

[1] Karen Armstrong, *Jerusalem: One City, Three Faiths* (New York: Ballantine Books Trade Paperback Edition/Random House. Inc., 2005), p. 229-230.

[2] "O People of the Book! Do not exaggerate in your religion nor utter aught concerning God save the truth. The Messiah, Jesus son of Mary, was only a Messenger of God, and His Word which He conveyed unto Mary, and a spirit from Him. So believe in God and His messengers, and say not 'Three,' (instead) cease! (it is) better for you! God is only One God. Far be it removed from His transcendent majesty that He should have a son. Whoso disbelieveth the revelations of God (will find that) lo! God is swift at reckoning!" ... based on a translation by *Islamic Awareness* (www.islamic-awareness.org).

[3] By denying the Sonship of Jesus, the Dome of the Rock inscription meets the definition for anti-Christ: *"He is antichrist, that denieth the Father and the Son"* ~ 1 John 2:22 (KJV).

CHAPTER SEVEN

HE SHALL CONFIRM THE COVENANT

READ DANIEL 9:24-27 ON PAGE 228 | SEE TIME LINE ❼ ON PLATE 1

The prophecy of the seventy weeks in Daniel, chapter 9, verses 24-27, sets forth three time periods that together total seventy weeks—an initial period of seven weeks, followed by a period of sixty-two weeks, followed by a third period of one week—all of which have already happened in history as explained in the last chapter. The first time period was comprised of seven weeks that coincided with a seven-year sabbath cycle, beginning with the Day of Pentecost in 42 BCE and ending with the Day of Pentecost in 36 BCE. The second time period of sixty-two weeks followed the first time period, beginning with the Day of Pentecost in 35 BCE and continuing for sixty-two Pentecosts, ending with the Day of Pentecost in 27 CE. Those two time periods accounted for sixty-nine of the seventy weeks. The third time period followed immediately after the sixty-nine weeks, beginning with events in Jewish history that happened after the Day of Pentecost of 27 CE and ending before the seventieth week was brought to a conclusion by the Day of Pentecost in 28 CE. After which, according to verse 27, a covenant was to be confirmed for one week by an anointed one. The logical question to ask at this point is: What covenant was introduced to the Jewish people in the year 28 CE or thereabout and confirmed by an anointed one for one week afterwards? The remainder of this chapter will be devoted to identifying that covenant and the anointed one by examining the six items in verse 24 that had to happen before the week of covenant confirmation could commence.

The New Covenant

The key to identifying the covenant described in verse 27 is contained in verse 24, the opening verse of the prophecy of the seventy weeks, which states *"Seventy weeks are determined upon thy people and upon thy holy city, to finish the transgression, and to make an end of sins, and to make reconciliation for iniquity, and to bring in everlasting righteousness, and to seal up the vision and prophecy, and to anoint the most Holy"* (KJV). In this verse, six items are specified that must happen before the conclusion of the seventy weeks in 28 CE. The first item, *"to finish the transgression,"* was accomplished when Herod the Great besieged

– 95 –

and captured Jerusalem from Antigonus and the Parthians before Pentecost in 36 BCE, bringing the civil and religious revolt in Jerusalem and Judea to a close. The next two items, *"to make an end of sins"* and *"to make reconciliation for iniquity,"* are the keys to identifying the covenant in question by pointing to the Book of Jeremiah, chapter 31, verses 31-34, which say:

> *"Behold, the days come, saith the Lord, that I will make a new covenant with the house of Israel, and with the house of Judah: Not according to the covenant that I made with their fathers in the day that I took them by the hand to bring them out of the land of Egypt; which my covenant they brake, although I was an husband unto them, saith the Lord: But this shall be the covenant that I will make with the house of Israel; After those days, saith the Lord, I will put my law in their inward parts, and write it in their hearts; and will be their God, and they shall be my people. And they shall teach no more every man his neighbour, and every man his brother, saying, Know the Lord: for they shall all know me, from the least of them unto the greatest of them, saith the Lord; for I will forgive their iniquity, and I will remember their sin no more"* (KJV).

Notice the promises at the end, *"for I will forgive their iniquity"* and *"I will remember their sin no more."* The wording of those two phrases is identical in meaning to the wording in the second and third items of the six items listed as having to be accomplished during the seventy weeks, namely, *"... to make an end of sins, and to make reconciliation for iniquity ..."* (KJV). The fact that the wording in Daniel, chapter 9, verse 24, mirrors the wording used in Jeremiah, chapter 31, verse 34, is the key to identifying the covenant in question. By using essentially the same words, the covenant in Daniel's ninth chapter is identified as being the "new covenant" that was promised by God through Jeremiah.

Some expositors object to this interpretation, saying that Jeremiah's new covenant was established when the Jews returned from Babylon. However, the biblical record indicates otherwise. The Jews rebuilt the Temple in Jerusalem after they returned and began offering the traditional Temple-centered sacrifices instituted by the Mosaic covenant, exactly as they had done before the exile. They were not operating under a new covenant. They were continuing to operate under the Mosaic covenant, and did so until the Temple was destroyed in the year 70 CE. Obviously, the resumption of the Mosaic covenant cannot be what was meant. Other expositors claim that the new covenant was established by the rabbis after the Romans destroyed the Temple, but that argument ignores the time frame for confirming the covenant set forth in verse 25 and verse 27, which require that the anointed one had to be anointed as the confirmer of the covenant no later than Pentecost in 28 CE. So, according to the time line in Daniel, the introduction of the new covenant could not happen after the destruction of the Temple, denying what has been claimed by Jewish rabbis for centuries. As for modern Jewish expositors, most interpret the reference to the new covenant in Jeremiah as referring to the original Mosaic covenant made with the Israelites at Sinai, but placed anew in the hearts of the Jewish people by the Messiah, usually assuming that will happen when a third Jewish Temple is rebuilt on the Temple Mount in the future. However, this is another wrong interpretation that ignores the time constraints given in Daniel, chapter 9, verses 24-27. According to those verses, the anointed one must be introduced no later than the year 28 CE.

Fulfillment in History

The *Tanakh* was completed, according to Jewish tradition, sometime before 400 BCE, so it will not contain the record of the introduction of Jeremiah's "new covenant" to Israel, an event which had to occur after Pentecost in 27 CE, nor will it record the fulfillment of the last five items of the six items specified in verse 24 that must occur before the seventy weeks end in 28 CE. For that information, we must look to the continuation of the *Tanakh*, the *B'rit Hadashah*, also called the Book of the New Covenant (or New Testament). It contains the continuing record of God's revelation to the Jewish people, and, like the *Tanakh*, was written by Jews, making it a trustworthy testimony about the new covenant and the anointed one who confirms that covenant to Israel. The first of the six items specified in verse 24, *"to finish the transgression,"* identifies the time period and was discussed on pages 88 and 95. The remaining five items, which identify the new covenant and reveal the identity of the anointed one who confirms the covenant, are listed below (numbers match those on Diagram 6.1 on page 91):

"to make an end of sins" ❷
"to make reconciliation for iniquity" ❸ ⎬ 2-3 identify the covenant
"to bring in everlasting righteousness" ❹
"to seal up the vision and prophecy" ❺ ⎬ 4-6 identify the anointed one
"to anoint the most Holy" ❻

"to make an end of sins"
"to make reconciliation for iniquity"

The second and third items of the six items from verse 24 that are required to happen during the seventy weeks, *"to make an end of sins,"* and *"to make reconciliation for iniquity,"* were shown on pages 95-97 to be the indicators that identified the covenant mentioned in the prophecy of the seventy weeks as the new covenant foretold by Jeremiah. The introduction of the new covenant, which had to occur before the end of the seventy weeks on the Day of Pentecost in 28 CE, is described in the Gospels[1] of Matthew, Mark, and Luke. The following account is from the Gospel of Matthew, chapter 3, verses 1-12:

> *"In those days came John the Baptist, preaching in the wilderness of Judaea, And saying, Repent ye: for the kingdom of heaven is at hand. For this is he that was spoken of by the prophet Esaias, saying, The voice of one crying in the wilderness, Prepare ye the way of the Lord, make his paths straight. And the same John had his raiment of camel's hair, and a leathern girdle about his loins; and his meat was locusts and wild honey. Then went out to him Jerusalem, and all Judaea, and all the region round about Jordan, And were baptized of him in Jordan, confessing their sins. But when he saw many of the Pharisees and Sadducees come to his baptism, he said unto them, O generation of vipers, who hath warned you to flee from the wrath to come? Bring forth therefore fruits meet for repentance: And think not to say within yourselves, We have Abraham to our father: for I say unto you, that God is able of these stones to raise up children unto Abraham. And now also the axe is laid unto the root of the trees: therefore every tree which bringeth not forth good fruit is hewn down, and cast into the fire. I indeed baptize you with water unto repentance: but he that cometh after me is mightier than I, whose shoes I am not worthy to bear: he shall baptize you with the Holy Ghost, and with fire: Whose fan is in his hand, and he will throughly purge his floor, and gather his wheat into the garner; but he will burn up the chaff with unquenchable fire"* (KJV).

John the Baptist was the messenger of the new covenant, raised up to call the people of Israel to repentance for forgiveness of sins, and he did so without

---

[1] A Middle English word, derived from Old English *gōdspel* meaning "good news."

reference to the Temple and its system of sacrifices that were required by the Law of Moses. The symbolism of John's use of baptism by submersion in a body of water, a Jewish practice of purification called a *mikvah* that represented purification of the soul from most bodily sins, would have been well understood by the Jews who heard his message and sought his baptism. His use of the Jordan River for baptism—that is, his use of freely running water that ancient Jews viewed as "living water" having special powers of purification from **all** sins—made for a powerful message that challenged the established religious authorities and the efficacy and exclusivity of the atonement achieved through the Temple system of animal sacrifice required under the Mosaic covenant. However, the authorities did not hinder John. They were intimidated by him because the masses considered him to be a prophet, possibly the expected Messiah. Eventually, the Temple authorities sent priests and Levites seeking to know who he was, as recorded in the Gospel of John, chapter 1, verses 19-28:

> *"And this is the record of John, when the Jews sent priests and Levites from Jerusalem to ask him, Who art thou? And he confessed, and denied not; but confessed, I am not the Christ. And they asked him, What then? Art thou Elias? And he saith, I am not. Art thou that prophet? And he answered, No. Then said they unto him, Who art thou? that we may give an answer to them that sent us. What sayest thou of thyself? He said, I am the voice of one crying in the wilderness, Make straight the way of the Lord, as said the prophet Esaias. And they which were sent were of the Pharisees. And they asked him, and said unto him, Why baptizest thou then, if thou be not that Christ, nor Elias, neither that prophet? John answered them, saying, I baptize with water: but there standeth one among you, whom ye know not; He it is, who coming after me is preferred before me, whose shoe's latchet I am not worthy to unloose. These things were done in Bethabara beyond Jordan, where John was baptizing"* (KJV).

Thus, John the Baptist, when challenged by the authorities, stated emphatically that he was not the anointed one who would confirm the covenant after the seventy weeks ended in 28 CE, and revealed that the anointed one was that very day walking among the people of Israel. But, who was this anointed one who would confirm the new covenant? That question is answered by the fulfillment of the fourth, fifth and sixth required items in Daniel, chapter 9, verse 24.

"to bring in everlasting righteousness"

The fourth item of the six items from verse 24 that are required to happen during the seventy weeks, *"to bring in everlasting righteousness"* (KJV), was fulfilled during the baptism of Jesus in the Jordan River by John the Baptist. This event is described in each of the Gospels of Matthew, Mark, and Luke, and it had to occur before the end of the seventy weeks on the Day of Pentecost in 28 CE according to the chronological constraints spelled out in the prophecy of the seventy weeks. The account of the baptism that is most pertinent to verse 24, in that it identifies that event with the prophecy of the seventy weeks, is given in the Gospel of Matthew, chapter 3, verses 1-17:

> *"Then cometh Jesus from Galilee to Jordan unto John, to be baptized of him. But John forbad him, saying, I have need to be baptized of thee, and comest thou to me? And Jesus answering said unto him, Suffer it to be so now: for thus it becometh us* **to fulfil all righteousness***. Then he suffered him. And Jesus, when he was baptized, went up straightway out of the water: and, lo, the heavens were opened unto him, and he saw the Spirit of God descending like a dove, and lighting upon him: And lo a voice from heaven, saying, This is my beloved Son, in whom I am well pleased"* (KJV).

The Gospel of Mark contains a second account of the baptism of Jesus in chapter 1, verses 1-11:

> *"The beginning of the gospel of Jesus Christ, the Son of God; As it is written in the prophets, Behold, I send my messenger before thy face, which shall prepare thy way before thee. The voice of one crying in the wilderness, Prepare ye the way of the Lord, make his paths straight. John did baptize in the wilderness, and preach the baptism of repentance for the remission of sins. And there went out unto him all the land of Judaea, and they of Jerusalem, and were all baptized of him in the river of Jordan, confessing their sins. And John was clothed with camel's hair, and with a girdle of a skin about his loins; and he did eat locusts and wild honey; And preached, saying, There cometh one mightier than I after me, the latchet of whose shoes I am not worthy to stoop down and unloose. I indeed have baptized you with water: but he shall baptize you with the Holy Ghost. And it came to pass in those days, that Jesus came from Nazareth of*

Galilee, and was baptized of John in Jordan. And straightway coming up out of the water, he saw the heavens opened, and the Spirit like a dove descending upon him: And there came a voice from heaven, saying, Thou art my beloved Son, in whom I am well pleased" (KJV).

A third account of the baptism, one that contains important chronological information, is found in the Gospel of Luke, chapter 3, verses 1-22:

"Now in the fifteenth year of the reign of Tiberius Caesar, Pontius Pilate being governor of Judaea, and Herod being tetrarch of Galilee, and his brother Philip tetrarch of Ituraea and of the region of Trachonitis, and Lysanias the tetrarch of Abilene, Annas and Caiaphas being the high priests,[1] *the word of God came unto John the son of Zacharias in the wilderness. And he came into all the country about Jordan, preaching the baptism of repentance for the remission of sins; As it is written in the book of the words of Esaias the prophet, saying, The voice of one crying in the wilderness, Prepare ye the way of the Lord, make his paths straight. Every valley shall be filled, and every mountain and hill shall be brought low; and the crooked shall be made straight, and the rough ways shall be made smooth; And all flesh shall see the salvation of God. Then said he to the multitude that came forth to be baptized of him, O generation of vipers, who hath warned you to flee from the wrath to come? Bring forth therefore fruits worthy of repentance, and begin not to say within yourselves, We have Abraham to our father: for I say unto you, That God is able of these stones to raise up children unto Abraham. And now also the axe is laid unto the root of the trees: every tree therefore which bringeth not forth good fruit is hewn down, and cast into the fire. And the people asked him, saying, What shall we do then? He answereth and saith unto them, He that hath two coats, let him impart to him that hath none; and he that hath meat, let him do likewise. Then came also publicans to be baptized, and said*

---

[1] Luke also mentions Annas as high priest, which is unusual, since there was only one high priest at a time, and Caiaphas is known to have been the high priest between 18 CE and 36 CE. The mention of Annas can be explained by the fact that he was a high priest who preceded Caiaphas between 6 CE and 15 CE, and was the father-in-law of Caiaphas, making him a *high priest emeritus*, so to speak. Also, Annas may have served as high priest when Caiaphas was ritually impure for any reason. No mention of Lysanias, tetrarch of Abilene, has been found outside of Luke, so no dating is possible in his case.

unto him, Master, what shall we do? And he said unto them, Exact no more than that which is appointed you. And the soldiers likewise demanded of him, saying, And what shall we do? And he said unto them, Do violence to no man, neither accuse any falsely; and be content with your wages. And as the people were in expectation, and all men mused in their hearts of John, whether he were the Christ, or not; John answered, saying unto them all, I indeed baptize you with water; but one mightier than I cometh, the latchet of whose shoes I am not worthy to unloose: he shall baptize you with the Holy Ghost and with fire: Whose fan is in his hand, and he will throughly purge his floor, and will gather the wheat into his garner; but the chaff he will burn with fire unquenchable. And many other things in his exhortation preached he unto the people. But Herod the tetrarch, being reproved by him for Herodias his brother Philip's wife, and for all the evils which Herod had done, Added yet this above all, that he shut up John in prison. Now when all the people were baptized, it came to pass, that Jesus also being baptized, and praying, the heaven was opened, And the Holy Ghost descended in a bodily shape like a dove upon him, and a voice came from heaven, which said, Thou art my beloved Son; in thee I am well pleased" (KJV).

In the three Gospel accounts of the baptism of Jesus, there are two important pieces of information, one dealing with prophetic fulfillment and the other with chronology, that are particularly useful for interpretive purposes, as follows:

The first piece of information is found in the statement by Jesus recorded in the Gospel of Matthew that his baptism was being done *"to fulfil all righteousness."* The Greek word πληρῶσαι (NTG, Strong's NT: 4137), rendered as "fulfil" in the King James text, is most often used to indicate fulfillment of Scripture, and that is the case in this instance. Over the years, countless expositors have questioned the need for Jesus to be baptized by John the Baptist. If indeed his life was sinless, why was it necessary for Jesus to submit to a baptism of repentance for remission of sins? The answer is quite simple. The baptism of Jesus was done to fulfill the prophecy about everlasting righteousness that was specified in Daniel, chapter 9, verse 24, and it served as a public announcement of the identity of the anointed one specified in verse 27 as the one who would confirm the new covenant.

The second piece of information is the chronologically rich statement in the Gospel of Luke that the ministry of John the Baptist began in the fifteenth year of the reign of Tiberius Caesar, when Pilate was governor of Judea, and so on. The

Chapter Seven: He Shall Confirm the Covenant (Daniel 9:24-27)

baptism of Jesus had to occur before Pentecost in the year 28 CE, the year that marked the end of the seventy "weeks," so the chronological details in Luke can be used to pinpoint the start of the ministry of John the Baptist with accuracy and make sure a pre-Pentecost of 28 CE baptism was possible. Since Joseph Caiaphas was high priest from 18 CE until 36 CE, Pontius Pilate was governor of Judea from 26 CE until 36 CE, Herod Antipas was tetrarch of the Galilee from 4 BCE until 39 CE, Herod Philip II was tetrarch of Ituraea and the region of Trachonitis from 4 BCE until about 33/34 CE, all of those dates taken together produce a time frame that encompasses and includes the years 26 CE to 33/34 CE. A baptism happening between the Pentecosts of 27 CE and 28 CE can be seen to fall within that time frame. So far, so good. Next, some portion of *"the fifteenth year of the reign of Tiberius Caesar"* must be shown to have happened before the Pentecost in 28 CE, the time specified as the conclusion of the seventy weeks (see Diagram 6.1 on page 91). Many traditional expositors assign the fifteenth year of Tiberius to the year 29 CE, but the actual year is not quite as simple to fix with certainty as it might seem at first examination.

Biblical scholars specializing in ancient Roman chronology have researched the possible years that could be identified as the fifteenth year of the reign of Tiberius. The possibilities depend on whether one counts the first year of Tiberius' reign as an accession year followed by numbered years or counts numbered years with no accession year, on whether the count begins with the year of his coreign over the provinces with Augustus in 12 CE or with the year of his sole reign after Augustus died in 14 CE, and on the type of calendar used, either Roman, Syro-Macedonian, or Jewish. If Jewish, there is the added uncertainty about whether the calendar in use started the new year in the first month Nisan or the seventh month Tishri. Using these variables, sixteen different time periods have been identified by chronologists as including the fifteenth year of the reign of Tiberius, the time period stipulated for the start of the ministry of John the Baptist. They range in real time from the year 26 CE to the year 30 CE. Five of the sixteen configurations allow for the fifteenth year of Tiberius' reign to occur after Pentecost in the year 27 CE and before Pentecost in the year 28 CE, which is the Pentecost that concluded the prophecy of the seventy weeks. The dates for the five most probable time periods for the fifteenth year of Tiberius' reign are as follows: (1) If the factual regnal years of Tiberius are counted from his joint rule of the provinces with Augustus, his fifteenth regnal year was October, 26 CE to October, 27 CE, (2) If the regnal years of Tiberius from his joint rule of the provinces are counted as Julian calendar years according to the accession-year system, his fifteenth regnal year was January 1-December 31, 27 CE, (3) If the regnal years of Tiberius from his joint rule of the provinces are counted as Syro-Macedonian calendar years according to the non-accession-year system, his fifteenth regnal year was October 1, 26 CE to September 30, 27 CE, (4) If the regnal years of Tiberius from his joint rule of the provinces are counted as Jewish calendar years according to the non-accession-year system, his fifteenth regnal year was March-April, 26 CE to September 30, 27 CE, (5) If the regnal years of Tiberius from his joint rule of the provinces are counted as Jewish calendar years according to the accession-year system, his fifteenth regnal year was March-April, 26 CE to March-April, 28 CE.[1]

It is probable that the Gospel of Luke was written by a Jew,[2] a follower of Jesus, possibly even as a formal presentation to the former high priest Theophilus[3] for the purpose of explaining the growing branch of Judaism that was built on recognition of Jesus as the Messiah of Israel. Thus, it seems not unreasonable to assume that a Jewish calendar system was used to calculate the fifteenth year of Tiberius as a reference in Luke, using one of the methods employed by calendars mentioned in numbers four and five in the preceding paragraph. However, knowing which calendar was used is not really important. All that is needed at this point is to show that *"the fifteenth year of the reign of Tiberius Caesar"* could have been referring to a time period that occurred before Pentecost in the year 28 CE, which marks the end of the seventy weeks, and that has been shown.

Now that the ministry of John the Baptist has been located as beginning sometime after the Pentecost of 27 CE (May 17), can the year of Jesus' baptism be placed within the time frame defined by the start of John's ministry in early 27 CE and the end of the seventy weeks on the Pentecost in 28 CE? Yes, it can be so placed, at least indirectly. The age at which Jesus began his ministry shortly after his baptism is given in the Gospel of Luke, chapter 3, verse 23: *"And Jesus himself began to be about thirty years of age"* (KJV). Since Jesus was born sometime before the death of Herod the Great, who died in March of 4 BCE, it can be easily

---

[1] Jack Finegan, *Handbook of Biblical Chronology* (Peabody, Massachusetts: Hendrickson Publishers, Inc., 1998), p. 330-345.

[2] Based on Romans 3:1-2 and the fact that the rest of the Bible (*Tanakh* and *B'rit Hadashah*) was written by Jews, it seems only logical that the writer of the Gospel of Luke was a Jew.

[3] Theophilus, high priest from 37-41 CE, was the son of the high priest Annas, brother of the high priest Caiaphas, both mentioned in Luke, and grandfather of a woman named Johanna, possibly the one mentioned in the eighth chapter of Luke, verse 3.

Chapter Seven: He Shall Confirm the Covenant (Daniel 9:24-27)

Table 7.1 - Year of Jesus' Baptism				
1 year old - 3 BCE	2 years old - 2 BCE	3 years old - 1 BCE	4 years old - 1 CE	5 years old - 2 CE
6 years old - 3 CE	7 years old - 4 CE	8 years old - 5 CE	9 years old - 6 CE	10 years old - 7 CE
11 years old - 8 CE	12 years old - 9 CE	13 years old - 10 CE	14 years old - 11 CE	15 years old - 12 CE
16 years old - 13 CE	17 years old - 14 CE	18 years old - 15 CE	19 years old - 16 CE.	20 years old - 17 CE
21 years old - 18 CE	22 years old - 19 CE	23 years old - 20 CE	24 years old - 21 CE	25 years old - 22 CE
26 years old - 23 CE	27 years old - 24 CE	28 years old - 25 CE	29 years old - 26 CE	30 years old - 27 CE

confirmed by simple calculation that Jesus would have been *"about thirty years of age"* in the time period between the Pentecost in 27 CE that ended the sixty-ninth week of the prophecy of the seventy weeks and the Pentecost in the year 28 CE that ended the seventy weeks (see Table 7.1 above).

So far, four of the six items that were required to happen before the seventy weeks ended in the year 28 CE have now been demonstrated to have happened in history exactly in the order predicted. The new covenant was introduced by John the Baptist in early 27 CE, and the baptism of Jesus by John, which identified Jesus as the anointed one who would confirm the new covenant to Israel, happened sometime after John began his ministry in 27 CE and before the seventy weeks came to their end on Pentecost in the year 28 CE That leaves just the fifth and sixth items, *"to seal up the vision and prophecy"* (KJV) and *"to anoint the most Holy"* (KJV). These last two items will now be shown to have also been fulfilled at the time of the baptism of Jesus, setting the stage for his public ministry.

"to seal up the vision and prophecy"

The fifth of the six items set forth in verse 24, *"to seal up the vision and prophecy,"* (a strict translation of the Masoretic Text yields: *"to seal up the vision and prophet"*) was fulfilled at the time of the baptism of Jesus. After his baptism, as recorded in the Gospel of John, chapter 6, verse 27, Jesus revealed to his disciples that God had previously sealed him, saying: *"... for him* [*i.e.,* for the Son of Man, a messianic term Jesus often used to describe himself] *hath God the Father sealed"* (KJV). Jesus was revealing to them that his messiahship and his role as "The Prophet" had been attested by God, but that his message had been sealed away from the understanding of the Jewish religious leadership and the Jewish people, all except those Israelites who were chosen by God to understand Jesus' message of the new covenant. God had warned Israel through Moses about what would happen if the nation did not keep the commandments. Daniel himself called attention to Moses' warning in his prayer (see page 229), and the prophet Isaiah, repeating Moses, had foretold that the nation of Israel would be given spiritual blindness, as recorded in Isaiah, chapter 6, verses 9-10 (also, note the use of the phrases *"thine iniquity is taken away, and thy sin purged,"* which is essentially the terminology used in chapter 9, verse 24, to signal the new covenant):

"In the year that king Uzziah died I saw also the Lord sitting upon a throne, high and lifted up, and his train filled the temple. Above it stood the seraphims ... And one cried unto another, and said, Holy, holy, holy, is the Lord of hosts: the whole earth is full of his glory. And the posts of the door moved at the voice of him that cried, and the house was filled with smoke. Then said I, Woe is me! for I am undone; because I am a man of unclean lips, and I dwell in the midst of a people of unclean lips: for mine eyes have seen the King, the Lord of hosts. Then flew one of the seraphims unto me, having a live coal in his hand, which he had taken with the tongs from off the altar: And he laid it upon my mouth, and said, Lo, this hath touched thy lips; and thine iniquity is taken away, and thy sin purged. Also I heard the voice of the Lord, saying, Whom shall I send, and who will go for us? Then said I, Here am I; send me. And he said, Go, and tell this people, Hear ye indeed, but understand not; and see ye indeed, but perceive not. Make the heart of this people fat, and make their ears heavy, and shut their eyes; lest they see with their eyes, and hear with their ears, and understand with their heart, and convert, and be healed" (KJV).

The spiritual blindness given to Israel by God is further clarified in Isaiah, chapter 29, verses 10-14:

"For the Lord hath poured out upon you the spirit of deep sleep, and hath closed your eyes: the prophets and your rulers, the seers hath he covered. And the vision of all is become unto you as the words of a book that is sealed, which men deliver to one that is learned, saying, Read this, I pray thee: and he saith, I cannot; for it is sealed: And the book is delivered to him that is not learned, saying, Read this, I pray thee: and he saith, I am not learned. Wherefore the Lord said, Forasmuch as this people draw near me with their mouth, and with

their lips do honour me, but have removed their heart far from me, and their fear toward me is taught by the precept of men: Therefore, behold, I will proceed to do a marvellous work among this people, even a marvellous work and a wonder: for the wisdom of their wise men shall perish, and the understanding of their prudent men shall be hid" (KJV).

This latter passage from Isaiah makes clear that the vision of Isaiah was not the only vision that was sealed away from Israel, but that the blindness of Israel would be extended to include the wisdom of their wise men and the understanding of their prudent men about the entire testimony of Moses and the prophets, all of this to occur in the future, after the time of Isaiah, when God was prophesied to do a marvellous work and wonder among the people. During his ministry to introduce the new covenant, Jesus was restrained by the spiritual blindness that was imposed by God on the religious leadership and people of Israel, as indicated in the Gospel of Matthew, chapter 13, verses 10-17, where he specifically invokes the words of Isaiah:

"And the disciples came, and said unto him, Why speakest thou unto them in parables? He answered and said unto them. ... Therefore speak I to them in parables: because they seeing see not; and hearing they hear not, neither do they understand. And in them is fulfilled the prophecy of Esaias, which saith, By hearing ye shall hear, and shall not understand; and seeing ye shall see, and shall not perceive: For this people's heart is waxed gross, and their ears are dull of hearing, and their eyes they have closed; lest at any time they should see with their eyes, and hear with their ears, and should understand with their heart, and should be converted, and I should heal them. But blessed are your eyes, for they see: and your ears, for they hear. For verily I say unto you, That many prophets and righteous men have desired to see those things which ye see, and have not seen them; and to hear those things which ye hear, and have not heard them" (KJV).

Isaiah had specifically predicted the blindness of Israel with respect to the redemptive ministry of Jesus. In Isaiah, chapter 53, the prophet wrote:

"Who hath believed our report? and to whom is the arm of the Lord revealed? For he shall grow up before him as a tender plant, and as a root out of a dry

ground: he hath no form nor comeliness; and when we shall see him, there is no beauty that we should desire him. He is despised and rejected of men; a man of sorrows, and acquainted with grief: and we hid as it were our faces from him; he was despised, and we esteemed him not. Surely he hath borne our griefs, and carried our sorrows: yet we did esteem him stricken, smitten of God, and afflicted. But he was wounded for our transgressions, he was bruised for our iniquities: the chastisement of our peace was upon him; and with his stripes we are healed. All we like sheep have gone astray; we have turned every one to his own way; and the Lord hath laid on him the iniquity of us all. He was oppressed, and he was afflicted, yet he opened not his mouth: he is brought as a lamb to the slaughter, and as a sheep before her shearers is dumb, so he openeth not his mouth. He was taken from prison and from judgment: and who shall declare his generation? for he was cut off[1] *out of the land of the living: for the transgression of my people was he stricken. And he made his grave with the wicked, and with the rich in his death; because he had done no violence, neither was any deceit in his mouth. Yet it pleased the Lord to bruise him; he hath put him to grief: when thou shalt make his soul an offering for sin, he shall see his seed, he shall prolong his days, and the pleasure of the Lord shall prosper in his hand. He shall see of the travail of his soul, and shall be satisfied: by his knowledge shall my righteous servant justify many; for he shall bear their iniquities. Therefore will I divide him a portion with the great, and he shall divide the spoil with the strong; because he hath poured out his soul unto death: and he was numbered with the transgressors; and he bare the sin of many, and made intercession for the transgressors"* (KJV).

"to anoint the most Holy"

The last of the six items that had to be accomplished before the end of the seventy "weeks," namely, *"to anoint the most Holy,"* was also accomplished at the time of the baptism of Jesus. This event involved an anointing that would signify a Holy One being "cut off" (*i.e.*, confirming a covenant, see discussion of "cut off" יִכָּרֵת on page 92). The covenant was the "new covenant" that was prophesied by Jeremiah, as explained at the beginning of this chapter. In addition, the baptism was done in the context of Isaiah, chapter 42, verses 1-8a, which say:

---

[1] The word "cut off" גָּזַר (BHS, Strong's OT:1504) here is not the same word used in verse 26.

Chapter Seven: He Shall Confirm the Covenant (Daniel 9:24-27)

"Behold my servant, whom I uphold; mine elect, in whom my soul delighteth; I have put my spirit upon him: he shall bring forth judgment to the Gentiles. He shall not cry, nor lift up, nor cause his voice to be heard in the street. A bruised reed shall he not break, and the smoking flax shall he not quench: he shall bring forth judgment unto truth. He shall not fail nor be discouraged, till he have set judgment in the earth: and the isles shall wait for his law. Thus saith God the Lord, he that created the heavens, and stretched them out; he that spread forth the earth, and that which cometh out of it; he that giveth breath unto the people upon it, and spirit to them that walk therein: I the Lord have called thee in righteousness, and will hold thine hand, and will keep thee, and give thee for a covenant of the people, for a light of the Gentiles; To open the blind eyes, to bring out the prisoners from the prison, and them that sit in darkness out of the prison house. I am the Lord: that is my name" (KJV).

Thus, it can be seen that Jesus' anointing by the Spirit of God at his baptism was his identification as the suffering servant in Isaiah, chapter 53, who would bear the iniquities and justify many. By the very act of the immersion of his body in the living waters of the Jordan River, his death, burial, and resurrection to eternal life, which would take place at the end of his ministry, was portrayed for all to see at the beginning of his ministry. His anointing in the year 28 CE set the stage for his public ministry to begin, a ministry that would be completed by the giving of the Holy Spirit to dwell in the hearts of all who believed in him after his resurrection.[1] As part of his ministry as the messianic forerunner, John the Baptist explained the spiritual meaning of the baptism of Jesus to his own disciples, as recorded in the Gospel of John, chapter 1, verses 29-36:

"The next day John seeth Jesus coming unto him, and saith, Behold the Lamb of God, which taketh away the sin of the world. This is he of whom I said, After me

---

[1] The baptism of Jesus re-introduced and clarified the trinitarian concept of the One God, with the three distinct personalities of Father, Son, and Holy Spirit appearing together at the same time as the manifestation of the one Godhead. This trinitarian concept was first introduced in the *Tanakh*, in the Book of Genesis, chapter 18, verses 1-18, when Abraham was visited by three "men" who gave Abraham the promise of the son out of Sarah through whom all nations would be blessed. Abraham addressed the three visitors as "My Lord" in verse 3. During his baptism by John the Baptist in the Jordan River, God the Father, by the anointing with the Holy Spirit, recognized Jesus as the son of the promise, the seed of Abraham who would be a light to the nations and the glory of Israel.

cometh a man which is preferred before me: for he was before me. And I knew him not: but that he should be made manifest to Israel, therefore am I come baptizing with water. And John bare record, saying, I saw the Spirit descending from heaven like a dove, and it abode upon him. And I knew him not: but he that sent me to baptize with water, the same said unto me, Upon whom thou shalt see the Spirit descending, and remaining on him, the same is he which baptizeth with the Holy Ghost. And I saw, and bare record that this is the Son of God. Again the next day after John stood, and two of his disciples; And looking upon Jesus as he walked, he saith, Behold the Lamb of God!" (KJV).

When the Holy Spirit of God was placed on Jesus as prophesied in Isaiah, chapter 41, the sixth and final item required to be accomplished during the seventy "weeks," *"to anoint the most Holy"* (KJV) as specified in Daniel, chapter 9, verse 24, was accomplished. Immediately afterwards, Jesus was led into the Judean wilderness, where he was tempted by Satan for forty days and forty nights. Soon thereafter, Jesus began his public ministry in Jerusalem by "cleansing" the Temple during Passover, followed by a period of baptizing in Judea. He continued to baptize in Judea until John the Baptist was arrested, after which the seventy weeks were brought to a close on the Day of Pentecost in 28 CE. With the events of the seventy weeks completed, verse 27 moves the action events of the prophecy forward by telling what will happen thereafter:

"And he shall confirm the covenant with many for one week: and in the midst of the week he shall cause the sacrifice and oblation to cease. And the people of the prince that shall come shall destroy the city and the sanctuary, and the end thereof shall be with a flood, and unto the end of the war desolations are determined, and for the overspreading of abominations he shall make it desolate, even until the consummation, and that determined shall be poured upon the desolate" (KJV).

After John's arrest, Jesus began preaching the new covenant to his Jewish brethren in Galilee, as recorded in the Gospel of Luke, chapter 4, verses 13-21:

"And when the devil had ended all the temptation, he departed from him for a season. And Jesus returned in the power of the Spirit into Galilee: and there went out a fame of him through all the region round about. And he taught in

their synagogues, being glorified of all. And he came to Nazareth, where he had been brought up: and, as his custom was, he went into the synagogue on the sabbath day, and stood up for to read. And there was delivered unto him the book of the prophet Esaias. And when he had opened the book, he found the place where it was written, The Spirit of the Lord is upon me, because he hath anointed me to preach the gospel to the poor; he hath sent me to heal the brokenhearted, to preach deliverance to the captives, and recovering of sight to the blind, to set at liberty them that are bruised, To preach the acceptable year of the Lord. And he closed the book, and he gave it again to the minister, and sat down. And the eyes of all them that were in the synagogue were fastened on him. And he began to say unto them, This day is this scripture fulfilled in your ears"* (KJV).

During his public ministry, which lasted about twenty-seven months from baptism to ascension, Jesus preached the "good news" of the new covenant in Judea, Samaria, Galilee, and other parts of *Eretz-Israel*, including Jerusalem. A two-year-plus ministry is indicated by the Scriptural text. The Gospel of John specifically mentions three Passovers observed during Jesus' ministry, one in chapter 2, verse 13, *"And the Jews' passover was at hand"* (KJV); a second in chapter 6, verse 4, *"And the passover, a feast of the Jews, was nigh"* (KJV); and a third in chapter 11, verse 55, *"And the Jews' passover was nigh at hand"* (KJV). The reference in chapter 2 is to the Passover in 28 CE,[1] the one in chapter 6 to the Passover in 29 CE, and the one in chapter 11 to Jesus' last Passover in 30 CE.

Some Bible scholars have speculated that a fourth Passover is alluded to in chapter 4, verse 35, when, immediately before an unnamed feast mentioned in John, chapter 5, verse 1, Jesus tells his disciples, *"Say not ye, There are yet four months, and then cometh harvest? behold, I say unto you, Lift up your eyes, and look on the fields; for they are white already to harvest"* (KJV). They assume that the statement by Jesus was literal, made in the spring when the fields of barley were ready for harvesting, something that would be true around the time of Passover. However, the chronology of Jesus' ministry (see the chronology on page 179 and time line Diagram 7.1 on page 113) shows that his statement was made after the Day of Pentecost and before the Day of Atonement in the year 28 CE, during a

---

[1] The exact year can be derived from the reference in John, chapter 2, verse 20, to Herod's Temple having been under construction for forty-six years (see page 177).

sabbath year and prior to the start of the jubilee year, which would begin on the 10th of Tishri. Looking around, the disciples would have seen that the fields had already been harvested many months earlier, before the start of the sabbath year, and, since this was to be a jubilee year as well, the disciples would have known that the next sowing season could not begin until the jubilee had ended on the Day of Atonement in 29 CE, which would be at least twelve months in the future. So, it must have been obvious to the disciples that Jesus was not making a literal statement about sowing or harvesting conditions at that moment. The Gospel of John goes on to clarify that Jesus was teaching instead about the season for harvesting souls, and emphasizing that the time for gathering them was now.

As history shows, Jesus' authority as mediator of the new covenant promised to Israel by Jeremiah was not understood by Jewish religious and political leaders of that day, and his simple message of justification through repentance and faith was almost universally rejected by the Temple authorities, Pharisees, Sadducees, scribes, and rabbis of his time.[1] On the other hand, many ordinary Jewish people in the countryside, and even some Jewish leaders in Jerusalem (especially those who had been enlightened by the gospel of the coming kingdom preached by John the Baptist), responded to Jesus' message of salvation and were baptized into the new covenant, as recorded in the Gospel of John, chapter 3, verse 26:

> *"And they came unto John* [the Baptist], *and said unto him, Rabbi, he that was with thee beyond Jordan, to whom thou barest witness, behold, the same baptizeth, and all men come to him. John answered and said, A man can receive nothing, except it be given him from heaven. Ye yourselves bear me witness, that I said, I am not the Christ, but that I am sent before him. He that hath the bride is the bridegroom: but the friend of the bridegroom, which standeth and heareth him, rejoiceth greatly because of the bridegroom's voice: this my joy therefore is fulfilled. He must increase, but I must decrease. He that cometh from above is above all: he that is of the earth is earthly, and speaketh of the earth: he that cometh from heaven is above all. And what he hath seen and*

---

[1] Much harm has been done by those who have used the rejection of Jesus' ministry by the Jewish leadership that is recorded in the *B'rit Hadashah* (New Testament) to justify anti-Semitic views and actions against Jewish people, individually and collectively, over the centuries. A careful reading and correct interpretation of the Bible, both the *Tanakh* and *B'rit Hadashah*, will show that there is absolutely no theological justification whatsoever for anti-Semitic/anti-Jewish/anti-Israel views or actions.

Chapter Seven: He Shall Confirm the Covenant (Daniel 9:24-27)

Diagram 7.1 - The Ministry of Jesus
(for complete chronology, see page 179)

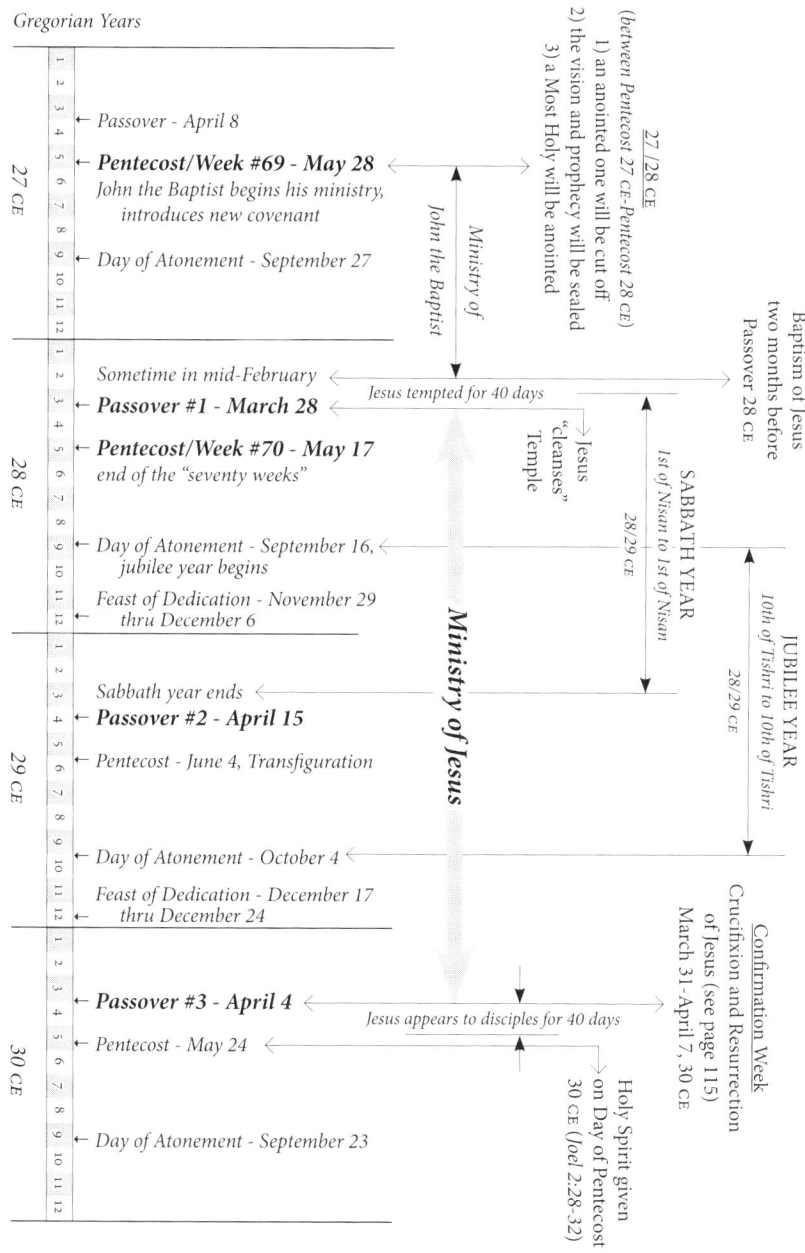

heard, that he testifieth; and no man receiveth his testimony. He that hath received his testimony hath set to his seal that God is true. For he whom God hath sent speaketh the words of God: for God giveth not the Spirit by measure unto him. The Father loveth the Son, and hath given all things into his hand. He that believeth on the Son hath everlasting life: and he that believeth not the Son shall not see life; but the wrath of God abideth on him" (KJV).

Confirmation of the Covenant

The public ministry of Jesus reached its climax during Passover week in the year 30 CE (see Diagram 7.2 on the opposite page), during which the first part of verse 27, which says *"And he shall confirm the covenant with many for one week: and in the midst of the week he shall cause the sacrifice and oblation to cease,"* was fulfilled. Jesus began the week by entering Jerusalem as the King of Israel, as recorded in the Gospel of Luke, chapter 19, verses 29-38:

"And it came to pass, when he was come nigh to Bethphage and Bethany, at the mount called the mount of Olives, he sent two of his disciples, Saying, Go ye into the village over against you; in the which at your entering ye shall find a colt tied, whereon yet never man sat: loose him, and bring him hither. And if any man ask you, Why do ye loose him? thus shall ye say unto him, Because the Lord hath need of him. And they that were sent went their way, and found even as he had said unto them. And as they were loosing the colt, the owners thereof said unto them, Why loose ye the colt? And they said, The Lord hath need of him. And they brought him to Jesus: and they cast their garments upon the colt, and they set Jesus thereon. And as he went, they spread their clothes in the way. And when he was come nigh, even now at the descent of the mount of Olives, the whole multitude of the disciples began to rejoice and praise God with a loud voice for all the mighty works that they had seen; Saying, Blessed be the King that cometh in the name of the Lord: peace in heaven, and glory in the highest" (KJV).

The kingship of Jesus was rejected by official Judaism from the beginning. During his entry into the city of Jerusalem on his way to the Temple area during the final week of his ministry, the Gospel of Luke, chapter 19, verses 39-44, records this exchange between some Pharisees and Jesus:

Chapter Seven: He Shall Confirm the Covenant (Daniel 9:24-27)

Diagram 7.2 - The Confirmation Week
(showing Galilean, Judean, and proleptic Gregorian rekoning for days)

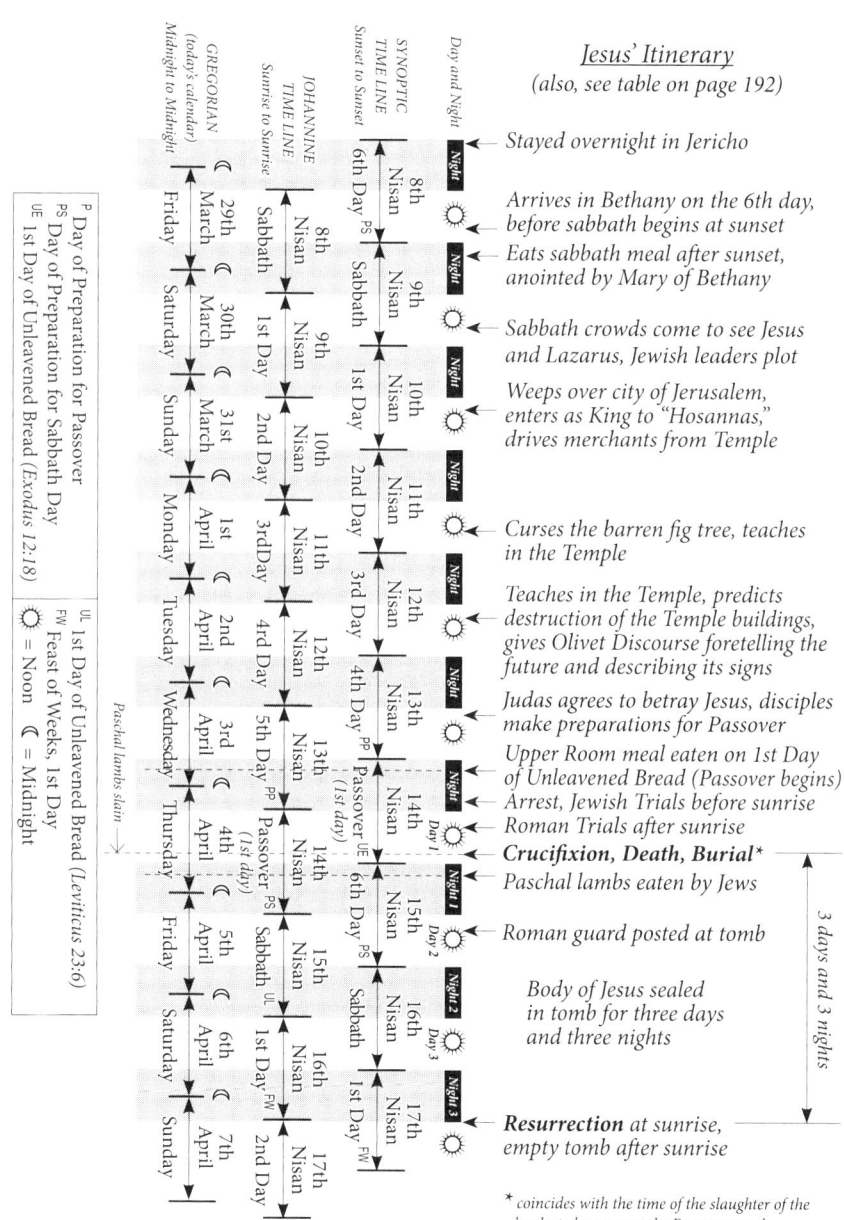

* coincides with the time of the slaughter of the lambs to be eaten at the Passover meal

> "And some of the Pharisees from among the multitude said unto him, Master, rebuke thy disciples. And he answered and said unto them, I tell you that, if these should hold their peace, the stones would immediately cry out. And when he was come near, he beheld the city, and wept over it, Saying, If thou hadst known, even thou, at least in this thy day, the things which belong unto thy peace! but now they are hid from thine eyes. For the days shall come upon thee, that thine enemies shall cast a trench about thee, and compass thee round, and keep thee in on every side, And shall lay thee even with the ground, and thy children within thee; and they shall not leave in thee one stone upon another; because thou knewest not the time of thy visitation" (KJV).

Jesus' entered Jerusalem on the 10th of Nisan, the day designated in the Scriptures for selecting the Passover lamb. His crucifixion four days later, on the fourteenth of Nisan, the eve of Passover, was on the day when the Paschal lamb was slain. At a supper with his disciples just hours before his arrest and trials by Jewish and Roman authorities, Jesus made it plain that his life blood that would be shed by his impending sacrifice on the cross was the blood that confirmed the new covenant, as recorded in the Gospel of Matthew, chapter 26, verses 26-28:

> "And as they were eating, Jesus took bread, and blessed it, and brake it, and gave it to the disciples, and said, Take, eat; this is my body. And he took the cup, and gave thanks, and gave it to them, saying, Drink ye all of it; For this is my blood of the new testament [covenant], which is shed for many for the remission of sins" (KJV).

The prophesied week of confirming the new covenant was brought to a close by the burial of Jesus in a rock-hewn tomb for three days and three nights, and then by his bodily resurrection to life on the third day, which was 17 Nisan by Sadducean reckoning or 16 Nisan by Pharisean reckoning, in both cases the resurrection occurring at sunrise on the first day of the Feast of Weeks (or First Fruits). Forty days later, after appearing to the eleven remaining disciples and many of his other followers for the purpose of creating multiple witnesses to the fact that he had been bodily resurrected, Jesus ascended to heaven from the Mount of Olives. On the fiftieth day following the morning of the resurrection of Jesus, on the Day of Pentecost, his followers were gathered together in Jerusalem as he had commanded them, where the Holy Spirit descended upon and indwelt each of them as Jesus had promised before ascending, an event that is recorded in the Book of Acts, chapter 2, as follows:

> "And when the day of Pentecost was fully come, they were all with one accord in one place. And suddenly there came a sound from heaven as of a rushing mighty wind, and it filled all the house where they were sitting. And there appeared unto them cloven tongues like as of fire, and it sat upon each of them. And they were all filled with the Holy Ghost, and began to speak with other tongues, as the Spirit gave them utterance. ... And they [the men of Jerusalem] were all amazed and marvelled, saying one to another, Behold, are not all these which speak Galilaeans? And how hear we every man in our own tongue, wherein we were born? ... What meaneth this? Others mocking said, These men are full of new wine. But [the apostle] Peter, standing up with the eleven, lifted up his voice, and said unto them, Ye men of Judaea, and all ye that dwell at Jerusalem, be this known unto you, and hearken to my words: For these are not drunken, as ye suppose, seeing it is but the third hour of the day. But this is that which was spoken by the prophet Joel; And it shall come to pass in the last days, saith God, I will pour out of my Spirit upon all flesh: and your sons and your daughters shall prophesy, and your young men shall see visions, and your old men shall dream dreams: And on my servants and on my handmaidens I will pour out in those days of my Spirit; and they shall prophesy: And I will shew wonders in heaven above, and signs in the earth beneath; blood, and fire, and vapour of smoke: The sun shall be turned into darkness, and the moon into blood, before that great and notable day of the Lord come: And it shall come to pass, that whosoever shall call on the name of the Lord shall be saved. Ye men of Israel, hear these words; Jesus of Nazareth, a man approved of God among you by miracles and wonders and signs, which God did by him in the midst of you, as ye yourselves also know: Him, being delivered by the determinate counsel and foreknowledge of God, ye have taken, and by wicked hands have crucified and slain: Whom God hath raised up, having loosed the pains of death: because it was not possible that he should be holden of it. For David speaketh concerning him, I foresaw the Lord always before my face, for he is on my right hand, that I should not be moved: Therefore did my heart rejoice, and my tongue was glad; moreover also my flesh shall rest in hope: Because thou wilt not leave my soul in hell, neither wilt thou suffer thine Holy One to see corruption. Thou hast made known to me

the ways of life; thou shalt make me full of joy with thy countenance. Men and brethren, let me freely speak unto you of the patriarch David, that he is both dead and buried, and his sepulchre is with us unto this day. Therefore being a prophet, and knowing that God had sworn with an oath to him, that of the fruit of his loins, according to the flesh, he would raise up Christ to sit on his throne; He seeing this before spake of the resurrection of Christ, that his soul was not left in hell, neither his flesh did see corruption. This Jesus hath God raised up, whereof we all are witnesses. Therefore being by the right hand of God exalted, and having received of the Father the promise of the Holy Ghost, he hath shed forth this, which ye now see and hear. For David is not ascended into the heavens: but he saith himself, The Lord said unto my Lord, Sit thou on my right hand, Until I make thy foes thy footstool. Therefore let all the house of Israel know assuredly, that God hath made that same Jesus, whom ye have crucified,[1] *both Lord and Christ"* (KJV).

From a theological standpoint, Jesus' crucifixion and resurrection during Passover week in the year 30 CE confirmed the new covenant and brought to an end the efficacy of Temple sacrifices for atonement. The cessation of the sacrificial system had been predicted in verse 27b, "*and in the midst of the week he shall cause the sacrifice and oblation to cease*" (KJV), and it was attested by ominous signs which were recorded in the Talmud.[2] The Temple continued to function for another forty years, until it was destroyed by Titus and the Romans in 70 CE as predicted, "*And the people of the prince that shall come shall destroy the city and the sanctuary*" (KJV). Verse 27c goes on to prophesy, "*and the end thereof shall be with a flood, and unto the end of the war desolations are determined, and for the overspreading of abominations he shall make it desolate, even until the consummation, and that determined shall be poured upon the desolate*" (KJV),[3] thus foretelling the state of perpetual spiritual desolation (no Temple) that would characterize Jerusalem and the Temple Mount to this very day.

---

[1] Jewish religious authority (the Sanhedrin) condemned Jesus for blasphemy, a capital offense under Jewish law; Roman civil authority executed him by means of crucifixion.

[2] *Jerusalem Talmud*, Tractate Yoma 6:3 [33b]: "It has been taught: For forty years before the destruction of the Temple the western menorah light darkened, the crimson thread did not turn white, and the lot for the Lord always came up in the left hand. The priests would close the gates of the Temple at night and get up in the morning and find them open" (Au).

[3] See previous exposition of verse 27 on page 92.

CONCLUSION

THE WISE SHALL UNDERSTAND

I have shared with you what I believe to be the most chronologically accurate and thus most authoritative exposition of the seven chrono-specific predictive prophecies recorded in the Book of Daniel, with clear and precise interpretations that supersede those offered by all previous expositors. Now that you have read the interpretations for yourself, you may have some reservations, perhaps feeling that my chronologically-based exposition reads too much like a technical manual to be truly spiritual, or you may be questioning whether projecting the efficacy of Hebrew prophecy into modern times is a valid exegetical extension. If so, I can relate. I, too, have a long history of reliance on the more traditional interpretive approaches used in commentaries written by Bible scholars whose works have become the standards for Danielic exposition, works that are built around some form of higher criticism or have a devotional focus as their basis, and which usually downplay or ignore chronology altogether. So, taking a fresh look at the Danielic prophecies from a chronological perspective and allowing for modern-day fulfillment of prophecy involved a departure from conventional biblical scholarship on my part. I had to set aside my biases favoring traditional interpretive approaches before I could begin to see the Danielic prophecies for what they are, namely, chrono-specific predictive prophecies that explain the history of the Jewish people and their eternal relationship to their God. Once I embraced that reality, the prophecies began to yield to understanding.

After the prophecies were understood and interpreted, I then had to decide how best to explain the new interpretations to you, whether to compare them to older interpretations, thus giving them a hermeneutic context, or to present them as novel interpretations standing on their own. I decided on the latter approach, choosing not to include synopses and critiques of the most quoted scholarly expositions of the Danielic prophecies, mainly because I found that the Daniel commentaries most in vogue today have been written by biblical scholars who seem to try their best to avoid mentioning the efficacy of divine providence with respect to the prophecies and their fulfillments. The resulting freedom from having to deal with that error allowed me to present my interpretations as simple explanations of predictive prophecy having exact real-time fulfillments in history, and to do so without the characteristic academic equivocations. I also decided to present the prophecies, not in the order in which they are set forth in the Bible, but in the order in which I had originally interpreted them. By rearranging the presentation, I was able to recreate for you the path of understanding that I had traveled from one Danielic prophecy to the next. Ultimately, though, I knew as I was writing down my explanations that the most I could accomplish was to present the interpretations as clearly as I could present them, then trust that God would open your eyes and ears in the same way he opened mine to understand the prophecies when I began my quest to know their meanings in 1974.

In the days to come, as you meditate on the interpretations of the chrono-specific predictive prophecies explained in this book, one previously unstated (or at least understated) but important point should be kept in mind: I did not have to employ any unique spiritual gifts to interpret the Danielic prophecies. The prophecies were unsealed by God acting providentially through Israel, not by me. Once they were unsealed, all I had to do was match the events described in the prophecies with events found in history, something relatively easy to do since all of the prophesied events had already occurred in history by the time I began to look at them. It is also worth noting that the fulfillment of every major chrono-specific prophecy in Daniel has now been fully explained in this book. This means that there are no things left unexplained, no predictions about events waiting to happen in the future. Apart from the resurrection of Daniel himself, an event that is implied at the end of the twelfth chapter, everything else prophesied by Daniel has now happened and can be so identified as residing in recorded history.

Of course, the interpretations set forth in this book, inasmuch as they fully explain all of the chrono-specific prophecies in Daniel by matching their biblical texts to events already documented in history, constitute a challenge to the field of biblical eschatology. Bible-believing Bible scholars (and, fortunately, there are still a few of them around) will need to reexamine basic assumptions about their sequence of end-time events, and do so without having a framework of future events from the Danielic prophecies to build upon. That process will be troubling for the more conservative Bible expositors among us, especially when they realize that some of their more cherished eschatological assumptions may have to be adjusted as a result. For non-Bible-believing Bible scholars (and, unfortunately, there are all too many of them around), the actuality of revelatory predictive prophecy validated by their later fulfillment in history, a sure sign of the reality of divine providence, will now have to be incorporated into their anti-theistic academic approach to biblical exposition. Sadly, even with the overwhelming evidence provided by the Danielic prophecies and their fulfillments, admitting

Conclusion: The Wise Shall Understand

the concept of transcendence into the halls of academia may seem too faith-based for those biblical scholars who choose to remain wise in their own eyes.

As for Jewish Bible scholars, the challenge offered by the new interpretations presented in this book will be even greater still. The chronological preciseness of the Danielic prophecies, especially the prophecy in Daniel, chapter 9, will demand that they give serious consideration to the evidence that Jesus, in whose name Jews have been unjustly persecuted and killed for almost two-thousand years, was, is, and will be the Anointed One that was foretold by Moses and the prophets in the *Tanakh*. Indeed, it is quite possible, even probable in my opinion, that the chrono-specific predictive prophecies in Daniel have been unsealed at this point in history especially for the edification of the Jewish people, to allow them to understand and approach the Holy One of Israel in the manner that the Scriptures ordain they will acknowledge and worship him at the time of the end.

In closing, I want to thank you for allowing me to share my understanding of the chrono-specific predictive prophecies recorded in the Book of Daniel with you. Now that you have read this book and the interpretations it presents, my hope is that the insights about God proffered herein will prove to have been spiritually illuminating, and that, by helping you to better understand God's faithfulness and steadfast love as evidenced through his most sure word of prophecy, your faith in his Word will have been increased, even to the point of belief if that was not already the case. I can testify from personal knowledge that the person who diligently seeks the God of the Bible and perseveres in seeking him to the point of belief will one day be rewarded with the gift of eternal life in his presence. Until that glorious day, God will freely give his earthly blessings, perhaps the greatest of which is that he will empower the believer to share the message of salvation through faith in him with a world that is desperately seeking to believe in something good and eternal and true.

> *"Blessed be the name of God for ever and ever: for wisdom and might are his: and he changeth the times and the seasons: he removeth kings, and setteth up kings: he giveth wisdom unto the wise, and knowledge to them that know understanding: he revealeth the deep and secret things: he knoweth what is in the darkness, and the light dwelleth with him."* - Daniel 2:20-22 (KJV)

Appendices

"The wise lay up knowledge." - Proverbs 10:14 (ESV)

APPENDIX ONE

Background Notes

ON THE BOOK OF DANIEL

The Book of Daniel is one of the most debated books in the Bible. Scholars seem unable to agree about who wrote it, when it was written, and what it means. In this book, the chrono-specific prophecies in Daniel are shown to be accurate and precise in their details, so it only follows that the things that the Book of Daniel says or implies about itself are taken at face value herein as well.

Author

The Book of Daniel, chapters 1-12, was written by Daniel, a Jewish man of supposed noble birth who was carried away as a captive from Judah to Babylon by Nebuchadnezzar in the year 605 BCE. In his book, Daniel records the revelation given to him by God, who communicated with him through visions, dreams, and angels. Interestingly, Daniel never refers to himself as a prophet, and his book is not included in the "Prophets" section of the *Tanakh*, being placed in the "Writings" section. In the *B'rit Hadashah,* Jesus specifically refers to him as "Daniel the prophet" (see Matthew 24:15, Mark 13:14), and his book is placed among those of the major prophets in most Christian Bibles. It can be inferred that Daniel was in his early teen years when taken to Babylon. There he lived and was schooled in the king's palace, and eventually held high office in the Babylonian Empire. Daniel spent most of his life removed from Jerusalem and Judah, but remained faithful to his Jewish heritage. He lived to see the fall of Babylon to Cyrus the Great of Persia, but nothing is known about his life thereafter. His death is assumed to have occurred soon after 536 BCE, with his place of burial unknown. In Hebrew, the name Daniel means "God is my judge."

Date Written

It is not known whether the vision-dream sequences in the Book of Daniel were recorded individually at the time they were experienced, or as a collection of several at a time, or perhaps even all together as one continuous work. It is certain that all were written down after the author was carried off to Babylon by

Nebuchadnezzar. In this book, the following chronology for each of the chrono-specific chapters is assumed: chapter 7 was written in the first year of Belshazzar, *ca.* 553 BCE, chapter 8 in the third year of Belshazzar, *ca.* 551 BCE, chapter 9 in the first year of Darius the Mede, son of Ahasuerus, *ca.* 538 BCE, chapters 10-12 in the third year of Cyrus the Great of Persia, *ca.* 536 BCE.

Languages Used

Biblical Hebrew was used for chapter 1, verse 1, through chapter 2, verse 3, and then it resumes in chapter 8, verse 1, through chapter 12, verse 13. Aramaic, the *lingua franca* of the Mesopotamian region in the 6th century BCE, was used for chapters 2, verse 4, through chapter 7, verse 28 (see illustration of language transition on opposite page). No expositor has come up with a good exegetical explanation for Daniel's use of two languages to write his book.

Historical Context

Daniel was born during the reign of Josiah (*r.* 640-609 BCE), who presided over a period of religious revival in the kingdom of Judah. Josiah restored the Temple and its priesthood to purity and re-instituted the biblical festivals. This return to righteousness followed the extreme wickedness of King Manasseh (*r.* 697-642 BCE), who provoked God to say in 2 Kings, chapter 21, verses 10-15: *"Because Manasseh king of Judah hath done these abominations, and hath done wickedly above all that the Amorites did, which were before him, and hath made Judah also to sin with his idols: Therefore thus saith the Lord God of Israel, Behold, I am bringing such evil upon Jerusalem and Judah, that whosoever heareth of it, both his ears shall tingle. And I will stretch over Jerusalem the line of Samaria, and the plummet of the house of Ahab: and I will wipe Jerusalem as a man wipeth a dish, wiping it, and turning it upside down. And I will forsake the remnant of mine inheritance, and deliver them into the hand of their enemies; and they shall become a prey and a spoil to all their enemies; Because they have done that which was evil in my sight, and have provoked me to anger, since the day their fathers came forth out of Egypt, even unto this day"* (KJV). However, God was so pleased with Josiah that he promised him that he would not see the wrath to come.

During Josiah's reign, Egypt was the great power to the south. To the north, the power of Assyria was on the wane and that of Babylon on the rise. In 609 BCE,

Appendix One: Background Notes on the Book of Daniel

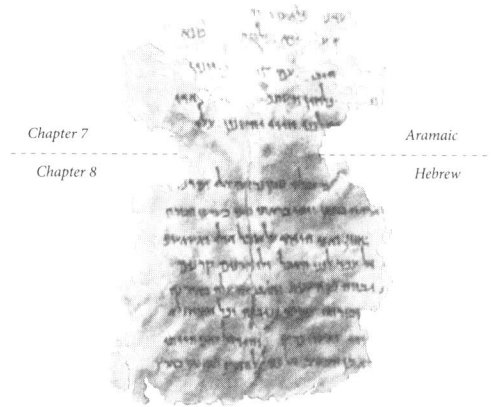

Fragment of a Daniel Scroll from the Dead Sea Scrolls (4Q112) showing the transition from Aramaic to Hebrew in the Book of Daniel when going from chapter 7 to chapter 8.

Josiah, who was allied with Babylon, in an attempt to block an Egyptian army that was passing through his territory to aid their Assyrian allies in their fight against Babylon, was killed by the Egyptians. As a consequence, the countdown to judgement against Judah that God had paused during Josiah's lifetime was resumed. In successive annual campaigns, the Babylonians moved southward to capture and subjugate cities in the Levant. In 605 BCE, the Babylonian army clashed with the Egyptian army in the Battle of Carchemish and were victorious, firmly securing Judah as a Babylonian vassal. It was during this time that Daniel and many Hebrew nobles were taken captive to Babylon and Judah came under the Babylonian hegemony. In 597 BCE, after a rebellion by King Jehoiachin of Judah, King Nebuchadnezzar of Babylon reacted with vigor. He seized Jerusalem and led the king, the prophet Ezekiel, and many Jews into exile in Babylon. Eleven years later, Nebuchadnezzar returned for a third time, entering Jerusalem in August of 586 BCE. It was at this time that Solomon's Temple and the walls of Jerusalem were destroyed and the rest of the people taken into captivity except for a small remnant left to their own devices in the countryside.

During the seventy years of the Babylonian Exile (605-536 BCE), a new power arrived on the scene which would challenge the supremacy of Babylon. As predicted in Isaiah, chapter 44, verse 28, and chapter 45, verse 1, Cyrus the Great unified the Medes and Persians, and in 539 BCE conquered Babylon under his banner as King of Persia. Cyrus was an enlightened ruler who tolerated and even encouraged retention of the customs and religious practices of conquered peoples. Not too long after conquering Babylon, Cyrus decreed that the Jews could return to their ancestral lands in Judah and rebuild their Temple. The first Jews returned in 536 BCE and began to rebuild Jerusalem and the Temple. Thus, the seventy years of Exile that had been predicted by the prophet Jeremiah came to an end. Prior to the return from Babylon, God had revealed to Daniel the history of the Jews from the end of the Exile until the end of days. However, because the prophecies were sealed, it is debatable how much of what God had revealed was understood by the Jewish people over the years.

Place in the Canon

In the Jewish Bible (the *Tanakh*), the Book of Daniel is not included in the Prophets, at least in the Masoretic and similar Hebrew texts, but is placed in the Writings, a section containing Psalms, Proverbs, Job, Song of Solomon, Ruth, Lamentations, Ecclesiastes, Esther, Ezra-Nehemiah, and Chronicles. On the other hand, the older Greek Septuagint includes Daniel with the major Prophets. Some have speculated that Daniel was moved from the Prophets section of the "official" Hebrew texts to the Writings section after early Christians made extensive use of Daniel to support their claims for the messiahship of Jesus. In the Christian Bible, the Book of Daniel is included as one of the Major Prophets, placed immediately after the Book of Ezekiel. The Roman Catholic version of Daniel contains two extra chapters not contained in the Protestant version, an account about Susanna added as chapter 13 and another about Bel and the Dragon added as chapter 14. In addition, the Catholic versions insert a "Prayer of Azariah" and the "Song of the Holy Children" into chapter 3. These two added chapters and the lengthy insertion in chapter 3 are found in various combinations in some of the earliest Greek versions of the Bible, but they are not recognized as Scripture by Protestants or Jews today. In this book, the Protestant/Jewish version, which is limited to chapters 1-12 of the Book of Daniel and is based on the Masoretic text, is considered authoritative and trustworthy as Scripture and is used exclusively herein for interpretive and illustrative purposes.

APPENDIX TWO

The Hebrew Calendar

in Ancient Times

The earliest reference to a calendar in the Bible is found in Genesis, chapter 1, verse 14: *"And God said, Let there be lights in the firmament of the heaven to divide the day from the night; and let them be for signs, and for seasons, and for days, and years"* (KJV). As this verse demonstrates, timekeeping was related to astronomy from the very beginning of biblical history. Unfortunately, the Bible does not describe the actual calendar system used by the ancients, so we can only guess about its structure, astronomical associations, and accuracy.

The first calendar component with a numerical notation is found in the Book of Exodus, when God commanded that the Passover be observed in the first month, which was called Abib. The early books of the Bible mention only four months by name: the first month Abib in Exodus, chapter 12, verse 2 and chapter 13, verse 4; the second month Zif in 1 Kings, chapter 6, verse 1; the seventh month Ethanim in 1 Kings, chapter 8, verse 2; and the eighth month Bul in 1 Kings, chapter 6, verse 38. From these mentions, it has been assumed that the early Hebrew calendar was a strict lunar calendar. There is evidence, however, that the movement of the sun was also taken into account by the early Hebrews. The Gezer Calendar, dating from the 10th century BCE, the earliest written example of a Hebrew calendar so far found by archeologists, shows a twelve-month year which is correlated with agricultural seasons (olive harvest, early grain planting, late grain planting, hoeing of flax, barley harvest, wheat harvest, *etc.*). This correlation of months to seasons confirms that the early Hebrew calendar was not exclusively lunar, but was instead lunisolar in practice, coordinated in some manner with the agricultural seasons as well as the movement of the moon, so as to keep the calendar aligned with the harvest seasons year after year.

After the Exodus, there were twelve months in the ancient calendar used by the Israelites, with months alternating between 29 and 30 days in length, which averages out to 29½ days per month. The resulting lunar year was composed of 354 days. Since this 354-day lunar year was eleven days shorter than the actual solar year, an adjustment by intercalation (probably a leap month added every three or four years, but the exact method is still unknown) was made to keep the seasons synchronized with the sun. While captive in Egypt, the Hebrews probably followed the Egyptian civil calendar, which had twelve-months, each having 30 days, then five leap days were added to prevent calendar creep, resulting in a year of 365 days. There is no evidence that the Israelites ever adopted the 365-day Egyptian calendar for sacred purposes after the Exodus, though. Some Bible expositors have postulated a 360-day "prophetic year" (and years other than the astronomically-correct 365¼-day year) that they claim can be used for interpreting biblical chronology and prophecies. However, the Bible itself does not stipulate any specific number of days in a Hebrew year, probably because its length had to be adjusted from time to time to reconcile the twelve lunar-determined Jewish festival months with their corresponding solar seasons.

Until the Exodus, the basic components of the Hebrew calendar were all derived from physical observation of the heavens—the day from the rising and setting of the sun, the month from the recurring crescent of the new moon, and the year from the seasons based on the equinoxes and solstices of the sun. After the Exodus, the new nation of Israel was given a non-astronomical time unit to add to its basic calendar system, the sabbath (seventh) day. It was to be observed by every Israelite as a reminder of their deliverance from bondage, as recorded in Deuteronomy, chapter 5, verses 12-15: *"Keep the sabbath day to sanctify it, as the Lord thy God hath commanded thee. Six days thou shalt labour, and do all thy work: But the seventh day is the sabbath of the Lord thy God: in it thou shalt not do any work, thou, nor thy son, nor thy daughter, nor thy manservant, nor thy maidservant, nor thine ox, nor thine ass, nor any of thy cattle, nor thy stranger that is within thy gates; that thy manservant and thy maidservant may rest as well as thou. And remember that thou wast a servant in the land of Egypt, and that the Lord thy God brought thee out thence through a mighty hand and by a stretched out arm: therefore the Lord thy God commanded thee to keep the sabbath day"* (KJV). Thus, the seven-day week became a unit of time in Jewish life.

In addition to the sabbath day, a sabbath year and a jubilee year were added to the calendar by God through Moses, as well as a system of festivals and religious days to be observed throughout the year. The Jewish new year was originally celebrated in the first month, as God had commanded, but when Israel became a kingdom there is evidence that a civil year was instituted with its new year observed in the seventh month. In later times, the religious and civil new years were combined into one Jewish new-year observance on the first day of the seventh month, and that holiday is called *Rosh Hashanah* (literally, "head of the year") today. Other changes were to happen over time as well. The Exile in

Appendix Two: The Hebrew Calendar in Ancient Times

Months of the Jewish Year			
Number	*English Name*	*Length (days)*	*Gregorian Equivalent*
1st	Nisan	30	March-April
2nd	Iyar	29	April-May
3rd	Sivan	30	May-June
4th	Tammuz	29	June-July
5th	Av	30	July-August
6th	Elul	29	August-September
7th	Tishri	30	September-October
8th	Heshvan	29 or 30	October-November
9th	Kislev	30 or 29	November-December
10th	Tevet	29	December-January
11th	Shevat	30	January-February
12th	Adar	29 (or 30 in LY)	February-March
13th (in LY)	Adar II	29	March-April

In a leap year (LY), the month of Adar II is inserted and all other months are moved back accordingly; a leap month is inserted in the 3rd, 6th, 8th, 11th, 14th, 17th and 19th years of the 19-year cycle.

Babylon that began in 605 BCE resulted in major changes to the Hebrew calendar. The most obvious change was the adoption of Babylonian names for the months, and those names are still being used today (see list of Jewish months above). The first month Abib became Nisan, the seventh month Ethanim became Tishri, and so on. More important for accuracy, the 19-year cycle of calendar synchronization (later called the Metonic cycle), with its schedule for adding leap months to seven specified years in every nineteen-year cycle, became standard, and it is reflected in the chronology of the Book of Daniel.

The ancient Hebrew calendar had a high degree of accuracy. Before 70 CE, it was based on priestly observations from Jerusalem, the sighting of the new moon being the most important calendric event. All other Jewish calendars were coordinated with the Temple calendar, so that the festivals would be celebrated on the correct day everywhere. After the Temple was destroyed in 70 CE and the priesthood ceased to function, the calendar was maintained by rabbis in various locations. Since observations from the Temple were no longer possible, and since the Jewish people were becoming so widely dispersed that timely dissemination

Major Festivals on the Ancient Jewish Priestly Calendar			
Month	*Post-Exilic Name*	*Day of Month and Festival*	*Pilgrimage*
1st Month	Nisan	14th - Passover (Pesach) and 15th - 22nd - Feast of Unleavened Bread 16th - First Day, Feast of Weeks, First Fruits (barley)	✓
2nd Month	Iyar	14th - Second Passover	
3rd Month	Sivan	50th Day, Feast of Weeks (Shavuot), First Fruits (wheat)	✓
4th Month	Tammuz	- - -	
5th Month	Av	- - -	
6th Month	Elul	First Fruits (figs, pomegranates, dates)	
7th Month	Tishri	1st - New Year (Rosh Hashanah) 10th - Day of Atonement (Yom Kippur) 15th-22nd - Feast of Tabernacles (Sukkot), First Fruits (wine and oil)	✓
8th Month	Heshvan	- - -	
9th Month	Kislev	25th - Feast of Dedication (Hanukkah)	
10th Month	Tevet	- - -	
11th Month	Shevat	- - -	
12th Month	Adar	14th - Purim (with Fast of Esther)	
Since the creation of the State of Israel in 1948, the Chief Rabbinate of Israel has established four new Jewish holidays: Jerusalem Day (Yom Yerushalayim); Holocaust Remembrance Day (Yom HaShoah); Memorial Day (Yom Hazikaron); Israel Independence Day (Yom Ha'atzmaut).			

of calendric information was impossible from one central location, a Hebrew calendar employing mathematical calculation was developed by Rabbi Hillel II in the 4th century CE. A derivative of that universal calendar is used by many Jews today. It standardized the length of months and the addition of leap months over the course of a 19-year cycle, so that the lunar calendar is regularly realigned with the solar years. In addition, the Hillel II calendar ensured that Yom Kippur would not fall adjacent to a Sabbath and Hoshanah Rabba would not fall on a Saturday. A day is added to the month of Heshvan or subtracted from the month of Kislev of the previous year to prevent those things from happening. In reality, the rules for computing the modern Jewish calendar are much more detailed than has been outlined here, but this presentation covers all aspects important for understanding the ancient Hebrew calendar system in the Bible.

APPENDIX THREE

Calculating Sabbath and Jubilee Years

Daniel 4

The Children of Israel were commanded to observe sabbath and jubilee years once they were settled in the promised land, as recorded in Leviticus, chapter 25, verses 1-10. Observance of the sabbath-jubilee commandment is rarely mentioned in the Bible, probably because the people of Israel frequently failed to keep it. In addition, the extra-biblical records of whatever observances did occur in ancient Israel were lost by the time of the destruction of the Temple in 70 CE. Even modern Jewish sources, which are based mainly on rabbinical writings and Josephus in addition to the Bible, disagree about the correct calendar for sabbath and jubilee years, and even about how the sabbath and jubilee years were related to one another, whether they were sequential or overlapping. So, the challenge for the modern biblical chronologist is to find a sabbath year and jubilee year with relative certainty, based only on the biblical text, and from those years calculate a calendar showing all sabbath and jubilee years in history. Fortunately, there is a way to do just that by using the chronological information in Daniel, chapter 4, together with information provided in the Book of 1 Kings, chapter 6, as a starting point.

Identifying the Sabbath-Jubilee Year of Solomon

Calculating a calendar of sabbath and jubilee years using the fourth chapter of Daniel begins with an understanding of how that chapter relates to the promises made to Solomon about the permanence of the kingdom to him and his posterity, as recorded in the Book of 1 Kings, beginning with chapter 9, verses 1-9:

"And it came to pass, when Solomon had finished the building of the house of the Lord, and the king's house, and all Solomon's desire which he was pleased to do, That the Lord appeared to Solomon the second time, as he had appeared unto him at Gibeon. And the Lord said unto him, I have heard thy prayer and thy supplication, that thou hast made before me: I have hallowed this house, which thou hast built, to put my name there for ever; and mine eyes and mine heart shall be there perpetually. And if thou wilt walk before me, as David thy father walked, in integrity of heart, and in uprightness, to do

according to all that I have commanded thee, and wilt keep my statutes and my judgments: Then I will establish the throne of thy kingdom upon Israel for ever, as I promised to David thy father, saying, There shall not fail thee a man upon the throne of Israel. But if ye shall at all turn from following me, ye or your children, and will not keep my commandments and my statutes which I have set before you, but go and serve other gods, and worship them: Then will I cut off Israel out of the land which I have given them; and this house, which I have hallowed for my name, will I cast out of my sight; and Israel shall be a proverb and a byword among all people: And at this house, which is high, every one that passeth by it shall be astonished, and shall hiss; and they shall say, Why hath the Lord done thus unto this land, and to this house? And they shall answer, Because they forsook the Lord their God, who brought forth their fathers out of the land of Egypt, and have taken hold upon other gods, and have worshipped them, and served them: therefore hath the Lord brought upon them all this evil" (KJV).

In his later years, Solomon did evil in the sight of the Lord by marrying many foreign women, this done in addition to the daughter of pharaoh who he had married in the early years of his reign, and his heart was turned away from God to worship their gods, which were the gods of the surrounding nations, as recorded in 1 Kings, chapter 11, verses 1-8:

"But king Solomon loved many strange women, together with the daughter of Pharaoh, women of the Moabites, Ammonites, Edomites, Zidonians, and Hittites; Of the nations concerning which the Lord said unto the children of Israel, Ye shall not go in to them, neither shall they come in unto you: for surely they will turn away your heart after their gods: Solomon clave unto these in love. And he had seven hundred wives, princesses, and three hundred concubines: and his wives turned away his heart. For it came to pass, when Solomon was old, that his wives turned away his heart after other gods: and his heart was not perfect with the Lord his God, as was the heart of David his father. For Solomon went after Ashtoreth the goddess of the Zidonians, and after Milcom the abomination of the Ammonites. And Solomon did evil in the sight of the Lord, and went not fully after the Lord, as did David his father. Then did Solomon build an high place for Chemosh, the abomination of Moab, in the hill that is before Jerusalem, and for Molech, the abomination

of the children of Ammon. And likewise did he for all his strange wives, which burnt incense and sacrificed unto their gods" (KJV).

Solomon's disobedience, together with the disobedience of the people of Israel who followed his example by worshipping at the high places dedicated to foreign gods, caused the Lord to pass judgement on the king and the nation, as recorded in 1 Kings, chapter 11, verses 9-13:

"And the Lord was angry with Solomon, because his heart was turned from the Lord God of Israel, which had appeared unto him twice, And had commanded him concerning this thing, that he should not go after other gods: but he kept not that which the Lord commanded. Wherefore the Lord said unto Solomon, Forasmuch as this is done of thee, and thou hast not kept my covenant and my statutes, which I have commanded thee, I will surely rend the kingdom from thee, and will give it to thy servant. Notwithstanding in thy days I will not do it for David thy father's sake: but I will rend it out of the hand of thy son. Howbeit I will not rend away all the kingdom; but will give one tribe to thy son for David my servant's sake, and for Jerusalem's sake which I have chosen" (KJV).

Solomon, when dedicating the Temple (and possibly recalling the prediction of Israel's unfaithfulness given by Moses in Deuteronomy, chapter 28) had asked for future forgiveness for the people of Israel, as recorded in 1 Kings, chapter 8, verses 46-53:

"If they sin against thee, (for there is no man that sinneth not,) and thou be angry with them, and deliver them to the enemy, so that they carry them away captives unto the land of the enemy, far or near; Yet if they shall bethink themselves [alternate translation, "come to their senses"][1] *in the land whither they were carried captives, and repent, and make supplication unto thee in the land of them that carried them captives, saying, We have sinned, and have done perversely, we have committed wickedness; And so return unto thee with all their heart, and with all their soul, in the land of their enemies, which led them away captive, and pray unto thee toward their land, which thou gavest unto their fathers, the city which thou hast chosen, and the house which I have*

---

[1] The NET Bible®, Copyright © 1996-2006 by Biblical Studies Press, www.bible.org.

built for thy name: Then hear thou their prayer and their supplication in heaven thy dwelling place, and maintain their cause, And forgive thy people that have sinned against thee and all their transgressions wherein they have transgressed against thee, and give them compassion before them who carried them captive, that they may have compassion on them: For they be thy people, and thine inheritance, which thou broughtest forth out of Egypt, from the midst of the furnace of iron: That thine eyes may be open unto the supplication of thy servant, and unto the supplication of thy people Israel, to hearken unto them in all that they call for unto thee. For thou didst separate them from among all the people of the earth, to be thine inheritance, as thou spakest by the hand of Moses thy servant, when thou broughtest our fathers out of Egypt, O Lord God" (KJV).

The above passages quoted from the Book of 1 Kings explain the meaning of Daniel, chapter 4 (read full text on page 223), which presents a chrono-specific prophecy about Israel as an allegory (that is, a parable), with King Nebuchadnezzar symbolically representing the kingship of Israel and its relationship to God.[1] In the allegory, the king has a dream, seeing himself as a tree that reaches into the heavens and is then cut down, as described in verses 10-16:

"Thus were the visions of mine head in my bed; I saw, and behold a tree in the midst of the earth, and the height thereof was great. The tree grew, and was strong, and the height thereof reached unto heaven, and the sight thereof to the end of all the earth: The leaves thereof were fair, and the fruit thereof much, and in it was meat for all: the beasts of the field had shadow under it, and the fowls of the heaven dwelt in the boughs thereof, and all flesh was fed of it. I saw

---

[1] Some expositors have proposed that Daniel, chapter 4, is a story from history. However, there is no evidence in the historical record of any of the events described in the fourth chapter (loss of kingdom, madness, return to sanity, *etc.*) ever happening to the historical Nebuchadnezzar. Other expositors have worked around this deficiency by proposing that the events refer to a later Babylonian king, Nabonidus (r. 556-539 BCE). Early in his reign, he did leave Babylon to live at the oasis of Tayma in Arabia for religious retreat, but no one knows for certain how long he stayed there (most estimates say ten years, and no historical documents say seven). Nabonidus seriously neglected the Marduk priesthood and festivals back in Babylon. However, during the period of uncertainty caused by the king's long absence from Babylon, the Marduk priests never accused him of being mad, nor is there any indication that he later adopted and worshipped the God of Israel, as required by the description at the end of the fourth chapter of Daniel.

in the visions of my head upon my bed, and, behold, a watcher and an holy one came down from heaven; He cried aloud, and said thus, Hew down the tree, and cut off his branches, shake off his leaves, and scatter his fruit: let the beasts get away from under it, and the fowls from his branches: Nevertheless leave the stump of his roots in the earth, even with a band of iron and brass, in the tender grass of the field; and let it be wet with the dew of heaven, and let his portion be with the beasts in the grass of the earth: Let his heart be changed from man's, and let a beast's heart be given unto him; and let seven times pass over him" (KJV).

Daniel (keeping in mind that Nebuchadnezzar is a character representing the kingship of Israel in the allegory) then interprets the dream in verses 20-26:

*"The tree that thou sawest, which grew, and was strong, whose height reached unto the heaven, and the sight thereof to all the earth; Whose leaves were fair, and the fruit thereof much, and in it was meat for all; under which the beasts of the field dwelt, and upon whose branches the fowls of the heaven had their habitation: It is thou, O king, that art grown and become strong: for thy greatness is grown, and reacheth unto heaven, and thy dominion to the end of the earth. And whereas the king saw a watcher and an holy one coming down from heaven, and saying, Hew the tree down, and destroy it; yet leave the stump of the roots thereof in the earth, even with a band of iron and brass, in the tender grass of the field; and let it be wet with the dew of heaven, and let his portion be with the beasts of the field, till seven times pass over him; This is the interpretation, O king, and this is the decree of the most High, which is come upon my lord the king: That they shall drive thee from men, and thy dwelling shall be with the beasts of the field, and they shall make thee to eat grass as oxen, and they shall wet thee with the dew of heaven, and **seven times** shall pass over him; This is the interpretation, O king, and this is the decree of the most High, which is come upon my lord the king: That they shall drive thee from men, and thy dwelling shall be with the beasts of the field, and they shall make thee to eat grass as oxen, and they shall wet thee with the dew of heaven, and **seven times** shall pass over thee, till thou know that the most High ruleth in the kingdom of men, and giveth it to whomsoever he will. And whereas they commanded to leave the stump of the tree roots; thy kingdom shall be sure unto thee, after that thou shalt have known that the heavens do rule"* (KJV).

At the end of the fourth chapter, verses 28-36 record the following calamities that happened to the king in the allegory:

> "All this came upon the king Nebuchadnezzar. **At the end of twelve months** he walked in the palace of the kingdom of Babylon. The king spake, and said, Is not this great Babylon, that I have built for the house of the kingdom by the might of my power, and for the honour of my majesty? While the word was in the king's mouth, there fell a voice from heaven, saying, O king Nebuchadnezzar, to thee it is spoken; **The kingdom is departed** from thee. And they shall drive thee from men, and thy dwelling shall be with the beasts of the field: they shall make thee to eat grass as oxen, and **seven times shall pass over thee**, until thou know that the most High ruleth in the kingdom of men, and giveth it to whomsoever he will. The same hour was the thing fulfilled upon Nebuchadnezzar: and he was driven from men, and did eat grass as oxen, and his body was wet with the dew of heaven, till his hairs were grown like eagles' feathers, and his nails like birds' claws. And **at the end of the days** I Nebuchadnezzar lifted up mine eyes unto heaven, and **mine understanding returned** unto me, and I blessed the most High, and I praised and honoured him that liveth for ever, whose dominion is an everlasting dominion, and his kingdom is from generation to generation: And all the inhabitants of the earth are reputed as nothing: and he doeth according to his will in the army of heaven, and among the inhabitants of the earth: and none can stay his hand, or say unto him, What doest thou? At the same time my reason returned unto me; and for the glory of my kingdom, mine honour and brightness returned unto me; and my counsellors and my lords sought unto me; and I was established in my kingdom, and excellent majesty was added unto me" (KJV).

Recapping the sequence of events in verses 28-36, verse 29 specifies that the king, after he had been walking in the palace for twelve months, had the kingdom taken from him for a period of seven "times" during which the king lived among the birds of the air and the beasts of the field. Verse 34 then says that, at the end of the "days," the king came to his senses, and, at the conclusion of the "days," he was restored to his former glory in the kingdom. Focusing only on the chronological aspects of the narrative, there are three elements specifying time, namely "months," "times," and "days." Two of the three elements are associated with a specific time period. Twelve months are specified, and seven "times" are

Appendix Three: Calculating Sabbath and Jubilee Years (Daniel 4)

Table A - How to Count the 7 "times" (1,596 Passovers)

P1 - 632 CE	P2 - 631 CE	P3 - 630 CE	P4 - 629 CE	P5 - 628 CE	P6 - 627 CE	P7 - 626 CE	P8 - 625 CE	P9 - 624 CE	P10 - 623 CE
1-10 see above									
P110 - 523 CE	P120 - 513 CE	P130 - 503 CE	P140 - 493 CE	P150 - 483 CE	P160 - 473 CE	P170 - 463 CE	P180 - 453 CE	P190 - 443 CE	P200 - 433 CE
P210 - 423 CE	P220 - 413 CE	P230 - 403 CE	P240 - 393 CE	P250 - 383 CE	P260 - 373 CE	P270 - 363 CE	P280 - 353 CE	P290 - 343 CE	P300 - 333 CE
P310 - 323 CE	P320 - 313 CE	P330 - 303 CE	P340 - 293 CE	P350 - 283 CE	P360 - 273 CE	P370 - 263 CE	P380 - 253 CE	P390 - 243 CE	P400 - 233 CE
P410 - 223 CE	P420 - 213 CE	P430 - 203 CE	P440 - 193 CE	P450 - 183 CE	P460 - 173 CE	P470 - 163 CE	P480 - 153 CE	P490 - 143 CE	P500 - 133 CE
P510 - 123 CE	P520 - 113 CE	P530 - 103 CE	P540 - 93 CE	P550 - 83 CE	P560 - 73 CE	P570 - 63 CE	P580 - 53 CE	P590 - 43 CE	P600 - 33 CE
P610 - 23 CE	P620 - 13 CE	P630 - 3 CE	P640 - 8 BCE	P650 - 18 BCE	P660 - 28 BCE	P670 - 38 BCE	P680 - 48 BCE	P690 - 58 BCE	P700 - 68 BCE
P710 - 78 BCE	P720 - 88 BCE	P730 - 98 BCE	P740 - 108 BCE	P750 - 118 BCE	P760 - 128 BCE	P770 - 138 BCE	P780 - 148 BCE	P790 - 158 BCE	P800 - 168 BCE
P810 - 178 BCE	P820 - 188 BCE	P830 - 198 BCE	P840 - 208 BCE	P850 - 218 BCE	P860 - 228 BCE	P870 - 238 BCE	P880 - 248 BCE	P890 - 258 BCE	P900 - 268 BCE
P910 - 278 BCE	P920 - 288 BCE	P930 - 298 BCE	P940 - 308 BCE	P950 - 318 BCE	P960 - 328 BCE	P970 - 338 BCE	P980 - 348 BCE	P990 - 358 BCE	P1000 - 368 BCE
P1010 - 378 BCE	P1020 - 388 BCE	P1030 - 398 BCE	P1040 - 408 BCE	P1050 - 418 BCE	P1060 - 428 BCE	P1070 - 438 BCE	P1080 - 448 BCE	P1090 - 458 BCE	P1100 - 468 BCE
P1110 - 478 BCE	P1120 - 488 BCE	P1130 - 498 BCE	P1140 - 508 BCE	P1150 - 518 BCE	P1160 - 528 BCE	P1170 - 538 BCE	P1180 - 548 BCE	P1190 - 558 BCE	P1200 - 568 BCE
P1210 - 578 BCE	P1220 - 588 BCE	P1230 - 598 BCE	P1240 - 608 BCE	P1250 - 618 BCE	P1260 - 628 BCE	P1270 - 638 BCE	P1280 - 648 BCE	P1290 - 658 BCE	P1300 - 668 BCE
P1310 - 678 BCE	P1320 - 688 BCE	P1330 - 698 BCE	P1340 - 708 BCE	P1350 - 718 BCE	P1360 - 728 BCE	P1370 - 738 BCE	P1380 - 748 BCE	P1390 - 758 BCE	P1400 - 768 BCE
P1410 - 778 BCE	P1420 - 788 BCE	P1430 - 798 BCE	P1440 - 808 BCE	P1450 - 818 BCE	P1460 - 828 BCE	P1470 - 838 BCE	P1480 - 848 BCE	P1490 - 858 BCE	P1500 - 868 BCE
P1510 - 878 BCE	P1520 - 888 BCE	P1530 - 898 BCE	P1540 - 908 BCE	P1550 - 918 BCE	P1560 - 928 BCE	P1570 - 938 BCE	P1580 - 948 BCE	P1590 - 958 BCE	P1591 see below
P1591 - 959 BCE	P1592 - 960 BCE	P1593 - 961 BCE	P1594 - 962 BCE	P1595 - 963 BCE	P1596 - 964 BCE	---	---	---	---

Note that there was no year "0" (zero) when going from CE to BCE, so the count for the Passovers in the transition decade from 3 CE to 8 BCE is determined as follows: Passover number 630 in the count (P630 above) occurred in the year 3 CE, P631 in 2 CE, P632 in 1 CE, P633 in 1 BCE, P634 in 2 BCE, P635 in 3 BCE, P636 in 4 BCE, P637 in 5 BCE, P638 in 6 BCE, P639 in 7 BCE, P640 in 8 BCE.

– 137 –

specified. The duration of the period of "days" is left unspecified, but emphasis is put on the restoration that happens at the end of them.

Step 1 - *Identifying the year the kingdom divided ...*

As I considered the three time elements in the allegory, and the sequence of events specified in the allegorical narrative, I recalled the time line developed during the interpretation of Daniel, chapter 12, which describes a *"time, times, and an half"* (3½ "times") followed by a period of 1,335 "days," after which (as the fulfillment event in 1967 has shown) Israel was restored to dominion over the Temple Mount. Based on the similarity between the two sequences in Daniel, chapters 4 and 12, it seemed logical to consider that both prophecies were describing the same historical events. So, the next step was to align the "3½ times" in the twelfth chapter (see Diagram A on opposite page, top time line) with the last half of the seven "times" described in the fourth chapter of Daniel. By so doing, the *terminus ad quem* of the *"time, times, and an half"* in the twelfth chapter, which is the date June 8, 632 CE, became the *terminus ad quem* of the *"seven times"* in the fourth chapter as well. With the *terminus ad quem* thus established as 632 CE, and recalling that a "time" equals 228 Passovers (see page 38), I was then able to count backwards for seven times, which is 7 x 228 Passovers = 1,596 Passovers, to identify the Passover in the year 964 BCE as the starting point in history for the "seven times" specified in the allegory. Table A (on the previous page) shows how to count the 1,596 Passovers. The count is initiated with the Passover in 632 CE, which was the last Passover before the death of Mohammed and the start of the Muslim Caliphate that marked the end of the "3½ times" in the twelfth chapter, and it proceeds backward in time until the 1,596th Passover is revealed as the one occurring in 964 BCE. Each Passover in the table is denoted as "P#" (where "#" is its number in the count), followed by its corresponding Gregorian year. After the initial ten Passovers (P1 through P10), shown on the top line, Passovers are shown in ten-year increments, which allows you to count along on your fingers to verify the count. Once the Passover of 964 BCE had been identified as the starting point of the seven "times" in Daniel, chapter 4, it was easy to see that the starting event in the allegory, the rending of the kingdom from the allegorical Nebuchadnezzar, was actually describing an event that had happened in the history of Israel, namely, the rending of the kingdom from Solomon's son and heir, Rehoboam. Thus, sometime on or before Passover

Appendix Three: Calculating Sabbath and Jubilee Years (Daniel 4)

Diagram A - Calculating Solomon's Regnal Years
(to reveal Nisan 1002 BCE to Nisan 1001 BCE as a sabbath year)

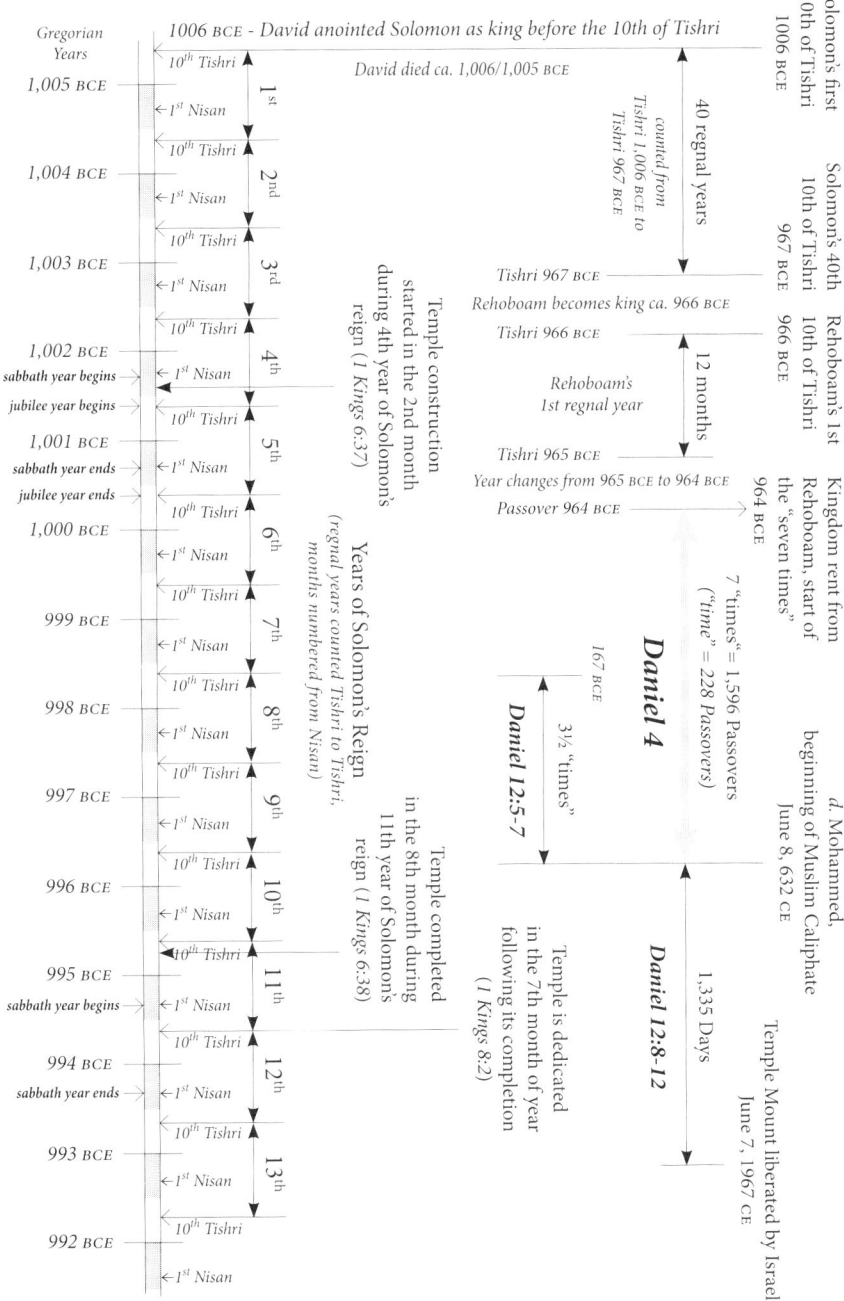

– 139 –

in the year 964 BCE, the Kingdom of Israel was rent from Rehoboam as foretold, and the separate kingdoms of Israel and Judah began soon thereafter.

Step 2 - Identifying the first year of Solomon's reign ...

Again focusing only on the chronological aspects of the allegorical narrative in Daniel, chapter 4, the first of the three time-related elements that are specified in that chapter, when projected into history, require that Rehoboam had to have been king "walking in the palace" at least twelve months (one complete Tishri to Tishri regnal year) prior to the rending of the kingdom that happened on the Passover of 964 BCE. That would mean that he had to have succeeded Solomon as king of the united kingdom of Israel sometime before the 10th of Tishri in 966 BCE, and then have ruled for one regnal year until the 10th of Tishri in 965 BCE, which would meet the requirement that, *"At the end of twelve months he walked in the palace of the kingdom,"* after which the kingdom was rent from him prior to Passover 964 BCE. And, this means that Solomon must have died in the year between the Tishri in the year 967 BCE and the Tishri in the year 966 BCE, a chronological clue that allows reasonable identification of Solomon's last Tishri as king before his death as the one that occurred in the year 967 BCE. The Bible preserves the length of Solomon's reign in 1 Kings, chapter 11, verse 42, recording that *"the time that Solomon reigned in Jerusalem over all Israel was forty years"* (KJV). Since Solomon reigned for forty years as king after David proclaimed him king of Israel in his place, and since regnal years were tabulated Tishri to Tishri during his days, this means that Solomon reigned as king for forty month-of-Tishris after his elevation to the throne by David. Counting back forty Tishris (see the table on the opposite page, which counts back forty Tishris from the last Tishri in Solomon's reign in the year 967 BCE), the first Tishri during which Solomon was ruler of Israel is identified as the one that occurred in the year 1,006 BCE. That Tishri marked the beginning of Solomon's first regnal year, and it is that year which allows the calculation that identifies the fourth year of Solomon's reign as the year 1,002 BCE.

Step 3 - Identifying the year Solomon began building the Temple ...

Of special importance for biblical chronology in general, and for the specific quest being pursued in this section, which is to identify the first sabbath year that occurred during Solomon's reign, is the identification of the year in which

Appendix Three: Calculating Sabbath and Jubilee Years (Daniel 4)

Counting the Years (Tishris) of Solomon's Reign				
40th - 967 BCE	39th - 968 BCE	38th - 969 BCE	37th - 970 BCE	36th - 971 BCE
35th - 972 BCE	34th - 973 BCE	33rd - 974 BCE	32nd - 975 BCE	31st - 976 BCE
30th - 977 BCE	29th - 978 BCE	28th - 979 BCE	27th - 980 BCE	26th - 981 BCE
25th - 982 BCE	24th - 983 BCE	23rd - 984 BCE	22nd - 985 BCE	21st - 986 BCE
20th - 987 BCE	19th - 988 BCE	18th - 989 BCE	17th - 990 BCE	16th - 991 BCE
15th - 992 BCE	14th - 993 BCE	13th - 994 BCE	12th - 995 BCE	11th - 996 BCE
10th - 997 BCE	9th - 998 BCE	8th - 999 BCE	7th - 1000 BCE	6th - 1001 BCE
5th - 1002 BCE	4th - 1003 BCE	3rd - 1004 BCE	2nd - 1005 BCE	1st - 1006 BCE

Solomon began to build the Temple, which is an event specified as occurring in his fourth regnal year. In the Book of 1 Kings, chapter 6, verses 37-38, and chapter 8, verse 2, the following details are given about building the Temple: 1) construction began in the second month in the fourth year of the reign of Solomon, 2) the Temple was completed in the eighth month in the eleventh year of the reign of Solomon, and 3) the Temple was dedicated on the tenth day of the seventh month in the year following its completion. From Diagram A on page 139, it can be seen that the fourth year of Solomon's reign began on the 10th of Tishri in the year 1,002 BCE. Although regnal years were counted from Tishri to Tishri, note that the Jewish months were still numbered in accordance with the religious calendar, starting with the first month Nisan, not with the seventh month Tishri. So, it can be determined that Temple construction was begun a few weeks after Passover (March-April) in the year 1,002 BCE, completed in the eighth month (October-November) seven years later, then dedicated on the Day of Atonement in the seventh month (September-October) of the year following its completion.

Step 4 - Identifying Solomon's first sabbath year ...

Although not stated directly in the Bible, it can be inferred that Solomon waited until 1,002 BCE, the fourth year of his reign, to start construction of the Temple for two very specific reasons. First, he could not begin building while David was still alive since God had decreed that David was to have no part in building the Temple, so David had to die before construction could begin. After a short coreign with Solomon, David died sometime between Tishri in the year 1,006 BCE and Tishri in the year 1,005 BCE. Second, Solomon needed a large workforce for gathering and preparing the huge quantities of materials needed for building the Temple, and for doing the actual construction once construction commenced, and that meant he had to wait for the first sabbath year when the land was at rest and the manpower of the nation was not devoted to its prime endeavor, agriculture.[1] Thus, the year 1,002 BCE, the year he started building the Temple, in his fourth regnal year, can be identified as the first sabbath year that occurred in Solomon's reign. Based on that one occurrence, all sabbath years can be calculated to produce a calendar of sabbath years.

Step 5 - Identifying all sabbath and jubilee years ...

The year 1,002 BCE was a jubilee year as well, providing Solomon with seven additional months of manpower for building the Temple, a circumstance that can be verified as follows: Every seventh sabbath cycle, the last year (in other words, every 49th year) sees the start of a jubilee year. However, aligning the jubilee years within the sabbath cycle involves knowing one jubilee year with certainty. Using information provided from the *B'rit Hadashah*, one jubilee year can be so identified. Jesus announced the start of a jubilee year in the first year of his ministry, which the chronological information in the Gospel of John, chapter 2, verses 13-21, identifies as the year 28 CE (see page 178). That beginning of the jubilee year in 28 BCE can be used to calculate a calendar of all jubilee years. Then, by combining the years from the sabbath calendar and the jubilee calendar, a single calendar of all sabbath and jubilee years can be derived. The result of that combination of sabbath and jubilee cycles is displayed in the tables that make up the *Calendar of Sabbath and Jubilee Years* in *Appendix Four* printed on the next three pages. In addition, several examples of crosschecks that verify the accuracy of the tables generated in this manner are included following the tables.

---

[1] Solomon used foreigners to do most of the construction on the Temple according to the Scriptures, as recorded in 2 Chronicles, chapter 2, verses 17-18, which says: *"And Solomon numbered all the strangers that were in the land of Israel, after the numbering wherewith David his father had numbered them; and they were found an hundred and fifty thousand and three thousand and six hundred. And he set threescore and ten thousand of them to be bearers of burdens, and fourscore thousand to be hewers in the mountain, and three thousand and six hundred overseers to set the people a work"* (KJV). The strangers were undoubtedly agricultural laborers and slaves who would normally be under-utilized during the sabbath year, since planting and harvesting of crops was prohibited by the Law of Moses.

APPENDIX FOUR

Calendar of Sabbath and Jubilee Years

The Children of Israel were commanded to observe sabbath and jubilee years once they had entered in the promised land (an event that happened in 1,442 BCE), as recorded in Leviticus, chapter 25, verses 1-12:

"And the Lord spake unto Moses in mount Sinai, saying, Speak unto the children of Israel, and say unto them, When ye come into the land which I give you, then shall the land keep a sabbath unto the Lord. Six years thou shalt sow thy field, and six years thou shalt prune thy vineyard, and gather in the fruit thereof; But in the seventh year shall be a sabbath of rest unto the land, a sabbath for the Lord: thou shalt neither sow thy field, nor prune thy vineyard. That which groweth of its own accord of thy harvest thou shalt not reap, neither gather the grapes of thy vine undressed: for it is a year of rest unto the land. And the sabbath of the land shall be meat for you; for thee, and for thy servant, and for thy maid, and for thy hired servant, and for thy stranger that sojourneth with thee, And for thy cattle, and for the beast that are in thy land, shall all the increase thereof be meat. And thou shalt number seven sabbaths of years unto thee, seven times seven years; and the space of the seven sabbaths of years shall be unto thee forty and nine years. Then shalt thou cause the trumpet of the jubilee to sound on the tenth day of the seventh month, in the day of atonement shall ye make the trumpet sound throughout all your land. And ye shall hallow the fiftieth year, and proclaim liberty throughout all the land unto all the inhabitants thereof: it shall be a jubilee unto you; and ye shall return every man unto his possession, and ye shall return every man unto his family. A jubilee shall that fiftieth year be unto you: ye shall not sow, neither reap that which groweth of itself in it, nor gather the grapes in it of thy vine undressed. For it is the jubilee; it shall be holy unto you: ye shall eat the increase thereof out of the field" (KJV).

Leviticus, chapter 25, verses 20-22, clarified that the people of Israel would not go hungry because of their obedience to the commandment:

"And if ye shall say, What shall we eat the seventh year? behold, we shall not sow, nor gather in our increase: Then I will command my blessing upon you in the sixth year, and it shall bring forth fruit for three years. And ye shall sow

Diagram A - Relationship of Seasons to Sabbath and Jubilee Years

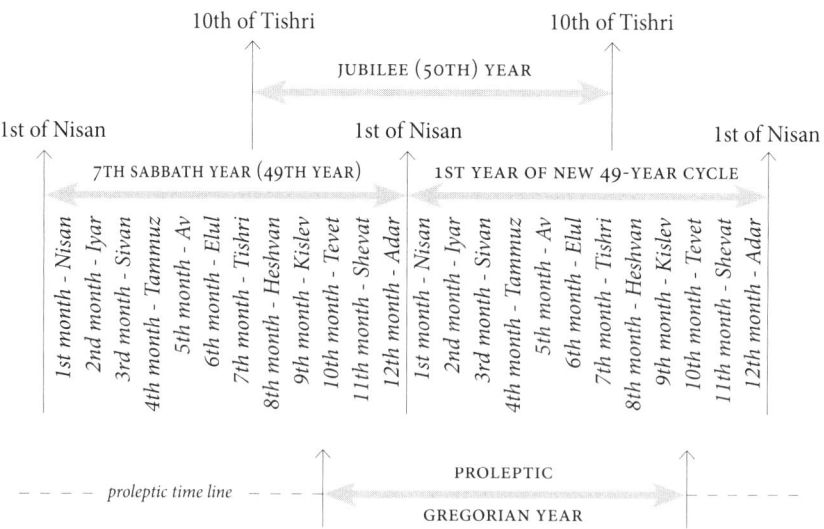

Jewish months are shown as numbers, with Nisan = 1; corresponding Gregorian months shown above.

Diagram B - Relationship of Sabbath, Jubilee, and Gregorian Years

(exact relationship to the Jewish year varies somewhat from year to year)

the eighth year, and eat yet of old fruit until the ninth year; until her fruits come in ye shall eat of the old store" (KJV).

In practical terms, the people would sow barley and wheat in November of the fifth year, then reap the bounteous threefold "sixth-year" yield of both grains during the following March through June harvest months, then sow barley again in November (the month for sowing) of the sixth year to harvest in early spring before the start of the seventh year on the 1st of Nisan (March-April). There would be no sowing at all in November of the seventh year, and thus no harvest of wheat or barley the following March through June harvest months in the eighth year. However, in November of the eighth year, both barley and wheat would once again be sown and then harvested in the spring and early summer of the ninth year. That schedule meant that there were two harvest seasons when no harvesting was done. Under that schedule, though, no additional provisions were needed for a sabbath-jubilee year since the jubilee ended on the 10th of Tishri (September-October in the eighth year), so sowing could still be done in November in the same manner as during the sabbath-only years. Sabbath years were to be observed every seventh year, beginning on the 1st of Nisan, and were to extend until the following 1st of Nisan, whereas a jubilee year began in the fall, on the 10th of Tishri in the forty-ninth year of a 49-year (seven seven-year) cycle, and it continued until the 10th of Tishri in the following year. Both sabbath and jubilee years began in one Gregorian year and ended in the following year. A Jubilee year, although called a "fiftieth year," was not a separate year, but overlapped the last five months in the forty-ninth year and the first seven months in the first year in the next 49-year cycle, as shown in Diagram B on the opposite page (bottom diagram).

Table of Sabbath and Jubilee Years from 1,700 CE to 2,037 CE							
JUBILEE	7th Sabbath	6th Sabbath	5th Sabbath	4th Sabbath	3rd Sabbath	2nd Sabbath	1st Sabbath
2037/2038	2037/2038	2030/2031	2023/2024	2016/2017	2009/2010	2002/2003	1995/1996
1988/1989	1988/1989	1981/1982	1974/1975	1967/1968	1960/1961	1953/1954	1946/1947
1939/1940	1939/1940	1932/1933	1925/1926	1918/1919	1911/1912	1904/1905	1897/1898
1890/1891	1890/1891	1883/1884	1876/1877	1869/1870	1862/1863	1855/1856	1848/1849
1841/1842	1841/1842	1834/1835	1827/1828	1820/1821	1813/1814	1806/1807	1799/1800
1792/1793	1792/1793	1785/1786	1778/1779	1771/1772	1764/1765	1757/1758	1750/1751
1743/1744	1743/1744	1736/1737	1729/1730	1722/1723	1715/1716	1708/1709	1701/1702

Table of Sabbath and Jubilee Years from 1 CE to 1,695 CE

JUBILEE	7th Sabbath	6th Sabbath	5th Sabbath	4th Sabbath	3rd Sabbath	2nd Sabbath	1st Sabbath
1694/1695	1694/1695	1687/1688	1680/1681	1673/1674	1666/1667	1659/1660	1652/1653
1645/1646	1645/1646	1638/1639	1631/1632	1624/1625	1617/1618	1610/1611	1603/1604
1596/1597	1596/1597	1589/1590	1582/1583	1575/1576	1568/1569	1561/1562	1654/1655
1547/1548	1547/1548	1540/1541	1533/1534	1526/1527	1519/1520	1512/1513	1505/1506
1498/1499	1498/1499	1491/1492	1484/1485	1477/1478	1470/1471	1463/1464	1456/1457
1449/1450	1449/1450	1442/1443	1435/1436	1428/1429	1421/1422	1414/1415	1407/1408
1400/1401	1400/1401	1393/1394	1386/1387	1379/1380	1372/1373	1365/1366	1358/1359
1351/1352	1351/1352	1344/1345	1337/1338	1330/1331	1323/1324	1316/1317	1309/1310
1302/1303	1302/1303	1295/1296	1288/1289	1281/1282	1274/1275	1267/1268	1260/1261
1253/1254	1253/1254	1246/1247	1239/1240	1232/1233	1225/1226	1218/1219	1211/1212
1204/1205	1204/1205	1197/1198	1190/1191	1183/1184	1176/1177	1169/1170	1162/1163
1155/1156	1155/1156	1148/1149	1141/1142	1134/1135	1127/1128	1120/1121	1113/1114
1106/1107	1106/1107	1099/1100	1092/1093	1085/1086	1078/1079	1071/1072	1064/1065
1057/1058	1057/1058	1050/1051	1043/1044	1036/1037	1029/1030	1022/1023	1015/1016
1008/1009	1008/1009	1001/1002	994/995	987/988	980/981	973/974	866/867
959/956	959/956	952/953	945/946	938/939	931/932	924/925	917/918
910/911	910/911	903/904	896/897	889/890	882/883	875/876	868/869
861/862	861/862	854/855	847/848	840/841	833/834	826/827	819/820
812/813	812/813	805/806	798/799	791/792	784/785	777/778	770/771
763/764	763/764	756/757	749/750	742/743	735/736	728/729	721/722
714/715	714/715	707/708	700/701	693/694	686/687	679/680	672/673
665/666	665/666	658/659	651/652	644/645	637/638	630/631	623/624
616/617	616/617	609/610	602/603	595/596	588/589	581/582	574/575
567/568	567/568	560/561	553/554	546/547	539/540	532/533	525/526
518/519	518/519	511/512	504/505	497/498	490/491	483/484	476/477
469/470	469/470	462/463	455/456	448/449	441/442	434/435	427/428
420/421	420/421	413/414	406/407	399/400	392/393	385/386	378/379
371/372	371/372	364/365	357/358	350/351	343/344	336/337	329/330
322/323	322/323	315/316	308/309	301/302	294/295	287/288	280/281
273/274	273/274	266/267	259/260	252/253	245/246	238/239	231/232
224/225	224/225	217/218	210/211	203/204	196/197	189/190	182/183
175/176	175/176	168/169	161/162	154/155	147/148	140/141	133/134
126/127	126/127	119/120	112/113	105/106	98/99	91/92	84/85
77/78	77/78	70/71	63/64	56/57	49/50	42/43	35/36
28/29	28/29	21/22	14/15	7/8	1 BCE/CE 1	- - -	- - -

Appendix Four: Calendar of Sabbath and Jubilee Years

Table of Sabbath and Jubilee Years from 1 BCE to 1,442 BCE

JUBILEE	7th Sabbath	6th Sabbath	5th Sabbath	4th Sabbath	3rd Sabbath	2nd Sabbath	1st Sabbath
- - -	- - -	- - -	- - -	- - -	CE 1/1 BCE	7/8	14/15
21/22	21/22	28/29	35/36	42/43	49/50	56/57	63/64
70/71	70/71	77/78	84/85	91/92	98/99	105/106	112/113
119/120	119/120	126/127	133/134	140/141	147/148	154/155	161/162
168/169	168/169	175/176	182/183	189/190	196/197	203/204	210/211
217/218	217/218	224/225	231/232	238/239	245/246	252/253	259/260
266/267	266/267	273/274	280/281	287/288	294/295	301/302	308/309
315/316	315/316	322/323	329/330	336/337	343/344	350/351	357/358
364/365	364/365	371/372	378/379	385/386	392/393	399/400	406/407
413/414	413/414	420/421	427/428	434/435	441/442	448/449	455/456
462/463	462/463	469/470	476/477	483/484	490/491	497/498	504/505
511/512	511/512	518/519	525/526	532/533	539/540	546/547	553/554
560/561	560/561	567/568	574/575	581/582	588/589	595/596	602/603
609/610	609/610	616/617	623/624	630/631	637/638	644/645	651/652
658/659	658/659	665/666	672/673	679/680	686/687	693/694	700/701
707/708	707/708	714/715	721/722	728/729	735/736	742/743	749/750
756/757	756/757	763/764	770/771	777/778	784/785	791/792	798/799
805/806	805/806	812/813	819/820	826/827	833/834	840/841	847/848
854/855	854/855	861/862	868/869	875/876	882/883	889/890	896/897
903/904	903/904	910/911	917/918	924/925	931/932	938/939	945/946
952/953	952/953	959/960	966/967	973/974	980/981	987/988	994/995
1001/1002	1001/1002	1008/1009	1015/1016	1022/1023	1029/1030	1036/1037	1043/1044
1050/1051	1050/1051	1057/1058	1064/1065	1071/1072	1078/1079	1085/1086	1092/1093
1099/1100	1099/1100	1106/1107	1113/1114	1120/1121	1127/1128	1134/1135	1141/1142
1148/1149	1148/1149	1155/1156	1162/1163	1169/1170	1176/1177	1183/1184	1190/1181
1197/1198	1197/1198	1204/1205	1211/1212	1218/1219	1225/1226	1232/1233	1239/1240
1246/1247	1246/1247	1253/1254	1260/1261	1267/1268	1274/1275	1281/1282	1288/1289
1295/1296	1295/1296	1302/1303	1309/1310	1316/1317	1323/1324	1330/1331	1337/1338
1344/1345	1344/1345	1351/1352	1358/1359	1365/1366	1372/1373	1379/1380	1386/1387
1393/1394	1393/1394	1400/1401	1407/1408	1414/1415	1421/1422	1428/1429	1435/1436

In the table for years BCE above, note that the year that started the sabbath cycle in the land of Canaan, 1441/1442 BCE, and the next five years in that first sabbath cycle after the land was settled (1440/1441 BCE, 1439/1440 BCE, 1438/1439 BCE, 1437/1438 BCE, 1436/1437 BCE) are not shown. Also, note that there was no year "0" (zero) when going from years BCE on this chart to years CE on the chart on the opposite page, since the year 1 BCE is followed by the year 1 CE as time moves forward in history.

Verifying the Sabbath and Jubilee Tables

The year that the Israelites entered the land of Canaan marked the beginning of their accounting to keep track of sabbath years and jubilee years, an exercise that was commanded in Leviticus as a show of obedience to God by the nation. The method used to identify the sabbath and jubilee years that occurred during Solomon's reign was explained earlier in this appendix. The sabbath and jubilee years revealed by employing that method were used to develop the tables in this book. The validity of the tables can be verified by comparing the years listed in them with the years in which the events of the Exodus and entry into the land of Canaan occurred. The two should agree if the tables are true.

Crosscheck #1 - The year of the first sabbath in the land ...

Seven years after crossing the Jordan River, the first sabbath year was observed, as recorded in the Book of Joshua, and that year can be identified from the year of the Exodus since the entry took place forty years after that event. The year of the Exodus can be identified from the chronological information in 1 Kings, chapter 6, verse 1, which says that the Exodus happened 480 years before Solomon began building the Temple in his fourth year. The fourth year of Solomon has already been identified as the year 1,002 BCE (see page 141), so the year of the Exodus was 1,482 BCE, and the Jordan River crossing into Canaan took place in 1,442 BCE. Counting back from that entry year in one-year increments reveals the proleptic Gregorian date for the first sabbath year observed by the Israelites in the land, as follows:

       1,442 BCE ... Israelites entered the land of Canaan in 1st year.
       1,441 BCE ... 2nd year in the seven-year sabbath cycle.
       1,440 BCE ... 3rd year in the seven-year sabbath cycle.
       1,439 BCE ... 4th year in the seven-year sabbath cycle.
       1,438 BCE ... 5th year in the seven-year sabbath cycle.
       1,437 BCE ... 6th year in the seven-year sabbath cycle.
       1,436 BCE ... **First sabbath year observed in the land** in 7th year.

The result of that calculation agrees with the first sabbath year shown in the sabbath and jubilee table for years BCE on the previous page (see bottom row, far right column), and, since it uses a different data set and method of calculation than those used to generate the tables, it serves as a crosscheck to verify the validity of the sabbath and jubilee tables.

Crosscheck #2 - The chronology of Caleb's sabbath request ...

A second crosscheck is provided by the chronology associated with Caleb as recorded in the Book of Joshua. In the year that the land was at rest and had been apportioned by lot to each tribe, Caleb asked for his share of land that had been promised specifically to him because of his faithfulness at Kadesh-Barnea. This incident is recorded in Joshua, chapter 14, verses 7-10: *"Forty years old was I when Moses the servant of the Lord sent me from Kadesh-barnea to espy out the land; and I brought him word again as it was in mine heart. Nevertheless my brethren that went up with me made the heart of the people melt: but I wholly followed the Lord my God. And Moses sware on that day, saying, Surely the land whereon thy feet have trodden shall be thine inheritance, and thy children's for ever, because thou hast wholly followed the Lord my God. And now, behold, the Lord hath kept me alive, as he said, these forty and five years, even since the Lord spake this word unto Moses, while the children of Israel wandered in the wilderness: and now, lo, I am this day fourscore and five years old"* (KJV). As stated in the quoted passage, Caleb was forty years old when he was sent by Moses from Kadesh-Barnea into the land of Canaan as a spy, and he was eighty-five years old when the land was assigned and at rest. That means there were forty-five years from the time when the land had been assigned and was at rest from war back to the time the spies were sent northward into Canaan. Since the spies were sent from Kadesh-Barnea early in the second year after the Exodus in 1,482 BCE, that would mean they were sent into Canaan in the year 1,481 BCE. Subtracting forty-five years from that year yields the year 1,436 BCE as the year that the land was at rest and Caleb made his request for his promised allotment of land. This result coincides with the year for the first sabbath and is a second crosscheck on the accuracy of the sabbath-jubilee tables presented in this book.

Crosscheck #3 - The destruction of the Temple in 70 CE ...

An ancient Jewish chronological source, the *Seder Olam*, which tradition says was written about the year 160 CE by Rabbi Yose ben Halafta (a student of

Rabbi Akiba and someone who was regarded as one of the foremost scholars of *halakha* and *aggadah* of his day), mentions in chapter 30 that the Temple and the city of Jerusalem were destroyed in a sabbath year.[1] Since we know from secular history that the destruction took place in August of the year 70 CE, that would mean that the Jewish year from Nisan 70 CE to Nisan 71 CE was a sabbath year, and that is in agreement with the sabbath and jubilee tables (see the table for years CE on page 146, second row from bottom).

Crosscheck #4 - *The renovations of the Temple by Joash and Josiah ...*

The *Seder Olam* has a two-step crosscheck based on the two renovations of the Temple mentioned in the Bible, the first undertaken by Joash of Judah (see 2 Chronicles, chapter 24) and the second done by Josiah of Judah (see 2 Kings, chapter 22), that identifies the year in which Solomon finished building the Temple. It says that Joash began his renovations in his twenty-third regnal year, 218 years before Josiah began his renovations, and 155 years after Solomon completed building the Temple.[2] Josiah began his renovations in his eighteenth regnal year, which was the year 622 BCE. Adding 218 years to that year gives the year 840 BCE as Joash's twenty-third regnal year. Adding 155 years to that year gives 995 BCE as the year Solomon finished building the Temple. Since it took Solomon seven years to build the Temple, that means the construction was begun in the year 1,002 BCE, which agrees with the calculations based on Daniel, chapter 4, shown earlier in *Appendix Three* (see page 140), that were used to formulate the sabbath and jubilee tables.

Crosscheck #5 - *The prophecy of the "seventy weeks" ...*

The prophecy of the "seventy weeks" in Daniel, chapter 9 (see Table 6.1 on page 89), provides indirect confirmation of the accuracy of the synchronization of the jubilee years with respect to sabbath years as displayed in the sabbath-jubilee tables insomuch as its ending year synchronizes with a year that is denoted as a sabbath-jubilee year in the tables.

---

[1] Guggenheimer, Heinrich W., *Seder Olam: The Rabbinic View of Biblical Chronology* (Lanham, Maryland: Rowman & Littlefield Publishers, Inc., 1998, 2005), p. 264.
[2] Guggenheimer, *Seder Olam*, p. 161-162.

APPENDIX FIVE

Chronology in the Book of Ezekiel

See Time Line ❽ on plate 1

An important chrono-specific prophecy is set forth in Ezekiel, chapter 4, verses 5-6: *"Also for your part lie on your left side and place the iniquity of the house of Israel on it. For the number of days you lie on your side you will bear their iniquity. I have determined that the number of the years of their iniquity are to be the number of days for you, 390 days. So bear the iniquity of the house of Israel. When you have completed these days, then lie down a second time, but on your right side, and bear the iniquity of the house of Judah 40 days. I have assigned one day for each year"* (KJV). It specifies a period of 430 days during which the prophet Ezekiel bears the iniquity of Israel and Judah by laying on his sides, a task that represented a "siege of Jerusalem" that would last for a period of 430 years. Since Ezekiel often dated events from the time when King Jehoiachin was taken into exile by Nebuchadnezzar,[1] it seemed logical that the staring point for counting the 430 years would be the same. Thus, it was necessary to identify the proleptic Gregorian year when the exile of Jehoiachin began.

Ezekiel gives chronological clues that help determine the year of Jehoiachin's exile. In chapter 40, verse 1, he writes: *"In the five and twentieth year of our captivity, in the beginning of the year ... in the fourteenth year after that the city was smitten"* (KJV). This equates the twenty-fifth year of the exile of Jehoiachin with the fourteenth year after the destruction of Jerusalem, which was destroyed on August 14, 586 BCE.[2] Since Jewish years at the time of Ezekiel were reckoned from the first month of the year in accordance with the command given in Exodus 12, verse 2, *"This month* [Nisan, the month of the Passover] *shall be unto you the beginning of months: it shall be the first month of the year to you"* (KJV), the observance of the Passover was a way of keeping track of the passage of years, as demonstrated in Daniel, chapter 8, verses 13-14. This method of using Passovers to keep track of years seems to apply to the chronological references in Ezekiel as well. Thus, Ezekiel's reference to the "fourteenth year" after the destruction of

---

[1] See examples of such dating in Ezek. 1:2; 8:1; 20:1; 24:1; 26:1; 29:1, 17; 30:20; 31:1; 32:1, 17; 33:21; 40:1.
[2] Jack Finegan, *Handbook of Biblical Chronology* (Peabody, Massachusetts: Hendrickson Publishers, Inc., 1998), p. 259.

Jerusalem in chapter 40, verse 1, would mean that fourteen Passovers had occurred after that event, and his reference to the "twenty-fifth year" after the beginning of the exile of Jehoiachin would mean that twenty-five Passovers had occurred after that event.

Table A (on the opposite page, top table) demonstrates how the Passovers that indicate the passage of years in Ezekiel, chapter 40, verse 1, should be counted. Each Passover in the table is denoted as "P#" (where "#" is its number in the count), followed by its corresponding Gregorian year. The table should be read backwards to arrive at the year of the first Passover celebrated in exile in Babylon, starting with the cell to the far right on the bottom row labeled "25th year of exile," representing the point in time when Ezekiel said that he wrote his chapter 40, verse 1. The cell labeled "Temple destroyed," representing the destruction of the Temple on August 14, 586 BCE, is reached by counting back fourteen Passovers (P1-P14) to reach the first Passover after the destruction (the one celebrated in 585 BCE). By resuming the count with the last Passover before the destruction of the Temple, the one in 586 BCE, and counting back eleven more Passovers (P15-P25), the twenty-fifth Passover is revealed as occurring in 596 BCE. As this calculation demonstrates, the exile of Jehoiachin had to begin before the Passover in 596 BCE. It also had to happen after the surrender of Jerusalem on March 16, 597 BCE, which the Babylonian Chronicles (tablet number 21946)[1] records as occurring on the second day of the month Addaru, just before the new year began. Adding another clue, II Chronicles, chapter 36, verse 10, says that Jehoiachin was ordered brought to Babylon *"when the year was expired"* (KJV), which pinpoints the time as sometime after the Jewish new year on the 1st of Nisan, which occurred on the 8th of March that year. Since II Kings, chapter 24, verses 13-14, say that ten-thousand people were taken captive to Babylon, along with the Temple treasures and large amounts of booty, at least a few weeks would have been required after the capture to assemble everything and leave Jerusalem. All of these time constraints indicate that Jehoiachin left Jerusalem several weeks after the Passover in 597 BCE, which occurred on March 22 in the year 597 BCE, less than a week after the surrender of the city.

---

[1] The Babylonian Chronicles are cuneiform tablets recording major events in the history of Babylon, written by Babylonian astronomers ("Chaldaeans") over a long period of time stretching from the reign of Nabonassar to the Parthian Period. Almost all of the tablets currently reside in the Middle East collection of the British Museum.

Appendix Five: Chronology in the Book of Ezekiel (Ezekiel 4)

Table A - How to count the 25 Passovers in Ezekiel 40:1

P26 - 597 BCE	Exile begins	P25 - 596 BCE	P24 - 595 BCE	P23 - 594 BCE	P22 - 593 BCE	P21 - 592 BCE	P20 - 591 BCE	P19 - 590 BCE	P18 - 589 BCE
P17 - 588 BCE	P16 - 587 BCE	P15 - 586 BCE	Temple destroyed	P14 - 585 BCE	P13 - 584 BCE	P12 - 583 BCE	P11 - 582 BCE	P10 - 581 BCE	P9 - 580 BCE
P8 - 579 BCE	P7 - 578 BCE	P6 - 577 BCE	P5 - 576 BCE	P4 - 575 BCE	P3 - 574 BCE	P2 - 573 BCE	P1 - 572 BCE	25th year of exile	---

Table B - How to count the 430 Passovers in Ezekiel 4:5-6

P1 - 596 BCE	P2 - 595 BCE	P3 - 594 BCE	P4 - 593 BCE	P5 - 592 BCE	P6 - 591 BCE	P7 - 590 BCE	P8 - 589 BCE	P9 - 588 BCE	P10 - 587 BCE
1-10 see above	P20 - 577 BCE	P30 - 567 BCE	P40 - 557 BCE	P50 - 547 BCE	P60 - 537 BCE	P70 - 527 BCE	P80 - 517 BCE	P90 - 507 BCE	P100 - 497 BCE
P110 - 487 BCE	P120 - 477 BCE	P130 - 467 BCE	P140 - 457 BCE	P150 - 447 BCE	P160 - 437 BCE	P170 - 427 BCE	P180 - 417 BCE	P190 - 407 BCE	P200 - 397 BCE
P210 - 387 BCE	P220 - 377 BCE	P230 - 367 BCE	P240 - 357 BCE	P250 - 347 BCE	P260 - 337 BCE	P270 - 327 BCE	P280 - 317 BCE	P290 - 307 BCE	P300 - 297 BCE
P310 - 287 BCE	P320 - 277 BCE	P330 - 267 BCE	P340 - 257 BCE	P350 - 247 BCE	P360 - 237 BCE	P370 - 227 BCE	P380 - 217 BCE	P390 - 207 BCE	P400 - 197 BCE
P410 - 187 BCE	P420 - 177 BCE	P430 - 167 BCE	---	---	---				

Table C - How to count the 30 Passovers in Ezekiel 40:1-2

P30 - 592 BCE	P29 - 593 BCE	P28 - 594 BCE	P27 - 595 BCE	P26 - 596 BCE	P25 - 597 BCE	P24 - 598 BCE	P23 - 599 BCE	P22 - 600 BCE	P21 - 601 BCE
P20 - 602 BCE	P19 - 603 BCE	P18 - 604 BCE	P17 - 605 BCE	P16 - 606 BCE	P15 - 607 BCE	P14 - 608 BCE	P13 - 609 BCE	P12 - 610 BCE	P11 - 611 BCE
P10 - 612 BCE	P9 - 613 BCE	P8 - 614 BCE	P7 - 615 BCE	P6 - 616 BCE	P5 - 617 BCE	P4 - 618 BCE	P3 - 619 BCE	P2 - 620 BCE	P1 - 621 BCE

Now that the year of the exile of King Jehoiachin has been identified, the 430 Passovers can be counted to reveal the time span specified in Ezekiel, chapter 4, verses 5-6. Table B (on the previous page, middle table) demonstrates how to count the Passovers. Note that the count begins with the Passover in 596 BCE, the first Passover after the departure of Jehoiachin from Jerusalem and thus the first Passover celebrated in exile. Each Passover in the table is denoted as "P#" (where "#" is its number in the count), followed by its corresponding Gregorian year. After the initial ten Passovers (P1 through P10), which are shown on the top line, Passovers are shown in ten-year increments, which allows you to count along on your fingers to verify the count. The count of 430 Passovers ends with the Passover that was celebrated in the year 167 BCE, the Passover after which Antiochus IV Epiphanes desecrated the Temple, sparking the Maccabean revolt later that same year. The revolt resulted in a self-governing Jewish nation, the first time the Jewish people had been ruled by a Jewish ruler in Jerusalem since the capture of the city and deportation of the last king of Judah, Jehoiachin, by Nebuchadnezzar 430 years before in the year 597 BCE. Thus, the 430-year time span between the exile of Jehoiachin and the beginning of the Maccabean revolt that led to Jerusalem's liberation and the subsequent reconsecration of the Temple was the fulfillment of the days of iniquity of Israel and Judah that was prophesied by the symbolic actions of Ezekiel described in Ezekiel, chapter 4.

As an added bonus, the information contained in Table A on the previous page can also be used to help interpret the chronologically ambiguous phrase *"the thirtieth year"* (KJV) that is referenced in Ezekiel, chapter 1, verses 1-2. The meaning of that phrase has long been a subject of speculation among Bible scholars. Note that in verse 2, Ezekiel equates the thirtieth year with the fifth year of Jehoiachin's captivity. That means that the fifth year would have been the Nisan-to-Nisan year that began just before the fifth Passover of Jehoiachin's captivity, which was the Passover that occurred in the year 592 BCE (denoted as "P21" in the table). As shown on Table C (on the previous page, bottom table), the thirtieth Passover back from the Passover in the year 592 BCE (using the Passover in that year as the first Passover in the count) would have been the Passover celebrated in 621 BCE. This indicates that Ezekiel considered that Passover, the one celebrated in 621 BCE, as identifying year number one of his thirty-year count. That reveals that the zero point for his count was the Passover observed in the previous year, 622 BCE, which was the year of the Great Passover celebrated by King Josiah of Judah (see II Kings 22:8, 23:1-23).

APPENDIX SIX

BIBLICAL CHRONOLOGY

SYNCHRONIZED WITH DANIEL

The chronology embedded in the Book of Daniel provides a framework for the history of the Jewish people from the time of the reign of Solomon down to events occurring in modern times. Using chronological information from other books of the Bible together with the anchor date provided by the chronology in Daniel, chapter 4, the biblical time line can be synchronized with the time line of secular history all the way back to the birth of Abram in Ur.[1]

The Anchor Date

The anchor date revealed by the chronology of Daniel, chapter 4, is the year 964 BCE, which is the year specified as the year the Kingdom of Israel was rent from Rehoboam (see *Appendix Three* on pages 138-139, note Diagram A). From that year, the 40 years of Solomon's reign can be identified, and 1,002 BCE can be identified as the fourth year of his reign. The fourth year in the reign of Solomon is an important year because that is when he began building the Temple. Thus, the chronological information in 1 Kings, chapter 6, verse 1, which says, *"And it*

---

[1] By limiting the chronology in this section back only to the birth of Abram in Ur and no further, I am deliberately choosing to avoid participation in the Old Earth *versus* Young Earth debate about the year of creation, mainly because I do not see any scientific or, more important, any spiritual benefit in fostering what I believe to be a needless controversy akin to comparing apples to oranges. My own position is that I accept on faith the biblical account of creation as being both inspired and accurate, and I also accept as credible the physical evidence that supports the theory of scientific creation, which currently posits a universe that came into existence with a Big Bang about 13.73±0.12 billion years ago. However, do not fault me for not attempting to explain how to reconcile the two seemingly disparate creation accounts and chronologies. Over the years, I have heard more than a few renowned scientists interpreting the Bible inaccurately in an attempt to discredit assumed religious opponents, and I have heard just as many respected theologians and preachers espousing pseudo-science to do the same to assumed scientific adversaries, and I wish to do neither. All that I can certify from my own experience is that the Bible is always dependable and true and, at the same time, that the observations and conclusions of modern science are basically trustworthy. Where both are correctly interpreted and understood, I have no doubt that any truth revealed by one will agree with the truth revealed by the other since, ultimately, truth is an inherent attribute of God, who is, by definition, One.

came to pass in the four hundred and eightieth year after the children of Israel were come out of the land of Egypt, in the fourth year of Solomon's reign over Israel, in the month Zif, which [is] the second month, that he began to build the house of the Lord"* (KJV), can be used to perform a simple calculation (1,002 BCE plus 480 years) that reveals the year of the Exodus from Egypt as 1,482 BCE.

Part 1 - Abraham to the Exodus (2,202-1,482 BCE)

Once the year of the Exodus is known, the information provided in Exodus, chapter 12, verses 40-41, *"Now the sojourning of the children of Israel, who dwelt in Egypt, [was] four hundred and thirty years. And it came to pass at the end of the four hundred and thirty years, even the selfsame day it came to pass, that all the hosts of the Lord went out from the land of Egypt"* (KJV), can be used to calculate the year that Jacob (Israel) and his descendants went down to Egypt. As shown on Time Line A on the opposite page, subtracting 430 years in time from the Exodus year 1,482 BCE yields the year 1,912 BCE as the date for the beginning of the sojourn of the Children of Israel in Egypt.

From the year that the sojourn began, the year of the birth of Jacob can be calculated from the information given in Genesis, chapter 47, verses 8-9, *"And Pharaoh said unto Jacob, How old [art] thou? And Jacob said unto Pharaoh, The days of the years of my pilgrimage [are] an hundred and thirty years ..."* (KJV). Subtracting 130 years in time from 1,913 BCE gives the year 2,042 BCE as the year for the birth of Jacob.

From the year of the birth of Jacob, the year of the birth of Isaac can be calculated from the information given in Genesis, chapter 25, verse 26, *"And after that came his brother out, and his hand took hold on Esau's heel; and his name was called Jacob: and Isaac was threescore years old when she bare them"* (KJV). Subtracting 60 years in time from 2,042 BCE gives the year 2,102 BCE as the year for the birth of Isaac.

From the year of the birth of Isaac, the year for the birth of Abram (later renamed Abraham) can be calculated from the information given in Genesis, chapter 21, verse 5, *"And Abraham was an hundred years old, when his son Isaac was born unto him"* (KJV). Subtracting 100 years from 2,102 BCE gives the year 2,202 BCE for the birth of Abram.

Other time periods shown on the diagram can be calculated as follows: In Genesis, chapter 15, verse 13, Abraham is told by God, *"Know of a surety that thy*

Appendix Six: Biblical Chronology Synchronized with Daniel

BCE		
	Time Line A - Abraham to Solomon	
	▲ *denotes a pharaoh; using High Chronology* after 1,900 BCE*	
2202	— b. Abram in Ur, *Genesis 11*. [**Abraham = 1st generation**]	
2127	— Abram (75 years old) leaves Haran, enters Canaan, *Genesis 12*.	
2102	— b. Isaac (Abraham 100 years old), *Genesis 21*. [**Isaac = 2nd generation**]	
2042	— b. Jacob (Isaac 60 years old), *Genesis 25*. [**Jacob = 3rd generation**]	*Time line*
1951	— b. Joseph (Jacob 91 years old), *Genesis 30*.	
1934	— Joseph (17 years old) to Egypt, *Genesis 37*.	
1929	— ▲ *Amenemhat II d. 1895 BCE.*	
1921	— Joseph (30 years old) stands before Pharaoh, *Genesis 41*.	
1912	— Israel (*aka* Jacob, 130 years old) to Egypt, *Genesis 47*.	
---	... Joseph about 39 years old (30+7+2), *Genesis 41-42*; sojourn of	
---	Children of Israel in Egypt begins [**Children of Israel = 4th generation**]	
1897	— ▲ *Senusret II d. 1878 BCE.*	
1895	— d. Israel (147 years old); "blessing" given, *Genesis 47, 49*.	
1882	— 400 years of affliction begins, *Genesis 15, Acts 7*.	
1878	— ▲ *Senusret III d. 1841 BCE.*	
---	... coregency with Amenemhat III ca.1860 BCE.	
1842	— ▲ *Amenemhat III d. 1797 BCE.*	
1841	— d. Joseph (110 years old), *Genesis 50*.	
1570	— ▲ *Ahmose I d. 1546 BCE.*	
1562	— b. Moses, *Exodus 2*.	
1551	— ▲ *Amenhotep I d. 1524 BCE.*	
1524	— ▲ *Thutmose I d. 1518 BCE.*	
1522	— Moses flees from Egypt to Midian, *Exodus 2*.	
1518	— ▲ *Thutmose II d. 1504 BCE.*	
1504	— ▲ *Thutmose III d. 1450 BCE (ruled after 1483 BCE).*	
1498	— ▲ *Hatshepsut d. 1483 (ruled until 1483 BCE).*	
1482	— **The Exodus from Egypt**, *Exodus 12*.	
1442	— Israelites cross Jordan River, nations tremble; *Joshua 3, 5*.	
1436	— Israelites inherit the promised land, *Joshua 12*.	
---	... using seven years as the time span it took the Israelites	
---	to enter and assign the land, a figure calculated from the ages	
---	of Caleb, 40 years old at Kadesh-Barnea in Joshua 14:7 and	
---	85 years old in Joshua 14:10 (40 + 38 + 7 = 85 years old).	
1002	— Solomon (4th year), begins First Temple, *1 Kings 6*.	

Side brackets: *Genesis 47:9* 130 years; *Genesis 15:13, Acts 7:6* 400 years; *Acts 13:20 - "about 450 years"* 453 years; *Exodus 12:40* 430 years; *1 Kings 6:1, 37* 480 years.

* from *Chronicle of the Pharaohs* by Peter A. Clayton (New York: Thames &Hudson; 2006)

seed shall be a stranger in a land [that is] not theirs, and shall serve them; and they shall afflict them four hundred years" (KJV). Subtracting 400 years from the year of the Exodus in 1,482 BCE gives the year 1,882 BCE as the year for the beginning of the affliction. This chronology from the *Tanakh* is verified by a cross-reference in the *B'rit Hadashah*, in the Book of Acts, chapter 13, verses 16-20, which reveal the chronology understood by the Apostle Paul,[1] who said: *"Men of Israel and you who fear God, listen. The God of this people Israel chose our fathers and made the people great during their stay in the land of Egypt, and a with uplifted arm he led them out of it. And for about forty years he put up with them in the wilderness. And after destroying seven nations in the land of Canaan, he gave them their land as an inheritance. All this took about 450 years. And after that he gave them judges until Samuel the prophet"* (ESV).[2] From the time the fathers were chosen by Israel (Jacob) when giving his death-bed blessing in 1,895 BCE until the Israelites crossed the Jordan River in 1,442 BCE, when the nations were defeated spiritually (see Joshua, chapter 5, verse 1), yields a period of 453 years, which is, as Paul says, **about** (but not exactly) 450 years in duration.

The chronological reference in Genesis, chapter 15, verse 16, which records what Abraham was told by God: *"But in the fourth generation they* [Abraham's seed] *shall come hither* [to Canaan] *again"* (KJV), gives insight as to the meaning of the word "generation" as applied to Israel as a people. The Bible lists at least twelve genetic generations of Israelites during the 430-year stay in Egypt prior to the Exodus, so it seems that the term "fourth generation" was used spiritually, with Abraham being the first generation, Isaac the second generation, Jacob the third generation, and all subsequent descendants of Jacob (*i.e.*, the Children of Israel) referred to collectively as the fourth generation thereafter.

Part 2 - The Exodus to the Divided Kingdom (1,482-961 BCE)

From the year of the Exodus in 1,482 BCE, which is derived from the fourth year of Solomon's reign (the year Temple construction was begun) plus 480 years,

---

[1] Paul had studied the Hebrew Scriptures at the feet of the esteemed Rabbi Gamaliel, so it can be assumed that he is recounting the chronological understanding that was being espoused by the most authoritative Jewish scribes and Pharisees of the first century CE.

[2] The translation for this verse from the ESV Bible quoted here is preferred, since the King James translation incorrectly indicates that the period of the judges was about 450 years in duration, a length of time that cannot be supported chronologically.

Appendix Six: Biblical Chronology Synchronized with Daniel

BCE		
	Time Line B - Exodus to Divided Kingdom	
		Time line
1482	— **The Exodus from Egypt**, *Exodus 12*.	
1442	— Israelites cross Jordan River, *Joshua 3*.	
1436	— Israelites inherit the promised land, *Joshua 21*.	
---	... first sabbath year *(observance not mentioned in Bible)*,	*Judges 11:26* — *300 years*
---	beginning of period of the judges *(Joshua to Samuel)*.	
1394	— First jubilee year *(observance not mentioned in Bible)*.	
1142	— Jephthah taunts king of Ammon, *Judges 11*.	
	First kingdom period ♛ *King Saul*	
1086	— Saul anointed king of Israel, *1 Samuel 10, 13*.	
1076	— b. David. *(birth not mentioned in Bible)*	*Acts 13:21* — *40 years* — *1 Kings 6:1,37* — *480 years*
ca. 1064	— David (12 years old) anointed by Samuel, *1 Samuel 16*.	
ca. 1061	— David (15 years old) slays Goliath; *1 Samuel 17*.	
1046	— d. Saul slain by the Philistines; *1 Samuel 31*.	
	Second kingdom period ♛ *King David*	
1046	— David (30 years old) anointed king of Judah, *2 Samuel 2*.	
---	... reigns as king in Hebron for 7½ years.	
1039	— David anointed as king of Israel *2 Samuel 5*.	*1 Kings 2:11* — *40 years*
ca. 1038	— David captures Jerusalem, *2 Samuel 5*.	
1006	— Solomon begins short coreign with David, *1 Kings 1*.	
1006	— d. David, *1 Kings 2*.	
	Third kingdom period ♛ *King Solomon*	
1006	— *(from above)* Solomon made king by David, *1 Kings 1*.	
1006	— Solomon reigns as sole king of Israel, *1 Kings 2*.	
1002	— Solomon begins First Temple (4th regnal year), *1 Kings 6*.	*1 Kings 11:42* — *40 years*
---	... Temple construction begun during jubilee year.	
995	— Solomon dedicates First Temple; *1 Kings 8*.	
---	... Temple dedicated during sabbath year.	
966	— d. Solomon, *1 Kings 11*.	
	Fourth kingdom period ♛ *Divided Kingdom*	
966	— Rehoboam succeeds Solomon as king of United Kingdom, *1 Kings 11*.	
964	— Jeroboam and the northern tribes reject Rehoboam as king,*1 Kings 12*.	
961	— 5th year of Rehoboam; Shishak takes Temple treasures to Egypt, *1 Kings 14*.	
	— ... Jeroboam king in the northern kingdom, sets up rival priest/temple system.	
961	— Rehoboam becomes king of southern kingdom of Judah, *1 Kings 12*.	

the duration of the period of the judges and the period of the united kingdom of Israel can be derived, as shown on Time Line B on the previous page. Using the diagram, several insights about the chronology of the two periods are worth commenting on here:

1. The chronological information given in Judges, chapter 11, verse 26, in which Jephthah the Gileadite, chosen to defend Israel against the Ammonites when the latter demanded return of lands taken from them when the Children of Israel crossed the Jordan River after the Exodus, is recorded as taunting the king of Ammon by asking, *"... Israel [has] dwelt in Heshbon and her towns, and in Aroer and her towns, and in all the cities that be along by the coasts of Arnon, three hundred years? why therefore did ye not recover them within that time?"* (KJV). Many chronologists, especially those who believe that the Exodus happened in the thirteenth century BCE (instead of the fifteenth-century BCE date used in this book) have raised doubts about the accuracy of the Jephthah statement, saying that there was not enough time between **their** Exodus (*ca.* 1,240 BCE) and **their** reign of Saul (*ca.* 1,045) so as to allow for a period of judges lasting more than three-hundred years, as Jephthah's boast requires. However, when all of the chronological information is correctly interpreted (*e.g.,* placing the Exodus in the fifteenth century, in the year 1,482 BCE) and arranged as shown on the diagram on the previous page, a three-hundred-year-plus period of judges is shown to fit nicely within the biblical chronology exactly as the Bible says, without having to assume biblical error about the Exodus chronology or period of the judges.

2. The biblical record shows that Solomon was anointed king before David's death, and that there was a period of coreign, as indicated in 1 Kings, chapter 1, but the Bible does not indicate how long the coreign lasted. From the sequence of events revealed in the biblical text describing the last years of David, a one-year coreign is indicated (any less and there would not have been enough time for all of the events mentioned in the text to have happened), during which, for all intents and purposes, Solomon ruled as king and David acknowledged him publicly as his sovereign and the primary ruler of Israel (see page 139).

3. The fifth year of Rehoboam (*i.e.,* the fifth year after Rehoboam succeeded Solomon) occurred in 961 BCE, three-plus years after the northern kingdom broke away in 964 BCE. The purpose of Shishak's invasion was to diminish the authority of Jerusalem. The biggest threat to his ally Jeroboam was the loyalty of the people to the Temple. By taking the Temple treasures away from Jerusalem, Shishak was undermining the primacy of its Temple and priesthood.

Appendix Six: Biblical Chronology Synchronized with Daniel

Part 3 - The Divided Kingdom (961-586 BCE)

A synchronized chronology for the reigns of the kings of Israel and Judah, one that takes into account all relevant Scripture references without sacrificing the accuracy of the Masoretic text, while at the same time respecting the chronologies of Egyptologists, Assyriologists, and the *Seder Olam*, has eluded Bible expositors since the earliest days. The key to getting the regnal years to align properly with the biblical text and its contemporary history is in knowing the correct time frame into which to fit the reigns. Since the kingdoms of Israel and Judah are known to have ended with the fall of Samaria in 721 BCE and the fall of Jerusalem in 586 BCE respectively, and with the identification of the year 964 BCE as the year for the rending of the United Kingdom from Rehoboam (as demonstrated in *Appendix Three* on page 131), the year 961 BCE can be shown to be the year for the start of the divided kingdoms and the year from which the regnal years must be calculated. The resulting synchronization of the reigns of the kings of Israel and Judah is shown in the tables that follow on pages 165-173. For the most part, the tables are self-explanatory, but the following assumptions and/or adjustments were used in the few instances where the traditional interpretation of the biblical text about the reigns of the kings was found to be problematical:

On page 165 ... Rehoboam succeeded Solomon as king of Israel sometime after the 10th day of Tishri in 967 BCE and before the 10th of Tishri in 966 BCE (see Diagram A in *Appendix Three* on page 139). In 964 BCE, the northern tribes rejected him as king and rallied behind his rival Jeroboam. Rehoboam tried to reassert rule over all of the tribes for the next three years. His main "weapon" was the Temple, which commanded loyalty transcending tribal affiliation. To counter this, Jeroboam established a competing temple system in the north. In 961 BCE, the fifth year after Rehoboam succeeded Solomon, Shishak of Egypt, who had previously provided sanctuary to Jeroboam from Solomon, invaded Canaan to strengthen his Israelite ally. After Shishak's show of force, and his taking of the sacred treasures from the Jerusalem Temple to weaken its appeal, Jeroboam's rule in the kingdom of Israel was made secure and Rehoboam was left with only a kingdom comprised of Judah and Benjamin. Note that the date for Shishak's invasion, 961 BCE, is thirty-six years earlier in history than the traditional date accepted by most scholars. This means that the Shishak of the Bible is Siamum, not Shoshenq I. The latter did invade Canaan, but thirty-six years later in 925 BCE during the reign of Asa (the record of which is recorded on the wall at Karnak).

On page 166 ... Baasha did not attack Judah in the thirty-sixth year of Asa as stated in 2 Chronicles, chapter 16, verse 1 (KJV), since that event would have occurred ten years after Baasha's death. Instead, the text means "in the thirty-sixth year (of the kingdom of Israel) during the reign of Asa."

On page 166 ... Omri ruled as king in Tirzah for two years, starting at the time of Elah's death in 914 BCE. When Zimri killed Elah, Omri was recognized by half of Israel as the legitimate king but was challenged by Tibni, who was recognized by the other half of Israel. Omri defeated Tibni in the thirty-first year of Asa, becoming sole ruler in Israel, then built Samaria and reigned from there for about six years, for a total reign of twelve years.

On page 167 ... Ahaziah died childless in his second regnal year, so the throne of Israel was filled by Jehoram of Judah, son of Jehoshaphat (and also husband of Ahab's daughter, thus he was the "son of Ahab"), as the mysterious text of 2 Kings, chapter 1, verse 17, seems to indicate. Apparently, after two years as "regent," Jehoram of Judah was replaced by Joram, who was the son of Ahab and younger brother of the former king Ahaziah (perhaps Joram had come of age during the two years of Jehoram of Judah's rule). In the fifth regnal year of Joram, Jehoram of Judah succeeded Jehoshaphat as king of Judah.

On page 168 ... 2 Kings, chapter 13, verse 5, says that Syria was oppressing Israel when the Lord raised up a deliverer (unnamed) who freed Israel from Syrian power. This deliverer was apparently the son of Jehoahaz, Jehoash, who was apparently "acting king" from the time when he assumed control of the army to deliver Israel from the Syrians in the thirty-seventh year of Joash of Judah.

On page 169 ... 2 Kings, chapter 15, verses 1-2, say that Uzziah began to reign in the twenty-seventh year of Jeroboam II, when he was sixteen years old. However, what is meant is that he began to reign in place of Amaziah when he was sixteen years old, and, when he was twenty seven years old, during the reign of Jeroboam II, Amariah died and Uzziah began to reign as sole ruler.

On page 171 ... In 2 Kings, chapter 15, verse 30, the Bible says that Hoshea conspired against Pekah in the twentieth year of Jotham of Judah. Based on the regnal years given for Jotham, this seems to be an error, since the text implies that Jotham died at the end of his sixteenth regnal year and thus could have had no "twentieth year." However, Jotham coreigned with Uzziah for four years, reigned as sole ruler for twelve years, then was alive (coreigned with Ahaz?) for four more years, allowing the reign of Jotham to be accurately described as both sixteen and twenty years, depending on how you look at it.

Appendix Six: Biblical Chronology Synchronized with Daniel

Reigns of Pharoahs of Egypt and Kings of Judah, 999-922 BCE

(years shown in left column are proleptic Gregorian years; A = accession or partial year; ▲ denotes a pharaoh)

YEAR BCE	REGNAL YEAR (JUDAH)		Notes	YEAR BCE	REGNAL YEAR (JUDAH)		Notes
999	7th		← Solomon (1,006-966 BCE) begins his 7th regnal year	960	1st		DIVIDED KINGDOM [2]
998	8th			959	2nd		← ▲ Psusennes II (959-940) [3]
997	9th		The identity of Shishak, mentioned in the Bible as moving against Jerusalem and taking the treasures of the Temple in the fifth year of Rehoboam, has been disputed for years by both biblical and secular scholars. Based on the chronology of the kings of Israel and Judah developed in this book, Shishak can be identified as the pharaoh named Siamun	958	3rd		[2] Rehoboam (961-944 BCE) begins reign as king of Judah and Benjamin, and Jeroboam (961-940 BCE) begins reign as king of the ten tribes of northern Israel
996	10th			957	4th		
995	11th			956	5th		
994	12th			955	6th		
993	13th			954	7th		[3] After a 14/15-year reign (as calculated by K.A. Kitchen), Psusennes II coreigned with Shoshenq I for at least five additional years, for a total reign of about 19 years
992	14th			953	8th		
991	15th			952	9th		
990	16th			951	10th		
989	17th			950	11th		
988	18th			949	12th		
987	19th		← Siamun (987-959) (alternate reign if his 17th year occurred in 970 BCE, as calculated by Rolf Krauss)	948	13th		DYNASTY 21
986	20th	1st		947	14th		DYNASTY 22
985	21st	2nd		946	15th		
984	22nd	3rd		945	16th		← ▲ Shoshenq I (945-924)
983	23rd	4th	Pharaohs not shown: Psusennes I (1,039-991), Amenemope (993-994) Orsokon the Elder (994-978)	944	17th/A	1st	← ♛ Abijah (944-942)
982	24th	5th		943	1st	2nd	
981	25th	6th		942	2nd	3rd	
980	26th	7th		941	3rd/A	4th	← ♛ Asa (942-900)
979	27th	8th		940	1st	5th	← Nadab of Israel (940-939)
978	28th	9th	← ▲ Siamun[1] (978-959)	939	2nd	6th	
977	29th	10th	Siamun is known to have campaigned in the Levant during his reign based on a triumphal scene inscribed on a temple wall in Tanis	938	3rd	7th	← Baasha of Israel (939-916)
976	30th	11th		937	4th	8th	
975	31st	12th		936	5th	9th	Zerah the Ethiopian is not identified as pharaoh in the Bible (his one mention in history), and was possibly only a general in charge of Ethiopian forces during the year-20 campaign of Shoshenq I into Canaan in 925 BCE; The Seder Olam says that Zerah returned the Temple treasures taken by Shishak during his earlier 961 BCE invasion, but this return is not mentioned in the biblical account.
974	32nd	13th		935	6th	10th	
973	33rd	14th		934	7th	11th	
972	34th	15th		933	8th	12th	
971	35th	16th	Jeroboam of Israel flees to Shishak of Egypt seeking sanctuary from Solomon sometime before the death of Solomon in 966 BCE	932	9th	13th	
970	36th	17th		931	10th	14th	
969	37th			930	11th	15th	
968	38th			929	12th	16th	
967	39th			928	13th	17th	
966	40th/A		← ♛ Rehoboam (966-961) Succeeds Solomon as king of (united) Israel	927	14th	18th	
965	1st			926	15th	19th	
964	2nd			925	16th	20th	← Zerah the Ethiopian invades Judah, Baasha of Israel attacks Judah, both in 926/925 BCE; d. Shoshenq 924 BCE
963	3rd		Shishak invades Judah in 5th year of Rehoboam, divided kingdom begins	924	17th	21st	
962	4th			923	18th		
961	5th			922	19th		

– 163 –

Chronology of the Kings of Israel and Judah

Year	Kings of Israel	Year	Kings of Judah
966-961 BCE - Rehoboam (2 years as king of United Israel + 3 years of disputed rule)			
961 BCE	Jeroboam (king of Israel, 22 years)	961 BCE	Rehoboam (king of Judah, 17 years)
	... and in his 18th year	944 BCE	Abijah (3 years)
	... and in his 20th year	942 BCE	Asa (41 years)
940 BCE	Nadab (2 years)		
939 BCE	Baasha (24 years)		
916 BCE	Elah (2 years)		
914 BCE	Zimri (7 days)		
914 BCE	Omri (12 years)		
904 BCE	Ahab (22 years)		
	... and in his 4th year	900 BCE	Jehoshaphat (25 years)
883 BCE	Ahaziah (2 years)		
881 BCE	Jehoram of Judah (2 years)		
879 BCE	Joram (12 years)		
	... and in his 5th year	875 BCE	Jehoram of Judah (8 years)
	... and in his 12th year	868 BCE	Ahaziah/Athaliah (7 years)
868 BCE	Jehu (28 years)		
	... and in his 7th year	862 BCE	Joash (40 years)
841 BCE	Jehoahaz (17 years)		
827 BCE	Jehoash (16 years)		
	... and in his 2nd year	823 BCE	Amaziah (29 years)
809 BCE	Jeroboam II (41 years)		
	... and in Uzziah's 27th year	795 BCE	Uzziah/Azariah (52 years)
769 BCE	Zachariah (6 months)		
768 BCE	Shallum (1 month)		
768 BCE	Menahem (10 years)		
758 BCE	Pekahiah (2 years)		
758 BCE	Pekah (20 years)		
	... and in his 2nd year	755 BCE	Jotham (16 years)
	... and in his 17th year	741 BCE	Ahaz (16 years)
730 BCE	Hoshea (9 years)		
	... and in his 3rd year	726 BCE	Hezekiah (29 years)
Kingdom of Israel (northern tribes) 961 BCE - 721 BCE 240 years - - - - - - - - - - - - - - - - - - Kingdom of Judah (southern tribes) 961 BCE - 586 BCE 375 years		697 BCE	Manasseh (55 years)
^		642 BCE	Amon (2 years)
^		640 BCE	Josiah (31 years)
^		609 BCE	Jehoahaz (3 months)
^		609 BCE	Jehoiakim (11 years)
^		598 BCE	Jehoiachin/Jeconiah (3 months)
^		597 BCE	Zedekiah (11 years)

Appendix Six: Biblical Chronology Synchronized with Daniel

Regnal Years of the Kings of Israel and Judah, 966-930 BCE

(years shown in center column are proleptic Gregorian years; A = accession or partial year; sabbath years in bold type)

Kingdom of Israel (regnal years counted Nisan to Nisan)		START HERE YEAR BCE		Kingdom of Judah (regnal years counted Tishri to Tishri)
		966	A	← ♛ **Rehoboam** (966-964) King of United Israel
	---	965	1st	
Northern ten tribes reject →	---	964	2nd	← Kingdom rent from Rehoboam
Rehoboam as king	---	963	3rd	1st yr. in 964 BCE, priests/Levites move
	---	962	4th	2nd yr. to Judah, Judah-Benjamin is
	---	961	5th	3rd yr. secured for next three years [1]
♛ **Jeroboam** (961-940) →	*1 yr.* 1st	**960**	1st	
King of Divided Israel	*2 yrs.* 2nd	959	2nd	Kingdoms are divided after
	3 yrs. 3rd	958	3rd	Shishak (Siamun) campaigns
	4 yrs. 4th	957	4th	in the 5th year of Rehoboam,
	5 yrs. 5th	956	5th	establishes Jeroboam as king
	6 yrs. 6th	955	6th	of Israel, Rehoboam remains
	7 yrs. 7th	954	7th	King of Judah-Benjamin and
	8 yrs. 8th	**953**	8th	becomes a vassal of Egypt [2]
	9 yrs. 9th	952	9th	
	10 yrs. 10th	951	10th	[1] *2 Chronicles 11:16-17*
	11 yrs. 11th	950	11th	[2] *2 Chronicles 12:1-2*
	12 yrs. 12th	949	12th	
	13 yrs. 13th	948	13th	
	14 yrs. 14th	947	14th	
	15 yrs. 15th	**946**	15th	
	16 yrs. 16th	945	16th	
	17 yrs. 17th	944	17th/A	← ♛ **Abijah** (944-942)
	18 yrs. 18th	943	1st	18th year of Jeroboam
	19 yrs. 19th	942	2nd	
	20 yrs. 20th	941	3rd/A	← ♛ **Asa** (942-900)
♛ **Nadab** (940-939) →	*21 yrs.* 21st	940	1st	20th year of Jeroboam
2nd year of Asa →	*22 yrs.* 22nd/1st	**939**	2nd	
♛ **Baasha** (939-916) →	*23 yrs.* 2nd/1st	938	3rd	
3rd year of Asa	*24 yrs.* 2nd	937	4th	
	25 yrs. 3rd	936	5th	
	26 yrs. 4th	935	6th	
	27 yrs. 5th	934	7th	
	28 yrs. 6th	933	8th	After ten years of rest from the
	29 yrs. 7th	**932**	9th	threat of war, Baasha of Israel
	30 yrs. 8th	931	10th	fortifies Ramah in Benjamin
	31 yrs. 9th	930	11th	← as a prelude to hostilities with
	32 yrs. 10th			Asa and the kingdom of Judah

– 165 –

Regnal Years of the Kings of Israel and Judah, 929-893 BCE

(years shown in center column are proleptic Gregorian years; A = accession or partial year; sabbath years in bold type)

Kingdom of Israel (regnal years counted Nisan to Nisan)			YEAR BCE		Kingdom of Judah (regnal years counted Tishri to Tishri)
Baasha continued	→ 33 yrs.	11th	929	12th	← Asa continued
	34 yrs.	12th	928	13th	
Baasha attacks Judah in the 36th year of the kingdom of Israel [1]	35 yrs.	13th	927	14th	
	→ 36 yrs.	14th	926	15th	
		15th	**925**	16th	← Asa repells attack from the Ethiopians and Lubims, [2]
[1] impossible for Baasha to have attacked in the 36th regnal year of Asa since Baasha was killed in Asa's 26th year; see 1 Kings 16:7-8		16th	924	17th	then with help from Syria repells attack by Baasha in the 36th year after the start of the kingdom of Israel
		17th	923	18th	
		18th	922	19th	
		19th	921	20th	
		20th	920	21st	
		21st	919	22nd	[2] The invasion of Canaan by pharaoh Shoshenq I in 925 BCE (as recorded on a temple wall at Karnak) is usually equated with the invasion of Shishak of Egypt during the reign of Rehoboam (as recorded in the Bible), but chronologically Shishak's invasion is better synchronized with the attack against Asa of Judah by Zerah the Ethiopian and his army, which attacked Judah and Jerusalem while Shoshenq's army bypassed the southern kingdom to raid into the Jordan valley and the cities of the north, and this invasion was coordinated with an attack from the northern kingdom of Israel, led by Baasha, causing Asa to appeal for aid from Ben-Haddad of Syria; see 2 Chronicles 16:8
♛ **Zimri** (914) for 7 days		22nd	**918**	23rd	
		23rd	917	24th	
♛ Elah (916-914) → 26th year of Asa		24th/1st	916	25th	
♛ Omri (914-904) recognized as king in 27th year of Asa		2nd/A/1st	915	26th	
		2nd	914	27th	
		3rd	913	28th	
		4th	912	29th	
Omri defeats Tibni, becomes sole ruler in 31st year of Asa [3]		5th	**911**	30th	
		6th	910	31st	
Omri begins his rule from Samaria in 909 BCE, during the 33rd year of Asa, reigns there for ~ 6 years		7th	909	32nd	
		8th	908	33rd	
		9th	907	34th	
		10th	906	35th	
		11th	905	36th	
♛ Ahab (904-883) → 38th year of Asa		12th/1st	**904**	37th	
		2nd	903	38th	
		3rd	902	39th	← Asa diseased in his feet
[3] Thw Seder Olam says that the struggle between Omri and Tibni for sole rule of the northern kingdom of Israel was resolved in favor of Omri after four years		4th	901	40th	
		5th	900	41st/A	← ♛ **Jehoshaphat** (900-875) 4th year of Ahab
		6th	899	1st	
		7th	898	2nd	
		8th	**897**	3rd	← In his 3rd year, Jehoshaphat sends officials and priests to the cities of Judah teaching from the Book of the Law
		9th	896	4th	
		10th	895	5th	
		11th	894	6th	
		12th	893	7th	

Appendix Six: Biblical Chronology Synchronized with Daniel

Regnal Years of the Kings of Israel and Judah, 892-856 BCE

(years shown in center column are proleptic Gregorian years; A = accession or partial year; sabbath years in bold type)

Kingdom of Israel
(regnal years counted Nisan to Nisan)

Kingdom of Judah
(regnal years counted Tishri to Tishri)

Israel		YEAR BCE	Judah	
Ahab continued →	13th	892	8th	← Jehoshaphat continued
	14th	891	9th	
	15th	**890**	10th	
	16th	889	11th	
	17th	888	12th	
	18th	887	13th	
	19th	886	14th	
	20th	885	15th	
♛ **Ahaziah** (883-882)	21st	884	16th	
17th year of Jehoshaphat →	22nd/1st	**883**	17th	
♛ **Jehoram**[1] (882-879)	2nd A	882	18th	
18th year of Jehoshaphat	1st	881	19th	
	2nd	880	20th	
♛ **Joram**[2] (879-868) → A	1st	879	21st	
also called Jehoram, son of Ahab, brother of Ahaziah 1st	2nd	878	22nd	
2nd	3rd	877	23rd	
[1] *Jehoram of Judah, married to Ahab's daughter, reigned* 3rd	4th	**876**	24th	
for two years as king of Israel in Samaria (with extended 4th	5th	875	25th/A	← ♛ **Jehoram** (875-868)
accession year and his regnal 5th	6th	874	1st	*5th year of Joram*
years counted Tishri to Tishri 6th	7th	873	2nd	
as they were in Judah) 7th	8th	872	3rd	
[2] *Joram reigned in Israel for* 8th	9th	871	4th	
twelve years (non-accession 9th	10th	870	5th	
year system) or eleven years	11th	**869**	6th	
(accession-year system) 10th		868	7th	
♛ **Jehu** (868-841) → 11th	12th/1st	867	8th/A/(1st)	← ♛ **Ahaziah** (868)
	2nd	866	(2nd)	*12th (or 11th) year of Joram*[3]
	3rd	865	(3rd)	♛ **Athaliah** (868-862)
	4th	864	(4th)	*1st year of Ahaziah*
	5th	863	(5th)	
	6th	**862**	(6th)/1st	← ♛ **Joash** (862-823)
	7th	861	2nd	*7th year of Jehu*
	8th	860	3rd	
	9th	859	4th	[3] *Ahaziah began his reign as king (and died) in the twelfth year of Joram (or the eleventh year using the accession-year regnal system of Judah); see 2 Kings 9:29, 2 Kings 8:25*
	10th	858	5th	
	11th	857	6th	
	12th	856	7th	
	13th			

Regnal Years of the Kings of Israel and Judah, 855-819 BCE

(years shown in center column are proleptic Gregorian years; A = accession or partial year; sabbath years in bold type)

Kingdom of Israel (regnal years counted Nisan to Nisan)	Israel	YEAR BCE	Judah	Kingdom of Judah (regnal years counted Tishri to Tishri)
Jehu continued →	14th	**855**	8th	← Joash continued
	15th	854	9th	*Battle of Qarqar*
	16th	853	10th	← Ahab is named on the Kurkh Monolith as one of twelve kings defeated by Shalmaneser III at Qarqar in 853 BCE, but Ahab had died thirty years prior to the battle and no other accounts of the battle from Assyrian sources mention Ahab but do mention the other battle participants, so the Kurkh Monolith inclusion of Ahab is a probable scribal gloss; on the other hand, the Black Obelisk shows Jehu bowing and paying tribute to Shalmaneser in 841 BCE, which does coincide with the final year of Jehu
	17th	852	11th	
	18th	851	12th	
	19th	850	13th	
	20th	849	14th	
	21st	**848**	15th	
	22nd	847	16th	
	23rd	846	17th	
	24th	845	18th	
	25th	844	19th	
	26th	843	20th	
	27th	842	21st	
♛ **Jehoahaz (841-825)** →	28th/1st	**841**	22nd	
23rd year of Joash	2nd	840	23rd	← The Seder Olam says that Joash began renovating the Temple during his 23rd regnal year (in 840 BCE), 155 years after Solomon completed the First Temple in 995 BCE and 218 years before Josiah began his renovation of the Temple during his 18th regnal year in the year 622 BCE
	3rd	839	24th	
	4th	838	25th	
	5th	837	26th	
	6th	836	27th	
	7th	835	28th	
	8th	**834**	29th	
	9th	833	30th	
	10th	832	31st	
	11th	831	32nd	
	12th	830	33rd	
	13th	829	34th	
	14th	828	35th	
♛ **Jehoash (827-809)** →	15th (1st)	**827**	36th	
Jehoash leads a revolt against Benhadad of Syria as "acting" king for three years, beginning in the thirty-seventh year of Joash, begins reign as the sole ruler in Samaria in 824 BCE	16th (2nd)	826	37th	
	17th/(3rd)	825	38th	
	1st	824	39th	
	2nd	823	40th/A	← ♛ **Amaziah (823-795)** 2nd year of Johoash
	3rd	822	1st	
	4th	821	2nd	
	5th	**820**	3rd	
	6th	819	4th	

– 168 –

Appendix Six: Biblical Chronology Synchronized with Daniel

Regnal Years of the Kings of Israel and Judah, 818-782 BCE

(years shown in center column are proleptic Gregorian years; A = accession or partial year; sabbath years in bold type)

Kingdom of Israel
(regnal years counted Nisan to Nisan)

Kingdom of Judah
(regnal years counted Tishri to Tishri)

Israel	YEAR BCE	Judah	
Jehoash continued → 7th	818	5th	← Amaziah continued
8th	817	6th	
9th	816	7th	
10th	815	8th	
11th	814	9th	
12th	**813**	10th	
13th	812	11th	
14th	811	12th	
15th	810	13th	
♛ **Jeroboam II** (809-769) → 16th/1st	809	14th	
15th year of Amaziah 2nd	808	15th	
3rd	807	16th	
4th	**806**	(17th)/1st 16 yo.	← Uzziah 16 years old,
5th	805	(18th)/2nd 17 yo.	began serving as king
6th	804	(19th)/3rd 18 yo.	in his father's place
7th	803	(20th)/4th 19 yo.	
8th	802	(21st)/5th 20 yo.	
9th	801	(22nd)/6th 21 yo.	
10th	800	(23rd)/7th 22 yo.	
11th	**799**	(24th)/8th 23 yo.	
12th	798	(25th)/9th 24 yo.	
13th	797	(26th)/10th 25 yo.	
14th	796	(27th)/11th 26 yo.	
Amaziah dies in fifteenth 15th	795	(28th)/12th 27 yo.	♛ **Uzziah** (795-755)[1]
year after death of Jehoash, 16th	794	(29th)/13th 28 yo.	*Uzziah 27 years old,*
who died in 809 BCE 17th	793	14th	*becomes king as sole*
18th	**792**	15th	*ruler during the reign*
19th	791	16th	*of Jeroboam II* [2]
20th	790	17th	
21st	789	18th	[1] also called Azariah
22nd	788	19th	[2] Uzziah became sole ruler
23rd	787	20th	in his 27th year of life, not
24th	786	21st	in the 27th regnal year of
25th	**785**	22nd	Jeroboan II as stated in
26th	784	23rd	2 Kings 15:1 (KJV)
27th	783	24th	
28th	782	25th	

– 169 –

Regnal Years of the Kings of Israel and Judah, 781-745 BCE

(years shown in center column are proleptic Gregorian years; A = accession or partial year; sabbath years in bold type)

Kingdom of Israel (regnal years counted Nisan to Nisan)		YEAR BCE		Kingdom of Judah (regnal years counted Tishri to Tishri)
Jeroboam II continued →	29th	781	26th	← Uzziah/Azariah continued
	30th	780	27th	
	31st	779	28th	
	32nd	**778**	29th	
	33rd	777	30th	
	34th	776	31st	
Note: Starting in 769 BCE, the kingdom of Israel adopted the accession-year system for recording regnal years, but retained the Nisan-to-Nisan system for counting years.	35th	775	32nd	
	36th	774	33rd	
	37th	773	34th	
	38th	772	35th	
	39th	**771**	36th	
	40th	770	37th	
♔ Zachariah¹ (769) →	41st/A	769	38th	
♔ Shallum² (768) ⇒	1st/A/A	768	39th	
♔ Menahem³ (768-757) 39th year of Uzziah	1st	767	40th	
	2nd	766	41st	
¹ Zachariah reigns 6 months starting in the 38th year of Uzziah into the 39th year	3rd	765	42nd	
	4th	**764**	43rd	
	5th	763	44th	
² Shallum reigns 1 month in the 39th year of Uzziah	6th	762	45th	
³ Menahem pays tribute to Pul (= Ashur-Dan III)	7th	761	46th	
	8th	760	47th	
	9th	759	48th	
♔ Pekahiah (758-755) 50th year of Uzziah	10th/A/A	758	49th	
			(50th)	Jotham begins judging Judah
	1st/1st	**757**	(51st)/1st	← as king in Uzziah's place
♔ Pekah (758-738) becomes sole ruler in 52nd year of Uzziah³	2nd/2nd	756	(52nd)/2nd	← ♔ Jotham (755-738) 2nd year of Pekah (and Pekahiah), Jotham becomes sole ruler
	3rd	755	3rd	
	4th	754	4th	
³ Pekahiah and Pekah each had control of part of Israel after 758 BCE until Pekah killed Pekahiah in 755 BCE and became sole ruler as king in Samaria, thus his regnal years were counted from 758 BCE; cities in the northern kingdom were attacked and annexed by Tiglath-Pileser III during the reign of Pekah	5th	753	5th	
	6th	752	6th	
	7th	751	7th	
	8th	**750**	8th	
	9th	749	9th	
	10th	748	10th	
	11th	747	11th	
	12th	746	12th	
	13th	745		

Appendix Six: Biblical Chronology Synchronized with Daniel

Regnal Years of the Kings of Israel and Judah, 744-721 BCE

(years shown in center column are proleptic Gregorian years; A = accession or partial year; sabbath years in bold type)

Kingdom of Israel (regnal years counted Nisan to Nisan)		YEAR BCE		Kingdom of Judah (regnal years counted Tishri to Tishri)
			13th	← Jotham continued
Pekah continued →	14th	744	14th	
	15th	**743**	15th	
	16th	742	16th/1st	← ♛ **Ahaz**[1] (741-726)
Reigns of Pekah and Ahaz → overlap 741 BCE to 738 BCE, see note on next page	17th	741	(17th)/2nd	*17th year of Pekah Ahaz becomes king, Jotham lives until at least 738 BCE, his twentieth year*
	18th	740	(18th)/3rd	
	19th	739	(19th)/4th	
Pekah killed by Hoshea → in 20th year of Jotham	20th/(?)	738	(20th)/5th	
	(?)	737	6th	
	(?)	**736**	6th	[1] *Ahaz is also called king of Israel, possibly had nominal rule over both the kingdoms of Judah and Israel as a vassal of Tiglath-pileser of Assyria from 738 BCE to 730 BCE*
(?) The Seder Olam posits that Hoshea was king of Gilead and the lands across the Jordan under Assyrian control for about eight years before becoming king of Israel in Samaria in the year 730 BCE	(?)	735	7th	
	(?)	734	8th	
	(?)	733	9th	
	(?)	732	10th	
	(?)	731	11th	
♛ **Hoshea** (730-721) → *12th year of Ahaz*	(?)/A	730	12th	
	1st	**729**	13th	
	2nd	728	14th	
Hoshea made a vassal king of Assyria by Tiglath-pileser, has 9-year reign in Samaria; rebels against Assyria after the death of Tiglath-pileser in 727 BCE	3rd	727	15th	
	4th	726	16th/A	← ♛ **Hezekiah** (726-697)
	5th	725	1st	*3rd year of Hoshea, Temple cleansed and Passover observed*
	6th	724	2nd	
Samaria besieged (723) →	7th	723	3rd	
	8th	**722**	4th	
Fall of Samaria (721) →	9th	721	5th	
			6th	

Regnal years for Kings of Judah after the fall of Samaria in 721 BCE are continued on the next page.

↓

– 171 –

Regnal Years of the Kings of Judah after the fall of Israel, 726-653 BCE

(years shown in left column are proleptic Gregorian years; A = accession or partial year; sabbath years in bold type)

(regnal years counted Tishri to Tishri)

YEAR BCE				YEAR BCE		
726	A	← ♛	**Hezekiah** (726-697)	689	8th	← Manasseh continued
725	1st		3rd year of Hoshea.	688	9th	
724	2nd		Temple cleansed and	**687**	10th	
723	3rd		Passover observed	686	11th	
722	4th			685	12th	
721	5th			684	13th	
720	6th	←	Fall of Samaria (721)	683	14th	
719	7th			682	15th	
718	8th			681	16th	
717	9th			**680**	17th	
716	10th			679	18th	
715	11th			678	19th	
714	12th	←	Hezekiah's life-threatening	677	20th	
713	13th		illness, God gives him fifteen	676	21st	← Manasseh taken to
712	14th		extra years; see page 175	675	22nd[1]	Babylon by captains of
711	15th			674	23rd	Esarhaddon between
710	16th			**673**	24th	676 BCE and 673 BCE,
709	17th	←	b. Manasseh (709)	672	25th	see 2 Chronicles 33
708	18th	*1 yo.*		671	26th	
707	19th	*2 yo.*		670	27th	[1] The Seder Olam says
706	20th	*3 yo.*		669	28th	that Manasseh was taken
705	21st	*4 yo.*		668	29th	captive to Babylon in his
704	22nd	*5 yo.*		667	30th	22nd regnal year
703	23rd	*6 yo.*		**666**	31st	
702	24th	*7 yo.*		665	32nd	*Note*
701	25th	*8 yo.*	← Sennacherib's invasion	664	33rd	During 676-673 BCE,
700	26th	*9 yo.*		663	34th	Esarhaddon deported
699	27th	*10 yo.*		662	35th	the remaining Jews in
698	28th	*11 yo.*		661	36th	the northern kingdom
697	29th/A	*12 yo.*	← ♛ **Manasseh** (697-642)	660	37th	to Assyria, replacing
696	1st	*13 yo.*		**659**	38th	them with foreigners;
695	2nd			658	39th	fulfilling the prophecy
694	3rd			657	40th	given by Isaiah during
693	4th			656	41st	the overlapping reigns
692	5th			655	42nd	of Ahaz of Judah and
691	6th			654	43rd	Pekah of Israel from
690	7th			653	44th	741 BCE to 738 BCE, see Isaiah 7:8.

Appendix Six: Biblical Chronology Synchronized with Daniel

Regnal Years of the Kings of Judah after the fall of Israel, 652-586 BCE

(years shown in left column are proleptic Gregorian years; A = accession or partial year; sabbath years in bold type)

(regnal years counted Tishri to Tishri)

YEAR BCE				YEAR BCE			
652	45th	← Manasseh continued		615	25th	← Josiah continued	
651	46th			614	26th		
650	47th			613	27th		
649	48th			612	28th		
648	49th	← b. Josiah		611	29th		
647	50th	*1 yo.*		**610**	30th		
646	51st	*2 yo.*		609	31st/A		← ♛ Jehoahaz (609)[1]
645	52nd	*3 yo.*		608	1st/A		♛ Jehoiakim (609-597)
644	53rd	*4 yo.*		607	1st		
643	54th	*5 yo.*		606	2nd		
642	55th/A	*6 yo.*	← ♛ Amon (642-640)	605	3rd	*1st*	← King Nebuchadnezzar
641	1st	*7 yo.*		604	4th	*2nd*	(r. 605-562) becomes
640	2nd/A	*8 yo.*	← ♛ Josiah (640-609)	**603**	5th	*3rd*	king shortly after the Battle of Carchemish,
639	1st	*9 yo.*	becomes king in his	602	6th	*4th*	Daniel taken hostage
638	2nd		eighth year	601	7th	*5th*	to Babylon in 605 BCE;
637	3rd			600	8th	*6th*	in the nineteenth year of Nebuchadnezzar,
636	4th			599	9th	*7th*	the Temple and city of
635	5th			598	10th	*8th*	Jerusalem are burned
634	6th			597	11th/A/A	*9th*	← ♛ Jehoiachin (598-597)[2]
633	7th		*The Babylonian Talmud (tractate Arakin 12b) says that Solomon's Temple was destroyed in the third year of a sabbath cycle, a cross check confirming that the year 586 BCE was the year that the Babylonian army destroyed the Temple.*	**596**	1st	*10th*	♛ Zedekiah (597-586)[3]
632	8th			595	2nd	*11th*	
631	9th			594	3rd	*12th*	
630	10th			593	4th	*13th*	
629	11th			592	5th	*14th*	
628	12th			591	6th	*15th*	
627	13th			590	7th	*16th*	
626	14th			**589**	8th	*17th*	
625	15th		*sabbath yr.*	588	9th	*18th*	← Siege of Jerusalem (588)
624	16th		*1st yr.*	587	10th	*19th*	(10th month of 9th year)
623	17th		*2nd yr.*	586	11th		← Fall of Jerusalem (586)
622	18th	← *Hilkiah finds the Book*	*3rd yr.*				(4th month of 11th year)
621	19th	*of the Law during repair of the Temple in Josiah's eighteenth regnal year; as a result, celebration of the "Great Passover" takes place in 622 BCE*					
620	20th						
619	21st						
618	22nd						
617	23rd						
616	24th						

[1] Jehoahaz ruled for 3 months in 609 BCE, including a month of Tishri to begin a regnal year, before being deposed by pharaoh Necho and exiled to Egypt.
[2] Jehoiachin was king for 3 months and 10 days in late 598 BCE-early 597 BCE, but not in a month of Tishri.
[3] Zedekiah was appointed king by Nebuchadnezzar sometime before Tishri in 597 BCE and had a short accession year before his first Tishri later that year.

Part 4 - The Reign of Hezekiah (726-697 BCE)

The Bible describes the chronological details of the reign of Hezekiah in three separate accounts, in the Books of 2 Kings, chapters 18-20; 2 Chronicles, chapters 29-32; and Isaiah, chapters 36-39. The tables on pages 171-172, show the years in the reign of Hezekiah, with the years 726 BCE and 697 BCE as the starting and ending years for a total reign of twenty-nine years. This latter figure includes the fifteen "extra" years added to the life of the king by God according to the biblical account. Most traditional interpretations of the chronology of the reign of Hezekiah have assumed that the details in the Bible are incorrect, and thus dismiss the "extra" fifteen years as fable or myth that should not be included in any serious chronology of the regnal years of the kings of Israel and Judah. This exposition shows that the biblical account makes perfect sense chronologically.

In addition to the extra fifteen years given to Hezekiah, the king is promised a sign about the deliverance of Jerusalem from the king of Assyria. That sign is described in Isaiah, chapter 37, verse 30, *"And this shall be a sign unto thee, Ye shall eat this year such as groweth of itself; and the second year that which springeth of the same: and in the third year sow ye, and reap, and plant vineyards, and eat the fruit thereof"* (KJV). Traditional interpretation assumes that the two years without crops were a sabbath year and jubilee year during which no crops could be planted or harvested for each of those years, followed by a third year in which crops were planted and harvested. It is also assumed that the observance of that two-year-long sabbath-jubilee cycle coincided with the invasion of Judah by Sennacherib of Assyria, which the Bible says took place in Hezekiah's fourteenth year. Since the invasion can be pinpointed to the year 701 BCE by using the Assyrian *limmu* list, which is anchored precisely in time by the solar eclipse that Assyriologists say took place on June 7 (June 15 Julian), 763 BCE, Hezekiah seemingly had to begin his reign fourteen years earlier in the year 715 BCE.

However, the Bible states that Hezekiah began his reign in the third regnal year of Hoshea, the last king of Israel, which can be identified by the chronology of the regnal years of the kings of Israel and Judah on pages 165-171 as occurring either late in the year 727 BCE or early in the year 726 BCE. Obviously, something is wrong with the traditional interpretation. Fortunately, this is where having accurate tables of sabbath and jubilee years comes in handy. The tables show that the sabbath-jubilee combination during the reign of Hezekiah began in 708 BCE, not in 701 BCE as is traditionally assumed. That discrepancy means that there

Appendix Six: Biblical Chronology Synchronized with Daniel

Hezekiah's Regnal Years and 3-Year Sign

(years shown in left column are proleptic Gregorian years, with sabbath years shown in bold type; A = accession or partial year; sabbath and jubilee observances shown below are not mentioned in the Bible)

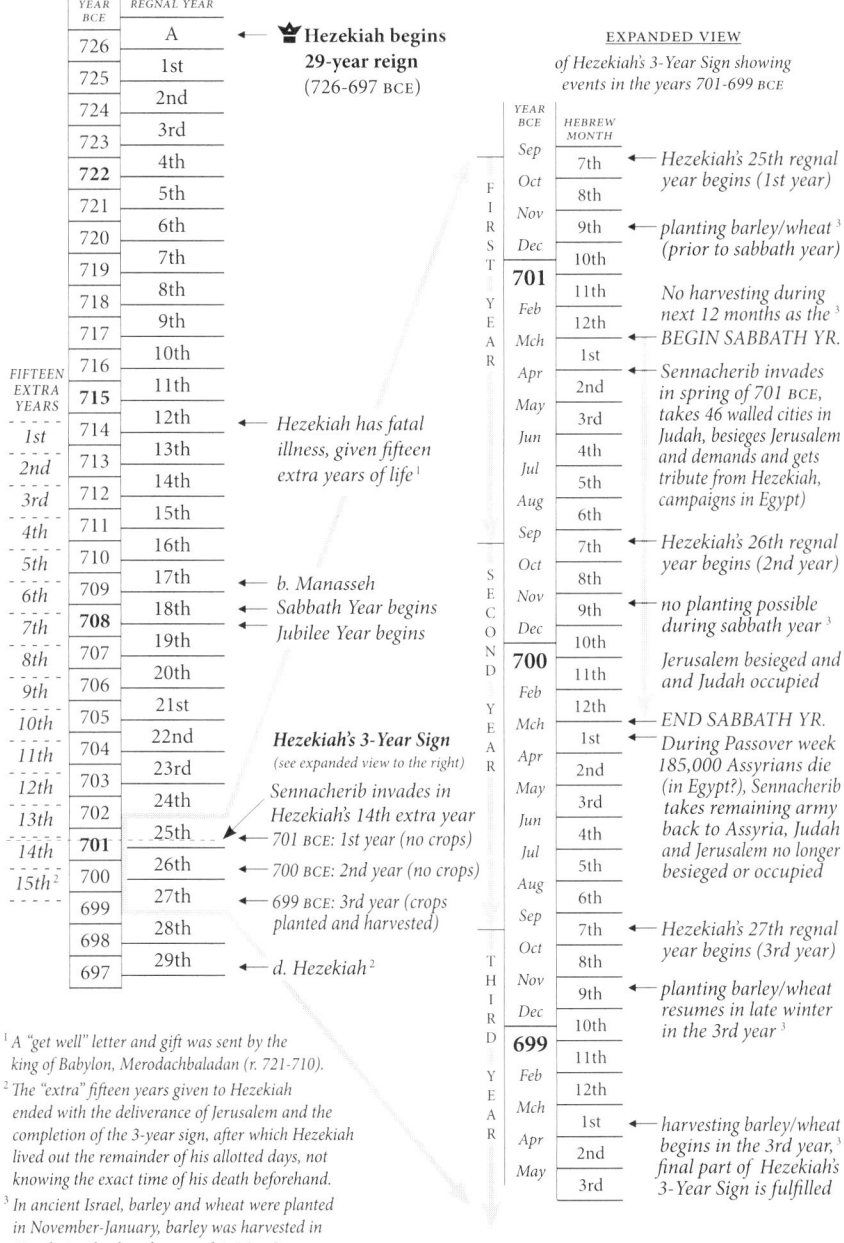

[1] A "get well" letter and gift was sent by the king of Babylon, Merodachbaladan (r. 721-710).

[2] The "extra" fifteen years given to Hezekiah ended with the deliverance of Jerusalem and the completion of the 3-year sign, after which Hezekiah lived out the remainder of his allotted days, not knowing the exact time of his death beforehand.

[3] In ancient Israel, barley and wheat were planted in November-January, barley was harvested in March-April, wheat harvested in May-June.

has to be another explanation besides the sabbath-jubilee cycle for why there would have been two successive years without crops, and there is. From the tables, it can be seen that the year 701 BCE featured the beginning of a sabbath year, which began in April that year, in the twenty-fifth regnal year of Hezekiah. That was the first year with no crops and no harvest. Soon thereafter, Sennacherib invaded and devastated Judah and began his siege of Jerusalem. The account of his campaign is given in the Scriptures and a secular account is recorded on the Taylor prism (also called Sennacherib's Prism, *ca.* 691 BCE) as follows:

> "Because Hezekiah, king of Judah, would not submit to my yoke, I came up against him, and by force of arms and by the might of my power I took 46 of his strong fenced cities; and of the smaller towns which were scattered about, I took and plundered a countless number. From these places I took and carried off 200,156 persons, old and young, male and female, together with horses and mules, asses and camels, oxen and sheep, a countless multitude; and Hezekiah himself I shut up in Jerusalem, his capital city, like a bird in a cage, building towers round the city to hem him in, and raising banks of earth against the gates, so as to prevent escape... Then upon Hezekiah there fell the fear of the power of my arms, and he sent out to me the chiefs and the elders of Jerusalem with 30 talents of gold and 800 talents of silver, and diverse treasures, a rich and immense booty... All these things were brought to me at Nineveh, the seat of my government" ... *translated by Daniel David Luckenbill.*

From the above, it is obvious that Sennacherib's invasion prevented planting of barley and wheat from being done in the fall and winter of 701 BCE, making those crops unavailable for harvest in the spring of 700 BCE, which means that both planting and harvesting would not have been carried out normally in Hezekiah's twenty-sixth regnal year, the second year with no crops. The Bible records that Sennacherib's army was later devastated by an angel of death that overnight killed 185,000 Assyrians and caused Sennacherib to withdraw back to his homeland, all of this taking place during Passover week in the year 700 BCE according to Jewish records. So, after two seasons with no crops, the land was at peace again in the third year, late in 700 BCE, and barley and wheat were planted that fall and harvested the following spring in 699 BCE. The "sign" given by God to Hezekiah was fulfilled exactly as promised. In Hezekiah's twenty-fifth and twenty-sixth regnal years, no crops could be planted or harvested. In his twenty-seventh regnal year (the third year), crops were both planted and harvested.

But, that scenario creates yet another chronological conundrum. If Hezekiah began his reign in the year 726 BCE and was invaded by Sennacherib in 701 BCE, how could the invasion have taken place in the fourteenth year of Hezekiah, as stated in 2 Kings, chapter 18, verse 13, and Isaiah, chapter 36, verse 1? The apparent conflict is easy to explain. The Hebrew text does not say fourteenth year of reign. It says only that Sennacherib invaded in the fourteenth year of Hezekiah. God extended Hezekiah's life by fifteen years, so the invasion of Sennacherib came in the fourteenth year of the fifteen-year extension, not in the fourteenth year of his total reign of twenty-nine years. That the deliverance of Jerusalem would signal the end of the "extra" fifteen years is indicated in 2 Kings, chapter 20, verse 6, which says: *"And I will add unto thy days fifteen years; and I will deliver thee and this city out of the hand of the king of Assyria; and I will defend this city for mine own sake, and for my servant David's sake"* (KJV}. The chronology of the reign of Hezekiah can thus be reconciled to incorporate all of the data given in the Bible, as shown by the diagram on page 175, without having to assume scribal error or myth-making on the part of the Hebrew scribes.

Part 5 - Construction of Herod's Temple (20 BCE-28 CE)

Herod the Great is perhaps most famous for rebuilding the Jewish Temple in Jerusalem, which was described by ancient historians as one of the architectural wonders of the world. The grandeur of the Temple building and its porticos and walls evoked admiration and praise from even the highly-resentful-of-Herod Jewish leaders and sages, who reportedly said, "He who has never seen Herod's Temple has never seen a beautiful building." According to Josephus (*Antiquities* 15:354 and 15:380), construction began after Herod had completed his seventeenth regnal year, which means that construction actually began during his eighteenth regnal year. Josephus also mentions that the year Herod began building the Temple was the same year that Augustus Caesar visited Syria, an event for which the year has been identified from a mention in Dio, who lists the consuls in office during that year, as occurring in the springtime of the year 20 BCE. Josephus also records that the Temple itself took one year and six months to complete, but that construction on the Temple complex continued for many decades.

The *B'rit Hadashah* (New Testament) contains a cross-reference that locates in history the ministry of Jesus in relationship to the above chronology of the Temple construction. At the beginning of his public ministry, Jesus went to the

How to Count the 46 Passovers					
20 BCE >>>>	P1 - 19 BCE	P2 - 18 BCE	P3 - 17 BCE	P4 - 16 BCE	P5 - 15 BCE
P6 - 14 BCE	P7 - 13 BCE	P8 - 12 BCE	P9 - 11 BCE	P10 - 10 BCE	P11 - 9 BCE
P12 - 8 BCE	P13 - 7 BCE	P14 - 6 BCE	P15 - 5 BCE	P16 - 4 BCE	P17 - 3 BCE
P18 - 2 BCE	P19 - 1 BCE	P20 - 1 CE	P21 - 2 CE	P22 - 3 CE	P23 - 4 CE
P24 - 5 CE	P25 - 6 CE	P26 - 7 CE	P27 - 8 CE	P28 - 9 CE	P29 - 10 CE
P30 - 11 CE	P31 - 12 CE	P32 - 13 CE	P33 - 14 CE	P34 - 15 CE	P35 - 16 CE
P36 - 17 CE	P37 - 18 CE	P38 - 19 CE	P39 - 20 CE	P40 - 21 CE	P41 - 22 CE
P42 - 23 CE	P43 - 24 CE	P44 - 25 CE	P45 - 26 CE	P46 - 27 CE	<<<< 28 CE

Temple during Passover and drove out the money changers and those selling animals, as recorded in the Gospel of John, chapter 2, verses 13-21:

> *"And the Jews' passover was at hand, and Jesus went up to Jerusalem, And found in the temple those that sold oxen and sheep and doves, and the changers of money sitting: And when he had made a scourge of small cords, he drove them all out of the temple, and the sheep, and the oxen; and poured out the changers' money, and overthrew the tables; And said unto them that sold doves, Take these things hence; make not my Father's house an house of merchandise. ... Then answered the Jews and said unto him, What sign shewest thou unto us, seeing that thou doest these things? Jesus answered and said unto them, Destroy this temple, and in three days I will raise it up. Then said the Jews,* **Forty and six years was this temple in building** [emphasis added], *and wilt thou rear it up in three days? But he spake of the temple of his body"* (KJV).

Jesus spoke his words of rebuke a few days before Passover in 28 BCE, the year being revealed by counting forward in time forty-six Passovers from the start of construction of the Temple by Herod in 20 BCE, as shown in the table above. The table shows that the interval between the start of construction of Herod's Temple after the Passover in 20 BCE and before the Passover in Jerusalem attended by Jesus in the year 28 CE, during which the crowd replied to him that the Temple had been under construction for forty-six years (Passovers), contains exactly forty-six Passovers. This synchronization provides an anchor date for the chronology of the ministry of Jesus. It also synchronizes the starting year of Jesus' ministry with the ending year of the prophecy of the "seventy weeks."

Appendix Six: Biblical Chronology Synchronized with Daniel

Part 6 - The Ministry of Jesus (28-30 CE)

The year when Jesus began his public ministry is revealed by the prophecy of the "seventy weeks" in Daniel, chapter 9, verses 24-27, which required that the "Most Holy" one who would confirm the covenant to Israel be anointed before the seventieth week ended on Pentecost in the year 28 CE (see page 91). That coincides with the baptism and "cleansing of the Temple" that Jesus performed at the beginning of his ministry, the latter being an event that occurred during Passover week in the year 28 CE as shown in the previous section about Herod's Temple (see "Part 5" on page 177). Thus, it can be said with absolute certainty that both the *Tanakh* and the *B'rit Hadashah* pinpoint 28 CE as the year when Jesus began his public ministry. Using the information given in the Gospels of Matthew, Mark, Luke, and John, the ministry of Jesus can be seen to have continued for about twenty-seven months after his baptism, a time period that includes three Passovers, as follows:

28 CE				
Events	*Matthew*	*Mark*	*Luke*	*John*
Jesus baptized by John the Baptist.	3:13-17	1:9-11	3:21-28	---
Jesus tempted by Satan for 40 days.	4:1-11	1:12-13	4:1-13	---
Jesus returns to Jordan R., Andrew hears John proclaim Jesus as the Lamb of God, two disciples follow him to Nazareth.	---	---	---	1:19-51
Jesus attends wedding at Cana, turns water to wine, the disciples believe.	---	---	---	2:1-11
Jesus goes to Capernaum with mother, brothers, and his disciples.	---	---	---	2:12
PASSOVER #1 - Feast of Unleavened Bread - March 28 to April 4, 28 CE				
Jesus goes to Jerusalem for the Passover, drives merchants and money changers out of Temple, challenged by Jewish leaders.	---	---	---	2:13-25
Nicodemus visits Jesus secretly at night and is told that he must be "born again."	---	---	---	3:1-21
Jesus and disciples baptize in Judea, John the Baptist continues to baptize at Aenon near Salim as his ministry diminishes.	---	---	---	3:22-36
Day of Pentecost - May 17, 28 CE - end of the "Seventy Weeks"				
Jesus hears that John the Baptist has been imprisoned, Jesus and his disciples decide to leave Judea, depart for Galilee.	4:12	1:14	4:14	4:1-3

28 CE				
Events (continued)	Matthew	Mark	Luke	John
Jesus passes through Samaria with his disciples, talks with woman at well, says the time to harvest (souls) is now.	---	---	---	4:4-42
Jesus leaves Samaria, arrives in Galilee, welcomed by Galileans.	---	---	---	4:43-45
Jesus moves to Capernaum, preaches in area synagogues, proclaims the kingdom.	4:13-17	1:15	4:15	---
Jesus, while he is visiting Cana, heals son of royal official back in Capernaum.	---	---	---	4:46-54
Day of Atonement - September 16, 28 CE				
Jesus reads from scroll at the synagogue in Nazareth on the sabbath, proclaims start of the jubilee ("acceptable") year, people take him to cliff to throw him down, he passes through their midst unharmed.	---	---	4:16-30	---
Jesus attends Feast of Tabernacles.	*This visit to Jerusalem is not mentioned in the Gospels.*			
Jesus returns to Capernaum, teaches in synagogue with authority, heals demoniac man, fame spreads throughout area.	---	1:21-28	4:31-37	---
Jesus visits Simon's house, cures Simon's mother-in-law of fever, heals many people.	8:14-17	1:29-34	4:38-41	---
Jesus calls Simon, Andrew, James, John.	4:18-22	1:16-20	5:1-11	---
Jesus preaches the kingdom and heals the sick in the synagogues of Galilee.	4:23-24	1:35-39	4:42-44	---
Jesus cleanses leper, crowds and reputation grow, often withdraws to wilderness to pray.	4:25 8:1-4	1:40-45	5:12-16	---
Matthew, chapters 5, 6, and 7 - Jesus goes up a mountain, privately teaching his disciples about the kingdom and publicly preaching the kingdom to the multitudes coming to him to be healed, topics covered include: The Beatitudes, salt and light, fulfillment of the Law and prophets, anger and murder, adultery and divorce, swearing of oaths, "eye for eye" and love for enemies, giving in secret, praying in private, fasting with joy, laying up treasure in heaven, do not worry about tomorrow, do not judge, ask-seek-knock, the narrow gate, tree known by its fruit, not all will enter the kingdom, heed and do his words, house built on rock stands.				
Jesus forgives paralytic man let down through roof, then heals him to confirm his authority to forgive sins.	9:1-8	2:1-12	5:17-26	---
Jesus calls Matthew (aka Levi), dines with him, tells Pharisees that he is called to save sinners, God requires mercy not sacrifice, sick need physician, new wine put into new wineskins, he is bridegroom.	9:9-17	2:13-22	5:27-39	---

Appendix Six: Biblical Chronology Synchronized with Daniel

28/29 CE					
Events (continued)	Matthew	Mark	Luke	John
Jesus and his disciples walk through a field picking wheat on sabbath, he says that Son of Man is Lord of the sabbath.[1]	12:1-8	2:23-28	6:1-5	---
Jesus heals man with withered hand in a synagogue on sabbath, Pharisees plot with Herodians about how they can kill him.	12:9-14	3:1-6	6:6-11	---
Feast of Dedication - November 29 to December 6, 28 CE				
Jesus attends feast in Jerusalem, heals paralytic man at pool of Bethesda on the sabbath, Jewish leaders criticize the man for picking up his mat on the sabbath.	---	---	---	5:1-15
Jesus confirms his authority as the Son, says deeds and Moses testify about him, hostility of Jewish leaders increases.	---	---	---	5:16-47
Jesus leaves Jerusalem to avoid wrath of Jewish leaders and withdraws to the Sea of Galilee to preach and heal the people.	12:15-16	3:7-12	---	---
Jesus is presented by Matthew as the chosen servant who fulfills Isaiah 42:1-4, the one who will show judgement to the nations, and in whom they will trust.	12:17-21	---	---	---
Jesus ordains the Twelve Apostles to preach the kingdom and heal the sick.	---	3:13-19	6:12-16	---
Jesus delivers sermon (often called the Sermon on the Mount) on a coastal plain of Sea of Galilee at base of a mountain.[2]	---	---	6:17-49	---
Jesus returns to Capernaum, heals a centurion's servant, marvels at centurion's display of faith not seen so far in Israel.	8:5-13	---	7:1-10	---
Jesus raises widow's son at Nain, people declare Jesus a prophet, report circulates through Judea and surrounding country.	---	---	7:11-17	---
John the Baptist sends his disciples to question Jesus about his identity after hearing reports of Jesus' ministry, Jesus confirms John is the herald of Messiah, thus confirming his own mission, says woe to cities that have rejected it.	11:2-24	---	7:18-35	---

[1] The year 28 CE was a sabbath/jubilee year, so grain would still be unharvested in early winter.
[2] The topics and the order of presentation in this sermon are almost identical to those recorded in Matthew, chapters 5-7. Some speculate that the two accounts are about the same event, but it is more likely that Jesus preached the same message, in whole or in part, on many occasions.

29 CE				
Events (continued)	Matthew	Mark	Luke	John
Jesus gives thanks to God for revealing him to the children, and for hiding him from the wise, gives invitation to weary.	11:25-30	---	---	---
Jesus dines with Pharisee, sinful woman anoints his feet with tears, wipes them with her hair, Jesus rebukes his host.	---	---	7:36-50	---
Jesus and his disciples go through towns and villages in the Galilee preaching and healing, women provide for them.	---	---	8:1-3	---
Jesus heals blind and mute man, crowd asks if Jesus is the Son of David, family says Jesus is deranged, Pharisees say Jesus is possessed by Beelzebub, Jesus warns about blasphemy against the Holy Spirit.	12:22-37 12:46-50	3:20-35	8:19-21	---
Pharisees ask for a sign of authority, Jesus replies that the only sign they will get will be the "sign of Jonah."	12:38-45	---	---	---
Jesus teaches mysteries of the kingdom, speaks to crowd in parables, explains the mysteries to his disciples in private; parable of the Sower, parable of the Tares, parable of the Mustard Seed, parable of the Yeast in Three Measures, parable of the Sickle and Harvest, parable of the Lamp on a Lampstand, parables of the Kingdom of Heaven.	13:1-9 13:18-33 13:36-52	4:1-9 4:13-32	8:4-18	---
Jesus reveals the reason for using parables to teach the crowds.	13:10-17 13:34-35	4:10-12 4:33-34	---	---
Jesus sails to the other side of the Sea of Galilee, calms storm, disciples awed.	8:18 8:23-27	4:35-41	8:22-25	---
Jesus heals demoniac man in region of the Gadarenes, sends demons into pigs, people urge Jesus to leave the region.	8:28-34	5:1-20	8:26-39	---
Jesus returns to Capernaum, heals daughter of a synagogue official named Jairus, woman with issue of blood cured by touching the hem of his garment.	9:18-26	5:21-43	8:40-56	---
Jesus gives sight to two blind men, gives voice to a mute man, Pharisees attribute his power to the "prince of demons."	9:27-34	---	---	---
Jesus teaches in synagogues in Galilee.	9:35-38	6:6b	---	---

Appendix Six: Biblical Chronology Synchronized with Daniel

29 CE				
Events (continued)	Matthew	Mark	Luke	John
Jesus teaches in synagogue at Nazareth, has his disciples with him, the people are offended, Jesus does no miracles there.	13:53-58	6:1-6a	---	---
Jesus sends the twelve out two by two to preach the kingdom and heal the sick, gives them authority over demons.	10:1-11:1	6:7-13	9:1-6	---
Herod Antipas mistakes Jesus for John the Baptist, who he had earlier beheaded.	14:1-12	6:14-29	9:7-9	---
The twelve report back to Jesus.	---	6:30	9:10a	---
Jesus goes off privately by boat with his disciples to Bethsaida for rest (and after hearing that John the Baptist is dead), crowds run ahead and meet them.	14:13-14	6:31-34	9:10b-11	6:1-3
Jesus has compassion on the crowd and heals the sick, then feeds 5,000 people (just before the week of the Passover).	14:15-21	6:35-44	9:12-17	6:4-13
People want to make Jesus king because of miraculous signs, Jesus sends crowds away, disciples wait below while Jesus goes up a mountainside to pray alone.	14:22-23	6:45-46	---	6:14-15
Jesus walks on the water of Sea of Galilee, startles disciples, Peter sinks and prays.	14:24-33	6:47-52	---	6:16-21
Jesus heals many people at Gennesaret.	14:34-36	6:53-56	---	---
Jesus is found in Capernaum by crowds seeking more bread, Jesus reveals that he is the true bread from heaven and that anyone who eats his flesh and drinks his blood will have eternal life.	---	---	---	6:22-59
Many disciples cannot accept Jesus' new teaching and depart.	---	---	---	6:60-65
Simon Peter says that he and the eleven believe that he is the Holy One of Israel, Jesus reveals one of them will betray him.	---	---	---	6:66-71
PASSOVER #2 - Feast of Unleavened Bread - April 15-22, 29 CE				
Jesus disputes with Pharisees about their man-made tradition and the word of God, says defilement comes from the heart, not by what food is eaten, Jesus explains the parable of Defilement and afterwards he explains that all foods are clean.	15:1-20	7:1-23	---	---

29 CE				
Events (continued)	Matthew	Mark	Luke	John
Jesus decides to stay out of Judea to avoid being killed by Jewish leaders.	---	---	---	7:1
Jesus goes to Tyre, heals the demoniac daughter of a Syrophoenician woman.	15:21-28	7:24-30	---	---
Jesus travels through Sidon to the region of the Decapolis on the Sea of Galilee, opens the ears and loosens the tongue of a man who could not hear or talk easily, people are astounded by his works.	15:29-31	7:31-37	---	---
Jesus has compassion on a crowd that has been listening to him for three days, feeds the crowd numbering about 4,000 men, plus women and children.	15:32-38	8:1-9	---	---
Jesus and his disciples go by boat to Dalmanutha, Pharisees ask Jesus for a sign of his authority, none is given.	15:39-16:4	8:10-12	---	---
Jesus and his disciples go back by boat across the Sea of Galilee, he warns the disciples to beware the leaven of the Pharisees (their man-made teachings).	16:5-12	8:13-21	---	---
Jesus and his disciples arrive at Bethsaida, Jesus heals a blind man, demonstrates that healing by him is always total, not partial.	---	8:22-26	---	---
Jesus and his disciples go to Caesarea Philippi, Jesus asks the disciples who people think he is, Simon (who is named Peter by Jesus) answers that Jesus is the Messiah, the Son of God, and Jesus says that on "this rock" his church will be built and it will have the keys of the kingdom.	16:13-20	8:27-30	9:18-21	---
Jesus reveals that he must go to Jerusalem and suffer many things at the hands of the elders, chief priests, and experts in the law, be killed, and on the third day be raised, Peter objects, Jesus rebukes him.[1]	16:21-26	8:31-33	9:22-25	---
Jesus reveals that if anyone wants to save his life, he must lose it, predicts that some listening will not see death before they see the coming of the Son of Man in glory.	16:27-28	8:34-9:1	9:26-27	---

[1] This is the first time Jesus predicts that he will suffer abuse at the hands of Jewish authorities and be killed in Jerusalem. He repeats the prediction two more times, repeating the prophecy immediately prior to each subsequent pilgrimage festival.

Appendix Six: Biblical Chronology Synchronized with Daniel

29 CE				
Events (continued)	*Matthew*	*Mark*	*Luke*	*John*
Day of Pentecost - June 4, 29 CE				
Jesus takes Peter, James, and John up a mountain where they witness his Transfiguration, see Moses and Elijah, hear the voice of God confirm Jesus as his Son.[1]	17:1-9	9:2-10	9:28-36	---
Jesus equates the ministry of John the Baptist with Elijah's coming, adding that the Son of Man will have to suffer at the hands of Jewish and Roman authorities.	17:10-13	9:11-13	---	---
Jesus heals a demoniac boy who the disciples could not heal, gives a discourse on faith, uses mustard seed as an example of the power of faith to move mountains.	17:14-21	9:14-29	9:37-43a	---
Jesus reveals for the second time that he will be betrayed, killed, and resurrected.	17:22-23	9:30-32	9:43b-45	---
Jesus and his disciples return to Capernaum, collectors of Temple tax come to Peter, Jesus sends him to find a coin in the mouth of a fish.	17:24-27	---	---	---
Jesus' disciples ask who will be greatest in the kingdom of heaven, Jesus tells them to become as little children.	18:1-5	9:33-37	9:46-48	---
Jesus warns about causing others to stumble, says not to stop others using his name since they are not against him.	18:6-14	9:38-50	9:49-50	---
Jesus teaches about kingdom conduct in this life, how to solve disputes among believers, the power of two or more praying together, application of forgiveness, then compares faith to mustard seed.	18:15-35	---	---	---
Jesus is taunted by his unbelieving brothers about going to Jerusalem for the Feast of Tabernacles, he says he will remain in Galilee, they leave, afterward he goes to Jerusalem secretly.	---	---	---	7:2-10

[1] The Transfiguration during Pentecost in 29 CE is an event based on the events in Exodus 24, which describe Moses going up the mountain of God to receive the covenant, with Aaron, Nadab, Abihu, and the seventy elders allowed to watch from a distance. After Moses comes down, the people confirm that they will keep the covenant and are sprinkled with the covenant blood. Moses, Aaron, Nadab, Abihu, and the seventy elders are then allowed to go back up the mountain to see God and live. Jesus takes his three disciples, Peter, James, and John, up the mountain to see his face shine (see Psalms 80: 19) and to hear God confirm him as the Son of salvation.

29 CE				
Events (continued)	Matthew	Mark	Luke	John
Jesus sends seventy disciples to preach and heal ahead of him as goes through villages on his way to Jerusalem, many in a Samaritan village reject his message, he explains the cost of commitment to him.	---	---	9:51-62 10:1-16	---
The seventy disciples report back to Jesus that even the demons submit to his name, Jesus praises the Father for hiding things from the wise and making them known to the children, says disciples are blessed to see what prophets and kings longed to see.	---	---	10:17-24	---
Feast of Tabernacles - October 9-16, 29 CE				
Jesus returns to Jerusalem for the Feast of Tabernacles, Jewish leaders are looking for him, on the third day of the feast Jesus publicly teaches in the Temple courts.	---	---	---	7:11 7:14
Midway through the feast (fourth day), Jesus again teaches in the Temple, woman caught in adultery is brought to him for judgement, he writes in dirt,[1] says let he who is without sin cast the first stone.	---	---	---	7:53-8:11
Reactions to Jesus are mixed, Jewish authorities are astounded at the depth of his knowledge, Jesus says that his teaching is from the one who sent him, accuses the people of not keeping Law of Moses and wanting to kill him, they say Jesus is possessed by a demon.	---	---	---	7:12-13 7:15-24
People in Jerusalem are puzzled about Jesus' identity, ask if Jewish leaders really know that he is the Messiah, many believe in him because of miracles, chief priests and Pharisees try to arrest him, Jesus says they cannot go where he is going.	---	---	---	7:25-36
On last day of feast, Jesus says that out of him will flow rivers of living water so that any who thirst can drink and be refreshed.	---	---	---	7:37-38

[1] This was a sabbath day. Jesus probably wrote the Pharisaical rule against picking up a stone on the sabbath (writing in dirt was not a violation because it was not permanent writing). Under the Law of Moses, a woman caught in adultery and accused by two witnesses should be stoned. However, the crowd would not violate the Pharisaical law against picking up a stone in order to uphold the Law of Moses. Jesus in this way was pointing out their hypocrisy. Since there were not enough witnesses, Jesus did not violate the Law of Moses by not stoning the woman.

Appendix Six: Biblical Chronology Synchronized with Daniel

29 CE				
Events (continued)	*Matthew*	*Mark*	*Luke*	*John*
Many people believe Jesus is the Prophet or the Messiah, others question him, because he is from Galilee, Jewish leaders send Temple guards to arrest Jesus, but Nicodemus says Jesus must be heard before the council.	---	---	---	7:39-52
An expert in the Law asks what he must do to inherit eternal life, Jesus questions him, approves the expert's response that he must love God and his neighbor, then tells the parable of The Good Samaritan.	8:19-22	---	10:25-37	---
Jesus visits in home of Martha and her sister Mary, rebukes Martha for worrying about details while he is still with them.	---	---	10:38-42	---
Jesus proclaims himself the Light of the World just prior to the Feast of Lights (Dedication), then reveals that he is not of this world, predicts that they will know him when they lift him up, many people believe in him as the Messiah.	---	---	---	8:12-30
Jesus promises that those who follow his teachings will not die, calls the Judeans children of the devil, they say he is possessed by a demon, Jesus equates himself with the Father by claiming he predates Abraham, the people pick up stones to stone him, Jesus leaves Temple.	---	---	---	8:31-59
Jesus teaches his disciples how to pray, assures them that if men know to give their children good gifts, the Father will give the Holy Spirit even moreso.	---	---	11:1-13	---
Jesus cures a mute man, crowds are amazed, some say Jesus is using the power of the prince of darkness Beelzebub, Jesus teaches that a guarded house cannot be invaded, that an unclean spirit will leave and, if it returns to an empty house, will bring seven unclean spirits with it.	---	---	11:14-28	---
Jesus says that a wicked generation seeks after a sign, but will get no sign but that of Jonah, adds that his teachings and works are greater than the teachings and works of both Solomon and Jonah.	---	---	11:29-32	---

– 187 –

29 CE				
Events (continued)	Matthew	Mark	Luke	John
Jesus teaches that no one who has a lamp puts it under a basket but on a lampstand, that the eye is the light of the body, and urges people to empty their body of darkness so that it can reflect light.	---	---	11:33-36	---
Jesus dines with a Pharisee who criticizes him for not washing his hands, Jesus rebukes him for hypocrisy, experts in the law takes offense, Jesus says woe to the experts as well, Jewish religious leaders try to trap Jesus into saying something that can used to condemn him.	---	---	11:37-54	---
On sabbath Jesus heals a man born blind, Jewish leaders skeptical, Jesus says that he has come into the world so that those who cannot see can see and those who claim to see can become blind.	---	---	---	9:1-39
Jesus points out the guilt of the Pharisees who say they are not spiritually blind.	---	---	---	9:40-41
Jesus is asked about salvation, stresses the need for repentance, tells the parable of the Fig Tree that was cultivated to see if it would bear fruit in the third year.	---	---	13:1-9	---
Jesus tells the story of the Good Shepherd, explains the parable to his disciples.	---	---	---	10:1-18
Jesus heals woman infirmed for eighteen years, synagogue official objects to Jesus healing on the sabbath, tells people that they should not seek sabbath healing.	---	---	13:10-17	---
Some say Jesus is possessed by a demon, others ask how he can cast out demons and heal the sick if that is so, opinion is divided about his words and deeds.	---	---	---	10:19-21
Jesus compares the kingdom of heaven to a mustard seed that grows into a tree, and to leaven in three measures of bread, says that the door to the kingdom is narrow, and that some who are last will be first.	---	---	13:18-30	---
Some Pharisees warn Jesus to leave Jerusalem because Herod wants to kill him, Jesus replies that a prophet cannot be killed outside of Jerusalem, then he laments over Jerusalem.	---	---	13:31-35	---

Appendix Six: Biblical Chronology Synchronized with Daniel

29 CE				
Events (continued)	Matthew	Mark	Luke	John
Feast of Dedication - December 17-24, 29 CE				
Jesus teaches crowd of thousands in Jerusalem during the Feast of Dedication, discussing various topics (see below).	---	---	12:1-59	10:22-23
Topics taught during the feast: Gives warning against the yeast of the Pharisees (which is equated with hypocrisy), says that there is nothing hidden that will not be revealed, says that all words spoken in darkness will eventually be revealed by the light, gives promise that those who acknowledge him before men in this life will one day be acknowledged before the angels of God, gives strict warning about speaking against the Holy Spirit, tells the parable of the Rich Landowner, gives exhortation not to worry about daily needs but to pursue the kingdom and all needed things will be provided by God, instructs believers to be ever ready for service when the master returns because the Son of Man will come when he is not expected, reveals that he will not bring peace but division, laments that the people cannot read the signs of the times, urges people to make peace with their accusers.				
Jesus dines with a Pharisee in Jerusalem on the sabbath, Pharisees are watching him intently, Jesus heals man with dropsy, asks the Pharisees present who would not save their son or an ox if either fell into a well, Pharisees refuse to answer him.	---	---	14:1-6	---
Jesus tells parable of the Honored Guest, which says to seek an humble seat and let the master of the house move one to a place of honor as he sees fit, that when you give a banquet, invite the poor, not those from whom you expect a return.	---	---	14:7-14	---
Jesus tells the parable of the Banquet, which says to accept the invitation and go to the banquet without excuses or delay since the host will eventually close the door to those who refuse the invitation.	---	---	14:15-24	---
Jesus warns those who want to follow him to count the cost of discipleship, that salt that has lost its flavor is of no value.	---	---	14:25-35	---
Jesus tells parables to show how the Father rejoices over all who return, that riches have no eternal value, that those who are faithful in little will be given much; parable of the Lost Sheep and Lost Coin, parable of the Prodigal Son and Forgiving Father, parable of the Clever Steward.	---	---	15:1-16:15	---
Jesus says that the Law was in effect until John the Baptist, that it will not pass away.	---	---	16:16-17	---

29/30 CE					
Events (continued)	Matthew	Mark	Luke	John
Jesus comments on divorce and adultery.	---	---	16:18	---
Jesus tells parable of the Rich Man and Lazarus, says that if Israel will not believe Moses and the Prophets, they will not believe if one comes back from the dead.	---	---	16:19-31	---
Jesus warns against being a stumbling block, teaches on forgiveness.	---	---	17:1-6	---
Jesus teaches that a servant should not expect praise or reward from his master for doing what he is commanded to do.	---	---	17:7-10	---
Jesus heads to Jerusalem, passing through Samaria he heals ten lepers, one returns.	---	---	17:11-19	---
Jewish leaders try to get Jesus to say that he is the Messiah, he says that they have seen his deeds and that the deeds identify him, that his sheep hear his voice, reveals that the kingdom will not come with signs but is already in their midst, Jesus adds that he and the Father are one, Pharisees attempt to stone him for blasphemy.	---	---	17:20-21	10:24-39
Jesus reveals that the days are coming when they will desire to see the coming of the Son of Man but that first he must suffer many things.	---	---	17:22-37	---
Jesus tells two parables about prayer, parable of the Persistent Widow, parable of the Pharisee and Tax Collector.	---	---	18:1-14	---
Jesus teaches about divorce, changes the terms of divorce specified by Moses.	19:1-12	10:1-12	---	---
Jesus leaves Jerusalem and goes across the Jordan to the place where John the Baptist formerly baptized (Bethany in Perea).	---	---	---	10:40
Many people come to Jesus in Bethany, some bring their children to be blessed, the disciples try to stop them but Jesus says that of such is the kingdom of God.	19:13-15	10:13-16	18:15-17	10:41-42
Jesus tells young man to sell everything, give it to the poor, and follow him, then observes that it will be easier for a camel to go through the eye of a needle than for a rich man to enter the kingdom of God.	19:16-26	10:17-27	18:18-27	---

Appendix Six: Biblical Chronology Synchronized with Daniel

30 CE				
Events (continued)	Matthew	Mark	Luke	John
The disciples ask about their reward, Jesus says they will inherit eternal life and sit on twelve thrones judging the tribes of Israel.	19:27-30	10:28-31	18:28-30	---
Jesus tells the parable of the Owner of a Vineyard, a story about a man who hired workers throughout the day, then paid all the same amount no matter how long they worked, says that the last shall be first and the first shall be last in the kingdom.	20:1-16	---	---	---
On the journey back to Jerusalem, Jesus tells his disciples that he will be handed over to the Jewish and Roman authorities to be condemned, flogged, and killed, but will rise again on the third day.	20:17-19	10:32-34	18:31-34	---
The mother of James and John seek to gain favor for her sons, Jesus says that such positions are not his to give, that to be great one must be a servant.	20:20-28	10:35-45	---	---
Approaching Jericho on the way from Perea, Jesus heals blind Bartemaeus. Leaving Jericho to go up to Jerusalem, Jesus heals two more blind men.	20:29-34	10:46-52	18:35-43	---
Passing through Jericho, Jesus dines with the tax collector Zacchaeus, who believes.	---	---	19:1-10	---
Nearing Jerusalem, the people following Jesus expect that the kingdom of God will appear immediately upon his arrival, Jesus tells the parable of the Nobleman Who Goes to a Far Country to receive a kingdom, entrusting money to his three servants to use while he is gone, then comes back to settle accounts.	---	---	19:11-28	---
Jesus returns to Judea four days after Lazarus is buried, raises Lazarus from the dead, many believe, some tell Pharisees.	---	---	---	11:1-46
Passover near, Sanhedrin discuss Jesus, decide to have him killed, so Jesus and his disciples withdraw to Ephraim.	---	---	---	11:47-57
Six days before Passover				
Jesus comes to Bethany before the start of the sabbath day at sunset.	---	---	---	12:1

30 CE					
Events (continued)	Matthew	Mark	Luke	John	
Sabbath Day					
After sunset, Jesus eats a sabbath meal at the home of Martha, Mary, and Lazarus.	26:6	14:3a	---	12:2	
Mary anoints Jesus' feet with oil of nard, Judas objects, Jesus says her deed will be remembered wherever gospel is heard.	26:7-13	14:3b-9	---	12:3-8	
Crowds come from Jerusalem to see Jesus and Lazarus, Jewish leaders plot to kill both.	---	---	---	12:9-11	
THE CONFIRMATION WEEK - March 31-April 7, 30 CE See Diagram 7.2 on page 115; Synoptic days reckoned sunset to sunset, Johannine days sunrise to sunrise.					
1st Day of the Week - 10th of Nisan[1] - Saturday/Sunday					
Jesus sends disciples from Bethphage to secure a donkey and foal.	21:1-6	11:1-11	19:29-44	12:12-19	
Jesus enters Jerusalem as king seated on a donkey,[2] with the people rejoicing and the Pharisees telling him to stop them.	21:7-11	---	---	---	
Jesus drives money changers from Temple,[3] heals blind/lame, Jewish leaders indignant.	21:12-17	11:15-19	19:45-48	---	
Greeks seek to talk with Jesus, who reveals that the Son of Man is about to be glorified, says that a grain of wheat must die to produce much grain, prays that the Father will glorify his own name, a voice answers that it will be so, Jesus tells crowd that he will be lifted up, they ask how it is that the Son of Man will die.	---	---	---	12:20-36	
Many believe but are afraid to say so because of fear of the Pharisees, Jesus says those who believe will receive eternal life.	---	---	---	12:37-50	
2nd Day of the Week - 11th of Nisan - Sunday/Monday					
Jesus curses the barren fig tree as he and the disciples go into Jerusalem, disciples are amazed, Jesus teaches on faith.	21:18-22	11:12-14 11:20-26	---	---	
Jesus' authority is challenged by Jewish leaders, in return he asks them by whose authority John the Baptist did his works, they say that they do not know.	21:23-27	11:27-33	20:1-8	---	

[1] The 10th of Nisan was the traditional day for selecting the Paschal lamb.
[2] This was done in fulfillment of Zechariah 9:9, as noted in the Gospels of Matthew and John.
[3] According to Deuteronomy 16:3-4, having leaven in the house during Passover was prohibited, so Jesus was cleaning his Father's house of leaven (man-made "laws") before Passover.

30 CE				
Events (continued)	Matthew	Mark	Luke	John
Jesus focuses on Israel's failure to be a nation of priests, warns that kingdom will be taken from them and given to a people who will produce fruit; parable of the Two Sons, parable of the Wicked Tenants, Parable of the Marriage of the King's Son.	21:28-44 22:1-14	12:1-11	20:9-18	---
Chief priests and Pharisees want to arrest Jesus but fear the crowds, who think he is a prophet.	21:45-46	12:12	20:19	---
Jewish authorities question Jesus about tribute to Caesar, resurrection, and which is the greatest commandment.	22:15-40	12:13-34	20:20-40	---
Jesus asks question about the Messiah, Jewish leaders cannot answer.	22:41-46	12:35-37	20:41-44	---
Jesus specifies the eight woes, indicating what will befall the scribes and Pharisees.	23:1-39	12:38-40	20:45-47	---
Jesus comments on the widow's mites.		12:41-44	21:1-4	---
3rd Day of the Week - 12th of Nisan - Monday/Tuesday				
Jesus foretells destruction of the Temple.	24:1-2	13:1-2	21:5-6	---
Jesus gives the Olivet Discourse, tells his disciples about things to come; turmoil among nations, famines, earthquakes, persecution of disciples, great suffering, false messiahs, lightning from east and west, sun and moon darkened, all tribes mourn, Son of Man appears in clouds of heaven with power and glory, angels will be sent forth to gather elect; parable of Sprouting Fig Tree, parable of Faithful and Wise Servant, parable of the Ten Virgins, parable of the Talents.	24:3-25:30	13:3-37	21:7-38	---
Jesus explains the Last Judgement.	25:31-46	---	---	---
Jesus tells his disciples that he will be handed over to the chief priests, Jewish elders meet in Caiphus' house to plan how to have Jesus arrested, but do not want him killed during the Passover feast.	26:1-5	14:1-2	22:1-2	---
4th Day of the Week - 13th of Nisan - Tuesday/Wednesday				
Judas goes to the chief priests and agrees to betray Jesus, begins looking for a way.	26:14-16	14:10-11	22:3-6	---
Disciples make preparations for Passover (and 1st Day of Feast of Unleavened Bread).	26:17-19	14:12-16	22:7-13	---

30 CE				
Events (continued)	Matthew	Mark	Luke	John
PASSOVER #3 - 5th Day of the Week - 14th of Nisan - Wednesday/(lamb's slain on) Thursday				
Jesus and disciples eat meal in upper room after sunset *(same day Paschal lambs slain)*.	26:20-35	14:17-31	22:14-38	13:1-17:26
Events and topics taught in the upper room: Jesus washes the disciples feet, names Judas as his betrayer, institutes the Lord's Supper (changing the focus of the Passover from deliverance out of Egypt by Moses to deliverance from sin and death), foretells the denials by Peter, says that he himself is the way, the truth, and the life, promises to send the Comforter (the Holy Spirit), tells the parable of the Vine and Branches, reveals his going and his return, prays for the disciples and then prays for all who will believe after his resurrection.				
Jesus prays in Gethsemene.	26:36-46	14:32-42	22:39-46	18:1
Jesus is betrayed by Judas and arrested.	26:47-56	14:43-52	22:47-53	18:2-12
Jesus tried before Annas and Sanhedrin, Peter denies Jesus at daybreak, Sanhedrin condemns Jesus for blasphemy, delivers him to Romans for execution.	26:57-75 27:1-2	14:53-72	22:54-71	18:13-27
Judas hangs himself.	27:3-10	---	---	---
Jesus is tried before Roman officials, first Pilate, then Herod Antipas, then back to Pilate who condemns him to be crucified.	27:11-31	15:1-20	23:1-25	18:28-19:16
Jesus is crucified at noon, dies at 3pm. *Paschal lambs are being slain until sunset.*	27:32-56	15:21-41	23:26-49	19:17-37
Before sunset, Jesus' body is removed from the cross, placed in tomb by Joseph of Arimathea.	27:57-61	15:42-47	23:50-56	19:38-42
6th Day of the Week - 15th of Nisan - Thursday/Friday				
After sunset, the Paschal lambs are eaten by Jews to commemorate the Exodus, and by the disciples in remembrance of Jesus.	*This event is not mentioned in the Gospels, but Passover was kept by all observant Jews, and the eleven disciples would have been no exception.*			
Jewish leaders go to Pilate and demand a Roman guard be placed on Jesus' tomb, to prevent disciples from removing his body.	27:62-66	---	---	---
Sabbath Day - 16th of Nisan - Friday/Saturday				
Jesus' body lays in tomb; after sabbath ends at sunset, women purchase burial spices.	---	16:1	---	---
1st Day of the Week - 17th of Nisan - Saturday/Sunday **Also, 1st Day of the Feast of Weeks (First Fruits)**				
Jesus' body lays in tomb, at sunrise he is resurrected to life after three days and three nights in the tomb; during the next 40 days, Jesus appears to many Jewish witnesses as proof of his resurrection to life.	28:1-20	16:2-20	24:1-53	20:1-21:24

APPENDIX SEVEN

THE MODERN NATION OF ISRAEL

IS IT BIBLICAL?

The rebirth of Israel as a nation is a remarkable story, one which began in earnest when the First Zionist Congress was convened in Basel, Switzerland, in the year 1897. From the start, the stated purpose of Zionism was to achieve a political homeland in Palestine for the Jewish people. The new movement quickly gained traction among Jews and among Christian Restorationists in Europe, especially in England. As a result, several proposals to create a Jewish homeland were soon put forth, the most serious being the 1903 "Uganda Proposal" by Great Britain offering land in East Africa instead of Palestine, an offer that was considered but rejected at the Seventh Zionist Congress in 1905. During WWI, the focus again turned back to the Middle East when Great Britain, on the verge of capturing Jerusalem from the Ottoman Empire in 1917, issued the Balfour Declaration favoring a Jewish homeland in Palestine. Five years later, the League of Nations endorsed the idea by passing the Palestine Mandate of 1922, formalizing the territory of Palestine and making Great Britain its administrator. In 1928, the lands east of the Jordan River (about 77% of the original Palestine mandate) were given to the Arabs as the nation of Transjordan. No similar territorial action was taken on behalf of the Jews. In 1947, two years after the end of WWII, when the horror of the Holocaust had focused world attention on the suffering of the Jewish people and their need for a safe haven (which, incredibly, no established nation was offering), the United Nations, which had inherited authority for the mandate from the defunct League, passed Resolution 181 partitioning the remaining 23% of the original Palestine territory between Arabs and Jews. The Arab states rejected the resolution, but the Jews in Palestine accepted it. When the U.N. mandate expired on May 14, 1948, the Jewish leadership proclaimed the nation of Israel on their sliver of the partitioned land. The Arab nations attacked the new Jewish state and a fierce war of self-defense ensued for the next year until Israel had beaten back the combined Arab armies, in the process extending the territory under Israeli control. However, Jerusalem's Old City and Temple Mount remained in Arab hands.

In 1950, two years after the modern nation of Israel was established, Israel's legislature, the Knesset, passed the Law of Return, which said that any Jewish person living anywhere in the world could come to the new nation of Israel, be welcomed as a citizen, and thereafter live under Jewish majority rule in his or her ancestral homeland. Still, the spiritual meaning of this modern ingathering of Jews to Palestine, and the sudden Jewish national rebirth there after more than eighteen-hundred years of exile among the nations, was questioned by both Jews and non-Jews, who asked: Is the modern ingathering of Jews to *Eretz-Israel* simply a secular phenomenon with only coincidental biblical basis, or is the ingathering actually a fulfillment of Bible prophecy?

Patriarchal Covenants

To find a biblical reference to modern Israel, the promises and covenants made by God to the patriarchs Abraham, Isaac, and Jacob (and extended to Jacob-renamed-Israel's descendants, *i.e.*, to the Children of Israel) must be understood as providing the foundational context for any such reference.

The first promise God gave to Abram in Ur of the Chaldees is recorded in Genesis, chapter 12, verses 1-3:

> *"Now the Lord had said unto Abram, Get thee out of thy country, and from thy kindred, and from thy father's house, unto a land that I will shew thee: And I will make of thee a great nation, and I will bless thee, and make thy name great; and thou shalt be a blessing: And I will bless them that bless thee, and curse him that curseth thee: and in thee shall all families of the earth be blessed"* (KJV).

Abram obeyed God, left the city of Ur, and eventually arrived in the land of Canaan, where he remained until famine forced him to seek food in Egypt. When conditions improved, Abram returned to the land of Canaan, where God renewed the promises, as recorded in Genesis, chapter 13, verses 14-15:

> *"And the Lord said unto Abram ... Lift up now thine eyes, and look from the place where thou art northward, and southward, and eastward, and westward: For all the land which thou seest, to thee will I give it, and to thy seed for ever"* (KJV).

God further confirmed his promises by making them into an unconditional covenant with Abram, as recorded in Genesis, chapter 15, verses 1-18:

Appendix Seven: The Modern Nation of Israel - Is it Biblical?

"After these things the word of the Lord came unto Abram in a vision, saying, Fear not, Abram: I am thy shield, and thy exceeding great reward. And Abram said, Lord God, what wilt thou give me, seeing I go childless, and the steward of my house is this Eliezer of Damascus? And Abram said, Behold, to me thou hast given no seed: and, lo, one born in my house is mine heir. And, behold, the word of the Lord came unto him, saying, This shall not be thine heir; but he that shall come forth out of thine own bowels shall be thine heir. And he brought him forth abroad, and said, Look now toward heaven, and tell the stars, if thou be able to number them: and he said unto him, So shall thy seed be. And he believed in the Lord; and he counted it to him for righteousness. And he said unto him, I am the Lord that brought thee out of Ur of the Chaldees, to give thee this land to inherit it. And he said, Lord God, whereby shall I know that I shall inherit it? And he said unto him, Take me an heifer of three years old, and a she goat of three years old, and a ram of three years old, and a turtledove, and a young pigeon. And he took unto him all these, and divided them in the midst, and laid each piece one against another: but the birds divided he not. And when the fowls came down upon the carcases, Abram drove them away. And when the sun was going down, a deep sleep fell upon Abram; and, lo, an horror of great darkness fell upon him. And he said unto Abram, Know of a surety that thy seed shall be a stranger in a land that is not theirs, and shall serve them; and they shall afflict them four hundred years; And also that nation, whom they shall serve, will I judge: and afterward shall they come out with great substance. And thou shalt go to thy fathers in peace; thou shalt be buried in a good old age. But in the fourth generation they shall come hither again: for the iniquity of the Amorites is not yet full. And it came to pass, that, when the sun went down, and it was dark, behold a smoking furnace, and a burning lamp that passed between those pieces. In the same day the Lord made a covenant with Abram, saying, Unto thy seed have I given this land, from the river of Egypt unto the great river, the river Euphrates" (KJV).

Some years later, God reiterated his covenant with Abram, changing his name to Abraham, as recorded in Genesis, chapter 17, verses 1-13:

"And when Abram was ninety years old and nine, the Lord appeared to Abram, and said unto him, I am the Almighty God; walk before me, and be thou

perfect. And I will make my covenant between me and thee, and will multiply thee exceedingly. And Abram fell on his face: and God talked with him, saying, As for me, behold, my covenant is with thee, and thou shalt be a father of many nations. Neither shall thy name any more be called Abram, but thy name shall be Abraham; for a father of many nations have I made thee. And I will make thee exceeding fruitful, and I will make nations of thee, and kings shall come out of thee. And I will establish my covenant between me and thee and thy seed after thee in their generations for an everlasting covenant, to be a God unto thee, and to thy seed after thee. And I will give unto thee, and to thy seed after thee, the land wherein thou art a stranger, all the land of Canaan, for an everlasting possession; and I will be their God. And God said unto Abraham, Thou shalt keep my covenant therefore, thou, and thy seed after thee in their generations. This is my covenant, which ye shall keep, between me and you and thy seed after thee; Every man child among you shall be circumcised. And ye shall circumcise the flesh of your foreskin; and it shall be a token of the covenant betwixt me and you ... and my covenant shall be in your flesh for an everlasting covenant" (KJV).

After Abraham died, the blessings of the covenant God had made with him were passed on and confirmed to Isaac, the "seed of Abraham" designated by God, as recorded in Genesis, chapter 26, verses 1-5. Then, just prior his death, Isaac confirmed the blessings of the Abrahamic covenant to his son Jacob, as recorded in Genesis, chapter 28, verses 1-4. However, because he had obtained the blessing through deceit, fooling his father Isaac into giving him the blessing that should have gone to his older brother Esau, Jacob was forced by fear of retribution to avoid the wrath of his brother by fleeing from the promised covenant land of Canaan. As he was leaving, Jacob had a dream at Bethel in which God gave him assurances that the covenant with him would still be still binding, as recorded in Genesis, chapter 28, verses 10-15:

"And Jacob went out from Beer-sheba, and went toward Haran. And he lighted upon a certain place, and tarried there all night, because the sun was set; and he took of the stones of that place, and put them for his pillows, and lay down in that place to sleep. And he dreamed, and behold a ladder set up on the earth, and the top of it reached to heaven: and behold the angels of God ascending and descending on it. And, behold, the Lord stood above it, and said, I am the

Lord God of Abraham thy father, and the God of Isaac: the land whereon thou liest, to thee will I give it, and to thy seed; And thy seed shall be as the dust of the earth, and thou shalt spread abroad to the west, and to the east, and to the north, and to the south: and in thee and in thy seed shall all the families of the earth be blessed. And, behold, I am with thee, and will keep thee in all places whither thou goest, and will bring thee again into this land; for I will not leave thee, until I have done that which I have spoken to thee of" (KJV).

On his return to the land of Canaan twenty years later, Jacob was again met by God, who reminded him of the covenant and reconfirmed it by giving him the covenant name Israel, as recorded in Genesis, chapter 35, verses 9-15:

"And God appeared unto Jacob again, when he came out of Padan-aram, and blessed him. And God said unto him, Thy name is Jacob: thy name shall not be called any more Jacob, but Israel shall be thy name: and he called his name Israel. And God said unto him, I am God Almighty: be fruitful and multiply; a nation and a company of nations shall be of thee, and kings shall come out of thy loins; And the land which I gave Abraham and Isaac, to thee I will give it, and to thy seed after thee will I give the land. And God went up from him in the place where he talked with him. And Jacob set up a pillar in the place where he talked with him, even a pillar of stone: and he poured a drink offering thereon, and he poured oil thereon. And Jacob called the name of the place where God spake with him, Bethel" (KJV).

Thus, Jacob became Israel, and his descendants would be known as the Children of Israel. Based on the covenant made to Abraham, passed on to Isaac, then to Jacob, and confirmed by God to Jacob again at Bethel, the Children of Israel would become the rightful heirs to the promises of land and nationhood made by God to each of the patriarchs.

The National Covenant

Jacob and his family prospered in the land of Canaan until a famine caused all of them to seek relief in Egypt. There the Israelites grew into a multitude. Then, after four-hundred years of affliction at the hand of the Egyptians, God called Moses to lead the Children of Israel out of Egypt and into the desert of the

Sinai, where he would make them into the chosen nation. The Book of Exodus recounts the story of Israel's deliverance and the call to be God's chosen people at Mount Horeb, as recorded in Exodus, chapter 19, verses 1-8:

> *"In the third month, when the children of Israel were gone forth out of the land of Egypt, the same day came they into the wilderness of Sinai. For they were departed from Rephidim, and were come to the desert of Sinai, and had pitched in the wilderness; and there Israel camped before the mount. And Moses went up unto God, and the Lord called unto him out of the mountain, saying, Thus shalt thou say to the house of Jacob, and tell the children of Israel; Ye have seen what I did unto the Egyptians, and how I bare you on eagles' wings, and brought you unto myself. Now therefore, if ye will obey my voice indeed, and keep my covenant, then ye shall be a peculiar treasure unto me above all people: for all the earth is mine: And ye shall be unto me a kingdom of priests, and an holy nation. These are the words which thou shalt speak unto the children of Israel. And Moses came and called for the elders of the people, and laid before their faces all these words which the Lord commanded him. And all the people answered together, and said, All that the Lord hath spoken we will do. And Moses returned the words of the people unto the Lord"* (KJV).

Unlike the covenant with Abraham, Isaac, and Jacob, the covenant with the Children of Israel was conditional. It required that they obey God's voice and keep his commandments. To achieve this end, God gave them the *Torah*, the Tabernacle with its high priest who had access to Urim and Thummin,[1] and later judges and prophets to exhort and warn them. Unfortunately, when it came time to go up to possess the promised land of Canaan, the Children of Israel who had come out of Egypt were overcome by fear. God judged their lack of faith harshly, decreeing that the doubters would not see the promised land. All except Joshua and Caleb, who were spared because of their faith, died during the next thirty-eight years in the wilderness, during which time God raised up a new generation.

In Moab, just before the new generation that God had raised up crossed the Jordan to take possession of the land, God renewed the national covenant with the Children of Israel, as recorded in Deuteronomy, chapter 29, verses 1-13:

---

[1] Urim and Thummin are not fully explained in the Bible. They were objects worn by the high priest that provided direct counsel from God (see Ex. 28:30, Lev. 8:8, Num. 27:21).

> "These are the words of the covenant, which the Lord commanded Moses to make with the children of Israel in the land of Moab, beside the covenant which he made with them in Horeb. And Moses called unto all Israel, and said unto them, Ye have seen all that the Lord did before your eyes in the land of Egypt unto Pharaoh, and unto all his servants, and unto all his land; The great temptations which thine eyes have seen, the signs, and those great miracles: Yet the Lord hath not given you an heart to perceive, and eyes to see, and ears to hear, unto this day. And I have led you forty years in the wilderness: your clothes are not waxen old upon you, and thy shoe is not waxen old upon thy foot. Ye have not eaten bread, neither have ye drunk wine or strong drink: that ye might know that I am the Lord your God. And when ye came unto this place, Sihon the king of Heshbon, and Og the king of Bashan, came out against us unto battle, and we smote them: And we took their land, and gave it for an inheritance unto the Reubenites, and to the Gadites, and to the half tribe of Manasseh. Keep therefore the words of this covenant, and do them, that ye may prosper in all that ye do. Ye stand this day all of you before the Lord your God; your captains of your tribes, your elders, and your officers, with all the men of Israel, Your little ones, your wives, and thy stranger that is in thy camp, from the hewer of thy wood unto the drawer of thy water: That thou shouldest enter into covenant with the Lord thy God, and into his oath, which the Lord thy God maketh with thee this day: That he may establish thee to day for a people unto himself, and that he may be unto thee a God, as he hath said unto thee, and as he hath sworn unto thy fathers, to Abraham, to Isaac, and to Jacob (KJV).

Continuing in verses 14-29, God extended the covenant to all of the future descendants of those Israelites who came out of Egypt by saying:

> "Neither with you only do I make this covenant and this oath; But with him that standeth here with us this day before the Lord our God, and also with him that is not here with us this day: (For ye know how we have dwelt in the land of Egypt; and how we came through the nations which ye passed by; And ye have seen their abominations, and their idols, wood and stone, silver and gold, which were among them:) Lest there should be among you man, or woman, or family, or tribe, whose heart turneth away this day from the Lord our God, to go and serve the gods of these nations; lest there should be among you a root

that beareth gall and wormwood; And it come to pass, when he heareth the words of this curse, that he bless himself in his heart, saying, I shall have peace, though I walk in the imagination of mine heart, to add drunkenness to thirst: The Lord will not spare him, but then the anger of the Lord and his jealousy shall smoke against that man, and all the curses that are written in this book shall lie upon him, and the Lord shall blot out his name from under heaven. And the Lord shall separate him unto evil out of all the tribes of Israel, according to all the curses of the covenant that are written in this book of the law: So that the generation to come of your children that shall rise up after you, and the stranger that shall come from a far land, shall say, when they see the plagues of that land, and the sicknesses which the Lord hath laid upon it; And that the whole land thereof is brimstone, and salt, and burning, that it is not sown, nor beareth, nor any grass groweth therein, like the overthrow of Sodom, and Gomorrah, Admah, and Zeboim, which the Lord overthrew in his anger, and in his wrath: Even all nations shall say, Wherefore hath the Lord done thus unto this land? what meaneth the heat of this great anger? Then men shall say, Because they have forsaken the covenant of the Lord God of their fathers, which he made with them when he brought them forth out of the land of Egypt: For they went and served other gods, and worshipped them, gods whom they knew not, and whom he had not given unto them: And the anger of the Lord was kindled against this land, to bring upon it all the curses that are written in this book: And the Lord rooted them out of their land in anger, and in wrath, and in great indignation, and cast them into another land, as it is this day. The secret things belong unto the Lord our God: but those things which are revealed belong unto us and to our children for ever, that we may do all the words of this law"* (KJV).

Foreseeing and foretelling that the Children of Israel would be unfaithful to the commandments, God confirms that he will be faithful to keep his promises that he made to the descendants of Abraham, Isaac, and Jacob far into the future, as revealed in Deuteronomy 30:1-20:

"And it shall come to pass, when all these things are come upon thee, the blessing and the curse, which I have set before thee, and thou shalt call them to mind among all the nations, whither the Lord thy God hath driven thee, And shalt return unto the Lord thy God, and shalt obey his voice according to all

that I command thee this day, thou and thy children, with all thine heart, and with all thy soul; That then the Lord thy God will turn thy captivity, and have compassion upon thee, and will return and gather thee from all the nations, whither the Lord thy God hath scattered thee. If any of thine be driven out unto the outmost parts of heaven, from thence will the Lord thy God gather thee, and from thence will he fetch thee: And the Lord thy God will bring thee into the land which thy fathers possessed, and thou shalt possess it; and he will do thee good, and multiply thee above thy fathers. And the Lord thy God will circumcise thine heart, and the heart of thy seed, to love the Lord thy God with all thine heart, and with all thy soul, that thou mayest live. And the Lord thy God will put all these curses upon thine enemies, and on them that hate thee, which persecuted thee. And thou shalt return and obey the voice of the Lord, and do all his commandments which I command thee this day. And the Lord thy God will make thee plenteous in every work of thine hand, in the fruit of thy body, and in the fruit of thy cattle, and in the fruit of thy land, for good: for the Lord will again rejoice over thee for good, as he rejoiced over thy fathers: If thou shalt hearken unto the voice of the Lord thy God, to keep his commandments and his statutes which are written in this book of the law, and if thou turn unto the Lord thy God with all thine heart, and with all thy soul. For this commandment which I command thee this day, it is not hidden from thee, neither is it far off. It is not in heaven, that thou shouldest say, Who shall go up for us to heaven, and bring it unto us, that we may hear it, and do it? Neither is it beyond the sea, that thou shouldest say, Who shall go over the sea for us, and bring it unto us, that we may hear it, and do it? But the word is very nigh unto thee, in thy mouth, and in thy heart, that thou mayest do it. See, I have set before thee this day life and good, and death and evil; In that I command thee this day to love the Lord thy God, to walk in his ways, and to keep his commandments and his statutes and his judgments, that thou mayest live and multiply: and the Lord thy God shall bless thee in the land whither thou goest to possess it. But if thine heart turn away, so that thou wilt not hear, but shalt be drawn away, and worship other gods, and serve them; I denounce unto you this day, that ye shall surely perish, and that ye shall not prolong your days upon the land, whither thou passest over Jordan to go to possess it. I call heaven and earth to record this day against you, that I have set before you life and death, blessing and cursing: therefore choose life, that both thou and thy seed may live: That thou mayest love the Lord thy God, and that thou mayest *obey his voice, and that thou mayest cleave unto him: for he is thy life, and the length of thy days: that thou mayest dwell in the land which the Lord sware unto thy fathers, to Abraham, to Isaac, and to Jacob, to give them"* (KJV).

Thus, the promised land was given to the Children of Israel as a homeland conditionally, with the promise of blessing and curse, blessing from God if they were faithful to keep his commandments, the curse of exile if they were not. The remainder of the Hebrew Scriptures, everything after the five Books of Moses, is a record of the struggle of the nation of Israel to keep the commandments to ensure their stay in the land. Repeatedly through the period of the judges, and later under king after king, the people of Israel, then Judah alone after the northern kingdom of Israel was taken into exile, were increasingly unfaithful to the covenant. Prophet after prophet warned the people that they would be removed from the land if they did not repent. Finally, in 721 BCE, as an example to the southern kingdom of Judah, God permanently removed the more wicked northern kingdom of Israel from the land, using the Assyrians. Judah did not seem to take heed and failed to correct its ways, except for a brief period of faithfulness under the boy-king Josiah, who sought to do the will of God with all his heart. After his death in 609 BCE, though, the decline began again and continued until 605 BCE, when God began a three-staged exile of Judah from the land, using the Babylonians. The exile in Babylon lasted for seventy years, as foretold by the prophet Jeremiah. In 539 BCE and afterwards, using Cyrus the Great of Persia, God fulfilled his promise to restore the people to the land if they repented (see Daniel's prayer of repentance on page 229). Still, over the next six centuries, the Jewish nation grew increasingly unfaithful to the covenant, causing God to eventually remove them from the land once again, in 70 CE, this time using the Romans. For the next 1,800-plus years, the Jewish people would remain nationless in the *Diaspora*, dispersed among the nations.

Modern Israel - Is it Biblical?

The involuntary *Diaspora* of the Jews described above has now ended. The Bible predicted that it would eventually be brought to a close with an ingathering of Jews from all nations of the world to *Eretz-Israel* in the latter days, and so it has been, as any student of recent Middle East history can attest. With the birth of the modern nation of Israel in 1948 and passage of the Law of Return in 1950, the prophecies were fulfilled. Still, the prophecies in the *Tanakh* (Hebrew Scriptures) that predicted the ingathering, though definite about a future ingathering, were not very specific about the point in history when it would occur, that is, beyond saying that it would happen in the latter days. However, a chrono-specific prophecy foretelling the exact time of the rebirth of the nation of Israel and the end of the involuntary *Diaspora* is found in the continuation of the *Tanakh*, the *B'rit Hadashah*, in the Gospel of Luke, chapter 21, verses 5-24:

> *"And as some spake of the temple, how it was adorned with goodly stones and gifts, he* [Jesus] *said, As for these things which ye behold, the days will come, in the which there shall not be left one stone upon another, that shall not be thrown down. And they asked him, saying, Master, but when shall these things be? and what sign will there be when these things shall come to pass? ... Then said he unto them, Nation shall rise against nation, and kingdom against kingdom: And great earthquakes shall be in divers places, and famines, and pestilences; and fearful sights and great signs shall there be from heaven. ... And when ye shall see Jerusalem compassed with armies, then know that the desolation thereof is nigh ... For these be the days of vengeance, that all things which are written may be fulfilled. But woe unto them that are with child, and to them that give suck, in those days! for there shall be great distress in the land, and wrath upon this people. And they shall fall by the edge of the sword, and shall be led away captive into all nations: and Jerusalem shall be trodden down of the Gentiles, until the times of the Gentiles be fulfilled"* (KJV).

The above passage records the events that Jesus prophesied to his disciples while walking in the Temple a few days before his crucifixion in 30 CE. He was sharing his foreknowledge of the coming destruction of Jerusalem and Herod's Temple, events that occurred forty years later in 70 CE exactly as described (and as had been foretold in the seventh chapter of Daniel, see page 50). Jesus was also revealing a much longer chronology than his disciples could comprehend at the time. In addition to the prophecy about the destruction of Jerusalem and the Temple by Titus and the Roman army that would happen in the near future, Jesus added an important chrono-specific prophecy that projected the history of Jerusalem and the Jews far into the future when he prophesied *"and [the Jews]* **shall be led away captive into all nations**: *and Jerusalem shall be trodden down of the Gentiles,* **until the times of the Gentiles be fulfilled**.*"*

The chrono-specific prophecy of Jesus in Luke, chapter 21, can be interpreted by understanding the phrase *"times of the Gentiles"* as follows:

1) The phrase used by Jesus (the only occurrence of that phrase in the entire Bible) is better translated as "times among the nations." Many modern expositors incorrectly interpret the phrase from a non-Jewish viewpoint to emphasize the idea of Gentile political domination of history, but the more important concept being put forth is the one seen from a Jewish perspective, as Jesus would have seen it, which places the emphasis on the Jewish people being *"led away captive"* to live in exile among the nations of the world until the *"times among the nations"* are fulfilled.

2) The word "time" is being used by Jesus as a chronological marker in the same way that the prophet Daniel used the word "time" in his prophecies, *e.g.*, as in the prophecy recorded in the seventh chapter of Daniel, where *"a time and times and the dividing of time"* = 3½ "times" = (3½ x 228 Passovers) = 798 Passovers (see page 47). And, since the word "times" in the phrase used by Jesus is plural, the span of time during which the Jews would be dispersed among the nations that was specified in Jesus' prophecy should be calculated as some multiple of a "time" (= 228 Passovers) in duration.

With the above clarifications in mind, I quickly realized that, in order to find out the duration of the *"times of the Gentiles,"* a starting point for calculating the "times" was needed. Since the Battle of Granicus, in which Alexander the Great first defeated the Persians, had been the starting point for calculating the restoration of the Temple Mount in the eighth chapter of Daniel (and was the key that had allowed me to understand the rest of Daniel), I began with the starting date for that prophecy, May/June 334 BCE, and began counting forward in increments of 228 Passovers (*i.e.*, in multiples of "times") from the first Passover after the Battle of Granicus,[1] which was the Passover in 333 BCE, looking for a match with a modern event in Jewish history. To my surprise, I found that ten "times" (10 x 228 Passovers = 2,280 Passovers) forward in time from that Passover brought the count to the Passover in the year 1947. I knew from modern Jewish history that between the two Passovers in 1947 and 1948,

---

[1] Why God picked the Battle of Granicus in 334 BCE to anchor the prophecy in Daniel, chapter 8, is not explained, but he did so and that makes it a significant event in Jewish history. Perhaps Greek dominion over the Jews and *Eretz-Israel* differed from that of Babylon and Persia in its spiritual implications. It is a matter of record that the conflict between Hellenism and Judaism becomes a major focus of Jewish history after Granicus.

Appendix Seven: The Modern Nation of Israel - Is it Biblical?

Diagram 6A - The Times of the Gentiles

"time" is equal to twelve 19-year Metonic Cycles (12 x 19 years = 228 years/Passovers)

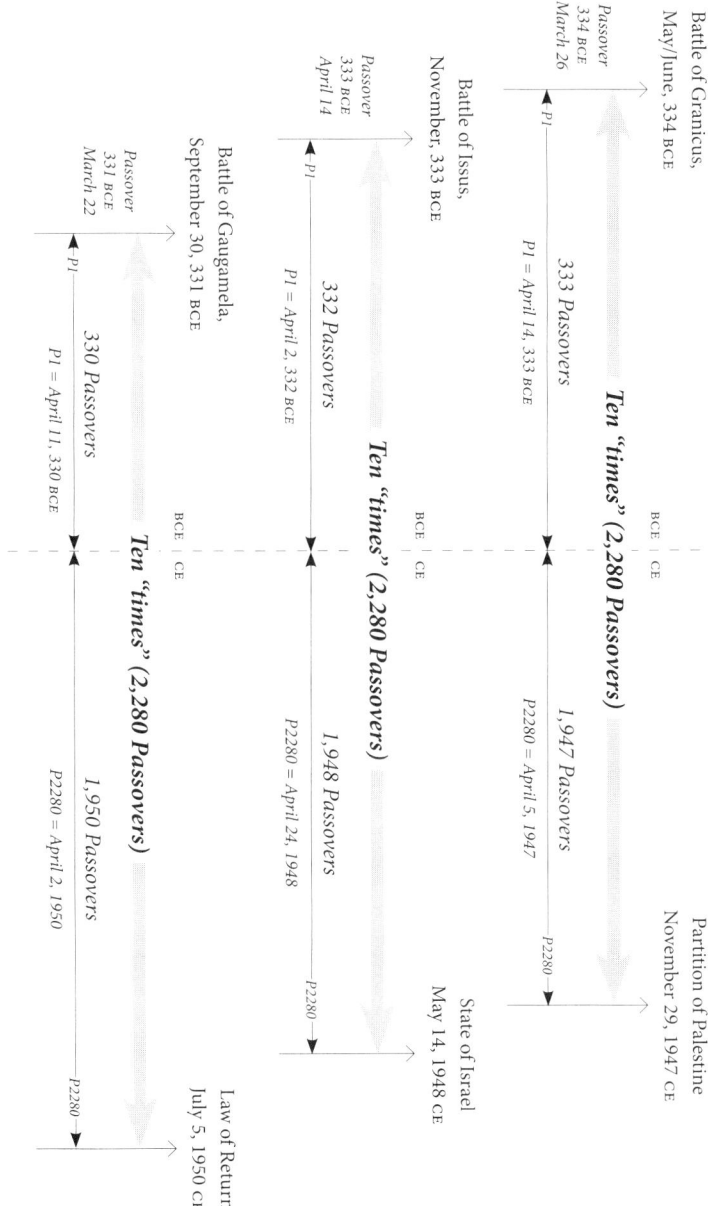

P = Passover (using Passover dates from "Calculating Easter using the Jewish Calendar in One Step" by Stephen P. Morse, available at www.stevemorse.org)

the United Nations had passed Resolution 181, which partitioned the remaining 23% of the original mandated territory in Palestine between the Arabs and Jews. For the first time, the political mechanism for establishing a Jewish homeland in *Eretz-Israel* was given official international sanction.

So, with the Battle of Granicus and the 1947 Jewish event "coincidence" fresh in mind, and aware that Alexander had defeated the Persians in two additional battles after the Battle of Granicus, I began counting again, this time from the second battle won by Alexander against Persia, the Battle of Issus in 333 BCE, and did the same calculation, using ten "times" as before, which brought the count to the Passover in 1948. I knew from modern Jewish history that shortly after that Passover, the nation of Israel had been proclaimed and established on May 14, 1948. Continuing in the same manner, I calculated ten "times" from the third and final battle against the Persians won by Alexander, the Battle of Gaugamela in 331 BCE. This third calculation brought the count to the Passover in 1950. I knew from modern Jewish history that shortly after that Passover the Israeli Knesset had passed the Law of Return, bringing the involuntary *Diaspora* to an official end after more than 1,800 years.

The occurrences of the three events in modern Jewish history that constitute the three-fold fulfillment of the chrono-specific predictive prophecy of Jesus in Luke, chapter 21, verses 5-24, are depicted graphically by Diagram 6A on the previous page. Each of the events was a major event in modern Jewish history. The final event, the passage of the Law of Return in 1950 ending the involuntary *Diaspora* that Jesus said would define the duration of the times of the Gentiles (*"and [the Jews] shall be led away captive into all nations ... until the times of the Gentiles be fulfilled"*), constitutes verification that the modern nation of Israel is the place of ingathering that was anticipated in the Bible, with the time of its rebirth in the year 1948 identified exactly. Thus, the modern nation of Israel is indeed biblical,[1] and the ingathering of the Jews to Palestine, culminating in the passage of the Law of Return in 1950 that marked the official end of the *Diaspora* as predicted, is a clear indicator that the *"times of the Gentiles"* have been completed and are being followed by the time of the end that is now underway.

---

[1] The term "biblical" in this case indicates that the modern nation of Israel was predicted in the Scriptures, and that its rebirth and existence is a reflection of the prophetic will of God being fulfilled in history. It should not be considered as a comment on the spiritual condition or covenantal status of the modern nation of Israel.

Appendix Seven: The Modern Nation of Israel - Is it Biblical?

Important Documents in Israel's Rebirth

The Balfour Declaration - November 2, 1917

Foreign Office,
November 2nd, 1917.

Dear Lord Rothschild.

    I have much pleasure in conveying to you, on behalf of His Majesty's Government, the following declaration of sympathy with Jewish Zionist aspirations which has been submitted to, and approved by, the Cabinet

    "His Majesty's Government view with favour the establishment in Palestine of a national home for the Jewish people, and will use their best endeavors to facilitate the achievement of this object, it being clearly understood that nothing shall be done which may prejudice the civil and religious rights of existing non-Jewish communities in Palestine, or the rights and political status enjoyed by Jews in any other country".

    I should be grateful if you would bring this declaration to the knowledge of the Zionist Federation.

Arthur James Balfour (signature)

Facsimile based on original letter in the British Library

The Palestine Mandate of the League of Nations in 1922 gave administration of Palestine to Great Britain, the nation that had gained possession of that territory from the Ottoman Empire in 1917, during WWI. This action by the nations of the world acting as one endorsed the Balfour Declaration and, for the first time, gave international approval to the idea of a modern Jewish homeland in Eretz-Israel.

Palestine Mandate - July 24, 1922

The Council of the League of Nations:

Whereas the Principal Allied Powers have agreed, for the purpose of giving effect to the provisions of Article 22 of the Covenant of the League of Nations, to entrust to a Mandatory selected by the said Powers the administration of the territory of Palestine, which formerly belonged to the Turkish Empire, within such boundaries as may be fixed by them; and

Whereas the Principal Allied Powers have also agreed that the Mandatory should be responsible for putting into effect the declaration originally made on November 2nd, 1917, by the Government of His Britannic Majesty, and adopted by the said Powers, in favor of the establishment in Palestine of a national home for the Jewish people, it being clearly understood that nothing should be done which might prejudice the civil and religious rights of existing nonJewish communities in Palestine, or the rights and political status enjoyed by Jews in any other country; and

Whereas recognition has thereby been given to the historical connection of the Jewish people with Palestine and to the grounds for reconstituting their national home in that country; and

Whereas the Principal Allied Powers have selected His Britannic Majesty as the Mandatory for Palestine; and

Whereas the mandate in respect of Palestine has been formulated in the following terms and submitted to the Council of the League for approval; and

Whereas His Britannic Majesty has accepted the mandate in respect of Palestine and undertaken to exercise it on behalf of the League of Nations in conformity with the following provisions; and

Whereas by the aforementioned Article 22 (paragraph 8), it is provided that the degree of authority, control or administration to be exercised by the Mandatory, not having been previously agreed upon by the Members of the League, shall be explicitly defined by the Council of the League Of Nations; confirming the said Mandate, defines its terms as follows:

ARTICLE 1. The Mandatory shall have full powers of legislation and of administration, save as they may be limited by the terms of this mandate.

ARTICLE 2. The Mandatory shall be responsible for placing the country under such political, administrative and economic conditions as will secure the establishment of the Jewish national home, as laid down in the preamble, and the development of self-governing institutions, and also for safeguarding the civil and religious rights of all the inhabitants of Palestine, irrespective of race and religion.

ARTICLE 3. The Mandatory shall, so far as circumstances permit, encourage local autonomy.

ARTICLE 4. An appropriate Jewish agency shall be recognised as a public body for the purpose of advising and cooperating with the Administration of Palestine in such

Appendix Seven: The Modern Nation of Israel - Is it Biblical?

economic, social and other matters as may affect the establishment of the Jewish national home and the interests of the Jewish population in Palestine, and, subject always to the control of the Administration to assist and take part in the development of the country. The Zionist organization, so long as its organization and constitution are in the opinion of the Mandatory appropriate, shall be recognised as such agency. It shall take steps in consultation with His Britannic Majesty's Government to secure the cooperation of all Jews who are willing to assist in the establishment of the Jewish national home.

ARTICLE 5. The Mandatory shall be responsible for seeing that no Palestine territory shall be ceded or leased to, or in any way placed under the control of the Government of any foreign Power.

ARTICLE 6. The Administration of Palestine, while ensuring that the rights and position of other sections of the population are not prejudiced, shall facilitate Jewish immigration under suitable conditions and shall encourage, in cooperation with the Jewish agency referred to in Article 4, close settlement by Jews on the land, including State lands and waste lands not required for public purposes.

ARTICLE 7. The Administration of Palestine shall be responsible for enacting a nationality law. There shall be included in this law provisions framed so as to facilitate the acquisition of Palestinian citizenship by Jews who take up their permanent residence in Palestine.

ARTICLE 8. The privileges and immunities of foreigners, including the benefits of consular jurisdiction and protection as formerly enjoyed by Capitulation or usage in the Ottoman Empire, shall not be applicable in Palestine. Unless the Powers whose nationals enjoyed the aforementioned privileges and immunities on August 1st, 1914, shall have previously renounced the right to their reestablishment, or shall have agreed to their non-application for a specified period, these privileges and immunities shall, at the expiration of the mandate, be immediately reestablished in their entirety or with such modifications as may have been agreed upon between the Powers concerned.

ARTICLE 9. The Mandatory shall be responsible for seeing that the judicial system established in Palestine shall assure to foreigners, as well as to natives, a complete guarantee of their rights. Respect for the personal status of the various peoples and communities and for their religious interests shall be fully guaranteed.

ARTICLE 11. The Administration of Palestine shall take all necessary measures to safeguard the interests of the community in connection with the development of the country, and, subject to any international obligations accepted by the Mandatory, shall have full power to provide for public ownership or control of any of the natural resources of the country or of the public works, services and utilities established or to be established therein. It shall introduce a land system appropriate to the needs of the country, having regard, among other things, to the desirability of promoting the close settlement and intensive cultivation of the land. The Administration may arrange with the Jewish agency mentioned in Article 4 to construct or operate, upon fair and equitable terms, any public works, services and utilities, and to develop any of the natural resources of the country, in so far as these matters are not directly undertaken by the Administration. Any such arrangements shall provide that no profits distributed by such agency, directly or indirectly, shall exceed a reasonable rate of interest on the capital, and any further profits shall be utilised by it for the benefit of the country in a manner approved by the Administration.

ARTICLE 12. The Mandatory shall be entrusted with the control of the foreign relations of Palestine and the right to issue exequaturs to consuls appointed by foreign Powers. He shall also be entitled to afford diplomatic and consular protection to citizens of Palestine when outside its territorial limits.

ARTICLE 13. All responsibility in connection with the Holy Places and religious buildings or sites in Palestine, including that of preserving existing rights and of securing free access to the Holy Places, religious buildings and sites and the free exercise of worship, while ensuring the requirements of public order and decorum, is assumed by the Mandatory, who shall be responsible solely to the League of Nations in all matters connected herewith, provided that nothing in this article shall prevent the Mandatory from entering into such arrangements as he may deem reasonable with the Administration for the purpose of carrying the provisions of this article into effect; and provided also that nothing in this mandate shall be construed as conferring upon the Mandatory authority to interfere with the fabric or the management of purely Moslem sacred shrines, the immunities of which are guaranteed.

ARTICLE 14. A special commission shall be appointed by the Mandatory to study, define and determine the rights and claims in connection with the Holy Places and the rights and claims relating to the different religious communities in Palestine. The method of nomination, the composition and the functions of this Commission shall be submitted to the Council of the League for its approval, and the Commission shall not be appointed or enter upon its functions without the approval of the Council.

ARTICLE 15. The Mandatory shall see that complete freedom of conscience and the free exercise of all forms of worship, subject only to the maintenance of public order and morals, are ensured to all. No discrimination of any kind shall be made between the inhabitants of Palestine on the ground of race, religion or language. No person shall be excluded from Palestine on the sole ground of his religious belief. The right of each community to maintain its own schools for the education of its own members in its own language, while conforming to such educational requirements of a general nature as the Administration may impose, shall not be denied or impaired.

ARTICLE 16. The Mandatory shall be responsible for exercising such supervision over religious or eleemosynary bodies of all faiths in Palestine as may be required for the maintenance of public order and good government. Subject to such supervision, no measures shall be taken in Palestine to obstruct or interfere with the enterprise of such bodies or to discriminate against any representative or member of them on the ground of his religion or nationality.

ARTICLE 17. The Administration of Palestine may organise on a voluntary basis the forces necessary for the preservation of peace and order, and also for the defence of the country, subject, however, to the supervision of the Mandatory, but shall not use them for purposes other than those above specified save with the consent of the Mandatory. Except for such purposes, no military, naval or air forces shall be raised or maintained by the Administration of Palestine. Nothing in this article shall preclude the Administration of Palestine from contributing to the cost of the maintenance of the forces of the Mandatory in Palestine. The Mandatory shall be entitled at all times to use the roads, railways and ports of Palestine for the movement of armed forces and the carriage of fuel and supplies.

ARTICLE 18. The Mandatory shall see that there is no discrimination in Palestine against the nationals of any State Member of the League of Nations (including companies incorporated under its laws) as compared with those of the Mandatory or of any foreign State in matters concerning taxation, commerce or navigation, the exercise of industries or professions, or in the treatment of merchant vessels or civil aircraft. Similarly, there shall be no discrimination in Palestine against goods originating in or destined for any of the said States, and there shall be freedom of transit under equitable conditions across the mandated area. Subject as aforesaid and to the other provisions of this mandate, the Administration of Palestine may, on the advice of the Mandatory, impose such taxes and customs duties as it may consider necessary, and take such steps as it may think best to promote the development of the natural resources of the country and to safeguard the interests of the population. It may also, on the advice of the Mandatory, conclude a special customs agreement with any State the territory of which in 1914 was wholly included in Asiatic Turkey or Arabia.

ARTICLE 19. The Mandatory shall adhere on behalf of the Administration of Palestine to any general international conventions already existing, or which may be concluded hereafter with the approval of the League of Nations, respecting the slave traffic, the traffic in arms and ammunition, or the traffic in drugs, or relating to commercial equality, freedom of transit and navigation, aerial navigation and postal, telegraphic and wireless communication or literary, artistic or industrial property.

ARTICLE 20. The Mandatory shall cooperate on behalf of the Administration of Palestine, so far as religious, social and other conditions may permit, in the execution of any common policy adopted by the League of Nations for preventing and combating disease, including diseases of plants and animals.

ARTICLE 21. The Mandatory shall secure the enactment within twelve months from this date, and shall ensure the execution of a Law of Antiquities based on the following rules. This law shall ensure equality of treatment in the matter of excavations and archaeological research to the nationals of all States Members of the League of Nations.

(1) "Antiquity" means any construction or any product of human activity earlier than the year 1700 A.D.

(2) The law for the protection of antiquities shall proceed by encouragement rather than by threat.
Any person who, having discovered an antiquity without being furnished with the authorization referred to in paragraph 5, reports the same to an official of the competent Department, shall be rewarded according to the value of the discovery.

(3) No antiquity may be disposed of except to the competent Department, unless this Department renounces the acquisition of any such antiquity.
No antiquity may leave the country without an export licence from the said Department.

(4) Any person who maliciously or negligently destroys or damages an antiquity shall be liable to a penalty to be fixed.

(5) No clearing of ground or digging with the object of finding antiquities shall be permitted, under penalty of fine, except to persons authorised by the competent Department.

(6) Equitable terms shall be fixed for expropriation, temporary or permanent, of lands which might be of historical or archaeological interest.

(7) Authorization to excavate shall only be granted to persons who show sufficient guarantees of archaeological experience. The Administration of Palestine shall not, in granting these authorizations, act in such a way as to exclude scholars of any nation without good grounds.

(8) The proceeds of excavations may be divided between the excavator and the competent Department in a proportion fixed by that Department. If division seems impossible for scientific reasons, the excavator shall receive a fair indemnity in lieu of a part of the find.

ARTICLE 22. English, Arabic and Hebrew shall be the official languages of Palestine.

Any statement or inscription in Arabic on stamps or money in Palestine shall be repeated in Hebrew and any statement or inscription in Hebrew shall be repeated in Arabic.

ARTICLE 23. The Administration of Palestine shall recognise the holy days of the respective communities in Palestine as legal days of rest for the members of such communities.

ARTICLE 24. The Mandatory shall make to the Council of the League of Nations an annual report to the satisfaction of the Council as to the measures taken during the year to carry out the provisions of the mandate. Copies of all laws and regulations promulgated or issued during the year shall be communicated with the report.

ARTICLE 25. In the territories lying between the Jordan and the eastern boundary of Palestine as ultimately determined, the Mandatory shall be entitled, with the consent of the Council of the League of Nations, to postpone or withhold application of such provisions of this mandate as he may consider inapplicable to the existing local conditions, and to make such provision for the administration of the territories as he may consider suitable to those conditions, provided that no action shall be taken which is inconsistent with the provisions of Articles 15, 16 and 18.

ARTICLE 26. The Mandatory agrees that, if any dispute whatever should arise between the Mandatory and another member of the League of Nations relating to the interpretation or the application of the provisions of the mandate, such dispute, if it cannot be settled by negotiation, shall be submitted to the Permanent Court of International Justice provided for by Article 14 of the Covenant of the League of Nations.

ARTICLE 27. The consent of the Council of the League of Nations is required for any modification of the terms of this mandate.

ARTICLE 28. In the event of the termination of the mandate hereby conferred upon the Mandatory, the Council of the League of Nations shall make such arrangements as may be deemed necessary for safeguarding in perpetuity, under guarantee of the League, the rights secured by Articles 13 and 14, and shall use its influence for securing, under the guarantee of the League, that the Government of Palestine will fully honour the financial obligations legitimately incurred by the Administration of Palestine during the period of the mandate, including the rights of public servants to pensions or gratuities.

The present instrument shall be deposited in original in the archives of the League of Nations and certified copies shall be forwarded by the Secretary General of the League of Nations to all members of the League. Done at London the twentyfourth day of July, one thousand nine hundred and twentytwo.

Text courtesy of The Avalon Project at Yale Law School

In 1928, 77% of the mandated territory was given to the Arabs so that they could form the nation of Transjordan (today's Jordan). In 1945, after WWII, the United Nations assumed control of the remaining 23% of the original mandated territory from the League of Nations. On November 29, 1947, by a two-thirds majority vote, U.N. General Assembly Resolution 181 was passed calling for the partition of the remaining territory into a Jewish state and an Arab state. The resolution was accepted by the Jews in Palestine, but rejected by the Arab states, whereupon they attacked the newly proclaimed nation of Israel. The text of Resolution 181 is available from the Yale Law School's online history archive (http://www.yale.edu/lawweb/avalon/un/res181.htm).

Appendix Seven: The Modern Nation of Israel - Is it Biblical?

On May 14, 1948, the day that the United Nations mandate for Palestine expired, the Jewish People's Council gathered at the Tel Aviv Museum, approved the following declaration, and proclaimed the establishment of the State of Israel ...

Declaration of the Establishment of the State of Israel
May 14, 1948

Eretz-Israel [the Land of Israel, Palestine] was the birthplace of the Jewish people. Here their spiritual, religious and political identity was shaped. Here they first attained to statehood, created cultural values of national and universal significance and gave to the world the eternal Book of Books.

After being forcibly exiled from their land, the people kept faith with it throughout their Dispersion and never ceased to pray and hope for their return to it and for the restoration in it of their political freedom.

Impelled by this historic and traditional attachment, Jews strove in every successive generation to re-establish themselves in their ancient homeland. In recent decades they returned in their masses. Pioneers, ma'pilim [(Hebrew) - immigrants coming to Eretz-Israel in defiance of restrictive legislation] and defenders, they made deserts bloom, revived the Hebrew language, built villages and towns, and created a thriving community controlling its own economy and culture, loving peace but knowing how to defend itself, bringing the blessings of progress to all the country's inhabitants, and aspiring towards independent nationhood.

In the year 5657 (1897), at the summons of the spiritual father of the Jewish State, Theodore Herzl, the First Zionist Congress convened and proclaimed the right of the Jewish people to national rebirth in its own country.

This right was recognized in the Balfour Declaration of the 2nd November, 1917, and re-affirmed in the Mandate of the League of Nations which, in particular, gave international sanction to the historic connection between the Jewish people and Eretz-Israel and to the right of the Jewish people to rebuild its National Home.

The catastrophe which recently befell the Jewish people - the massacre of millions of Jews in Europe - was another clear demonstration of the urgency of solving the problem of its homelessness by re-establishing in Eretz-Israel the Jewish State, which would open the gates of the homeland wide to every Jew and confer upon the Jewish people the status of a fully privileged member of the comity of nations.

Survivors of the Nazi holocaust in Europe, as well as Jews from other parts of the world, continued to migrate to Eretz-Israel, undaunted by difficulties, restrictions and dangers, and never ceased to assert their right to a life of dignity, freedom and honest toil in their national homeland.

In the Second World War, the Jewish community of this country contributed its full share to the struggle of the freedom- and peace-loving nations against the forces of Nazi wickedness and, by the blood of its soldiers and its war effort, gained the right to be reckoned among the peoples who founded the United Nations.

On the 29th November, 1947, the United Nations General Assembly passed a resolution calling for the establishment of a Jewish State in Eretz-Israel; the General Assembly required the inhabitants of Eretz-Israel to take such steps as were necessary on their part for the implementation of that resolution. This recognition by the United Nations of the right of the Jewish people to establish their State is irrevocable.

This right is the natural right of the Jewish people to be masters of their own fate, like all other nations, in their own sovereign State.

Accordingly, We, members of the People's Council, representatives of the Jewish Community in Eretz-Israel and of the Zionist movement, are here assembled on the day of the termination of the British Mandate over Eretz-Israel and, by virtue of our natural and historic right and on the strength of the resolution of the United Nations General Assembly, hereby declare the establishment of a Jewish state in Eretz-Israel, to be known as the State of Israel.

WE DECLARE that, with effect from the moment of the termination of the Mandate being tonight, the eve of Sabbath, the 6th Iyar, 5708 (15th May, 1948), until the establishment of the elected, regular authorities of the State in accordance with the Constitution which shall be adopted by the Elected Constituent Assembly not later than the 1st October 1948, the People's Council shall act as a Provisional Council of State, and its executive organ, the People's Administration, shall be the Provisional Government of the Jewish State, to be called "Israel."

THE STATE OF ISRAEL will be open for Jewish immigration and for the Ingathering of the Exiles; it will foster the development of the country for the benefit of all its inhabitants; it will be based on freedom, justice and peace as envisaged by the prophets of Israel; it will ensure complete equality of social and political rights to all its inhabitants irrespective of religion, race or sex; it will guarantee freedom of religion, conscience, language, education and culture; it will safeguard the Holy Places of all religions; and it will be faithful to the principles of the Charter of the United Nations.

THE STATE OF ISRAEL is prepared to cooperate with the agencies and representatives of the United Nations in implementing the resolution of the General Assembly of the 29th November, 1947, and will take steps to bring about the economic union of the whole of Eretz-Israel.

WE APPEAL to the United Nations to assist the Jewish people in the building-up of its State and to receive the State of Israel into the comity of nations.

WE APPEAL - in the very midst of the onslaught launched against us now for months - to the Arab inhabitants of the State of Israel to preserve peace and participate in the upbuilding of the State on the basis of full and equal citizenship and due representation in all its provisional and permanent institutions.

Appendix Seven: The Modern Nation of Israel - Is it Biblical?

WE EXTEND our hand to all neighbouring states and their peoples in an offer of peace and good neighbourliness, and appeal to them to establish bonds of cooperation and mutual help with the sovereign Jewish people settled in its own land. The State of Israel is prepared to do its share in a common effort for the advancement of the entire Middle East.

WE APPEAL to the Jewish people throughout the Diaspora to rally round the Jews of Eretz-Israel in the tasks of immigration and upbuilding and to stand by them in the great struggle for the realization of the age-old dream - the redemption of Israel.

Placing out trust in the "Rock of Israel," we affix our signatures to this proclamation at this session of the Provisional Council of State, on the soil of the homeland, in the city of Tel-Aviv, on this Sabbath Eve, the 5th day of Iyar, 5708 (14th May, 1948).

David Ben-Gurion

Daniel Auster	Herzl Vardi	Aharon Zisling
Mordekhai Bentov	Rachel Cohen	Moshe Kolodny
Yitzchak Ben Zvi	Rabbi Kalman Kahana	Eliezer Kaplan
Eliyahu Berligne	Saadia Kobashi	Abraham Katznelson
Fritz Bernstein	Rabbi Yitzchak Meir Levin	Felix Rosenblueth
Rabbi Wolf Gold	Meir David Loewenstein	David Remez
Meir Grabovsky	Zvi Luria	Berl Repetur
Yitzchak Gruenbaum	Golda Myerson	Mordekhai Shattner
Dr. Abraham Granovsky	Nachum Nir	Ben Zion Sternberg
Eliyahu Dobkin	Zvi Segal	Bekhor Shitreet
Meir Wilner-Kovner	Rabbi Yehuda Leib Hacohen Fishman	Moshe Shapira
Zerach Wahrhaftig	David Zvi Pinkas	Moshe Shertok

Published in the Official Gazette, No. 1 of the 5th Iyar, 5708 (14th May, 1948).

Text courtesy of the Ministry of Foreign Affairs, State of Israel

Law of Return, 5710 / 1950[1] - July 5, 1950

Right of aliyah[2]
1. Every Jew has the right to come to this country as an oleh.[3]

Oleh's visa
2. (a) Aliyah shall be by oleh's visa.
   (b) An oleh's visa shall be granted to every Jew who has expressed his desire to settle in Israel, unless the Minister of Immigration is satisfied that the applicant
      (1) is engaged in an activity directed against the Jewish people; or
      (2) is likely to endanger public health or the security of the State.

Oleh's certificate
3. (a) A Jew who has come to Israel and subsequent to his arrival has expressed his desire to settle in Israel may, while still in Israel, receive an oleh's certificate.
   (b) The restrictions specified in section 2(b) shall apply also to the grant of an oleh's certificate, but a person shall not be regarded as endangering public health on account of an illness contracted after his arrival in Israel.

Residents and persons born in this country
4. Every Jew who has immigrated into this country before the coming into force of this Law, and every Jew who was born in this country, whether before or after the coming into force of this Law, shall be deemed to be a person who has come to this country as an oleh under this Law.

Implementation and regulations
5. The Minister of Immigration is charged with the implementation of this Law and may make regulations as to any matter relating to such implementation and also as to the grant of oleh's visas and oleh's certificates to minors up to the age of 18 years.

David Ben-Gurion,	Moshe Shapira,	Yosef Sprinzak,
Prime Minister	Minister of Immigration	Acting President of the State Chairman of the Knesset

Text courtesy of the Ministry of Foreign Affairs, State of Israel

---

[1] Passed by the Knesset on the 20th Tammuz, 5710 (5th July, 1950) and published in Sefer Ha-Chukkim No. 51 of the 21st Tammuz, 5710 (5th July. 1950), p. 159; the Bill and an Explanatory Note were published in Hatza'ot Chok No. 48 of the 12th Tammuz, 5710 (27th June, 1950), p. 189.

[2] *Aliyah* means the immigration of Jews to the modern nation of Israel.

[3] *Oleh* (plural: *olim*) means a Jew who is immigrating to the modern nation of Israel.

Appendix Seven: The Modern Nation of Israel - Is it Biblical?

A Hebrew-to-English transcript of the Israel Defence Forces (IDF) radio traffic on the morning of June 7, 1967, recorded live as the 55th Paratroopers Brigade liberated the Temple Mount and Western Wall during the Six-Day War, is reproduced below. The following people are featured: **Col. Motta Gur** *commanded the 55th (Reserve) Paratroopers Brigade, the primary military unit deployed for the capture of the Temple Mount and Western Wall;* **Gen. Uzi Narkiss** *commanded the IDF central Region, which included Jerusalem, and was charged with defending against Jordanian aggression;* **Commander 89** *was unidentified by name;* **Yossi Ronen** *was an IDF radio reporter;* **Rabbi Gen. Shlomo Goren** *was the Orthodox Zionist (Ashkenazi) Chief Rabbi of the Israeli army ...*

Liberation of the Temple Mount and Western Wall during the Six-Day War - June 7, 1967

Colonel Motta Gur [on loudspeaker]: All company commanders, we're sitting right now on the ridge [Mount of Olives] and we're seeing the Old City. Shortly we're going to go in to the Old City of Jerusalem, that all generations have dreamed about. We will be the first to enter the Old City. Eitan's tanks will advance on the left and will enter the Lion's Gate. The final rendezvous will be on the open square [of the Temple Mount] above ...

Sound of applause by the soldiers ...

Yossi Ronen: We are now walking on one of the main streets of Jerusalem towards the Old City. The head of the force is about to enter the Old City ...

Gunfire ...

Yossi Ronen: There is still shooting from all directions; we're advancing towards the entrance of the Old City ...

Gunfire and sound of running soldiers' footsteps ...

Yelling of commands to soldiers ...

More running soldiers' footsteps ...

Yossi Ronen: The soldiers are keeping a distance of approximately five meters between them ... It's still dangerous to walk around here; there is still sniper shooting here and there ...

Gunfire ...

Yossi Ronen: We're all told to stop ... we're advancing towards the mountainside ... on our left is the Mount of Olives ... we're now in the Old City opposite the Russian church ... I'm right now lowering my head, we're running next to the mountainside ... We can see the stone walls ... They're still shooting at us ...

Gunfire ...

Yossi Ronen: Israeli tanks are at the entrance to the Old City, and we're going ahead, through the Lion's Gate. I'm with the first unit to break through into the Old City ... There is a Jordanian bus next to me, totally burnt; it is very hot here ... We're about to enter the Old City itself. We're standing below the Lion's Gate, the Gate is about to come crashing down, probably because of the previous shelling. Soldiers are taking cover next to the palm trees ...

Gunfire ...

Yossi Ronen: I'm also staying close to one of the trees ... We're getting further and further into the City ...

Gunfire ...

Colonel Motta Gur [on the army wireless]: The Temple Mount is in our hands! I repeat, the Temple Mount is in our hands! ...

Gunfire ...

Colonel Motta Gur [on the army wireless]: All forces, stop firing! This is the David Operations Room. I repeat, all forces, stop firing! Over ...

Commander 89: Commander eight-nine here, is this Motta talking? Over ...

Inaudible response on the army wireless by Motta Gur ...

Gen. Uzi Narkiss: Motta, there isn't anybody like you. You're next to the Mosque of Omar ...

Yossi Ronen: I'm driving fast through the Lion's Gate all the way inside the Old City ...

Command [on the army wireless]: Comb the area, discover the source of the firing. Protect every building, in every way. Do not touch anything, especially in the holy places ...

Lt.-Col. Uzi Eilam blows the Shofar ...

Soldiers are singing 'Jerusalem of Gold' [a patriotic song written by Naomi Shemer in 1967 and introduced at the Israel Song Festival just before the war] ...

Gen. Narkiss: Tell me, where is the Western Wall? How do we get there? ...

Yossi Ronen: I'm walking right now down the steps towards the Western Wall. I'm not a religious man, I never have been, but this is the Western Wall and I'm touching the stones of the Western Wall ...

Soldiers [reciting the 'Shehechianu' blessing]: Baruch ata Hashem, elokeinu melech haolam, she-hechianu ve-kiemanu ve-hegianu la-zman ha-zeh. [Translation: BLESSED ART THOU LORD GOD KING OF THE UNIVERSE WHO HAS SUSTAINED US AND KEPT US AND HAS BROUGHT US TO THIS DAY] ...

Appendix Seven: The Modern Nation of Israel - Is it Biblical?

Rabbi Shlomo Goren: Baruch ata Hashem, menachem tsion u-voneh Yerushalayim. [Translation: Blessed are thou, who comforts Zion and builds Jerusalem] ...

Soldiers: Amen! ...

Soldiers sing "HaTiqvah" next to the Western Wall ["HaTiqvah" is Israel's national anthem, see lyrics and comments on next page] ...

Rabbi Goren: We're now going to recite the prayer for the fallen soldiers of this war against all of the enemies of Israel ...

Soldiers weeping ...

Rabbi Goren: El male rahamim, shohen ba-meromim. Hamtse menuha nahona al kanfei hashina, be-maalot kedoshim, giborim ve-tehorim, kezohar harakiya meirim u-mazhirim. Ve-nishmot halalei tsava hagana le-yisrael, shenaflu be-maaraha zot, neged oievei yisrael, ve-shnaflu al kedushat Hashem ha-am ve-ha'arets, ve-shichrur Beit Hamikdash, Har Habayit, Hakotel ha-ma'aravi veyerushalayim ir ha-elokim. Be-gan eden tehe menuhatam. Lahen ba'al ha-rahamim, yastirem beseter knafav le-olamim. Ve-yitsror be-tsror ha-hayim et nishmatam adoshem hu nahlatam, ve-yanuhu be-shalom al mishkavam [soldiers weeping loud]ve-ya'amdu le-goralam le-kets ha-yamim ve-nomar amen! [Translation: Merciful God in heaven, may the heroes and the pure be under thy Divine wings, among the holy and the pure who shine bright as the sky, and the souls of soldiers of the Israeli army who fell in this war against the enemies of Israel, who fell for their loyalty to God and the land of Israel, who fell for the liberation of the Temple, the Temple Mount, the Western Wall and Jerusalem the city of the Lord. May their place of rest be in paradise. Merciful One, O keep their souls forever alive under Thy protective wings. The Lord being their heritage, may they rest in peace, for they shalt rest and stand up for their allotted portion at the end of the days, and let us say, Amen!] ...

Soldiers weeping ...

Rabbi Goren sounds the shofar ...

Sound of gunfire in the background ...

Rabbi Goren [holding Torah scroll]: Le-shana HA-ZOT be-Yerushalayim ha-b'nuya, be-yerushalayim ha-atika! [Translation: This year in a rebuilt Jerusalem! In the Jerusalem of old!]

Copyright © 2008 Isracast (www.isracast.com). All rights reserved. Used by permission.

HaTiqvah

As long as deep in the heart,
The soul of a Jew yearns,
And towards the East,
An eye looks to Zion,
Our hope is not yet lost,
The hope of two thousand years,
To be a free people in our land,
The land of Zion and Jerusalem.

Hebrew	Transliteration
כֹּל עוֹד בַּלֵּבָב פְּנִימָה	Kol 'od balleivav penimah
נֶפֶשׁ יְהוּדִי הוֹמִיָּה	Nefesh yehudi homiyah,
וּלְפַאֲתֵי מִזְרָח קָדִימָה	Ul(e)fa'atei mizrach kadimah,
עַיִן לְצִיּוֹן צוֹפִיָּה	'Ayin letziyon tzofiyah;
עוֹד לֹא אָבְדָה תִּקְוָתֵנוּ	'Od lo avdah tikvateinu,
הַתִּקְוָה בַּת שְׁנוֹת אַלְפַּיִם	Hatikvah bat shnot alpayim,
לִהְיוֹת עַם חָפְשִׁי בְּאַרְצֵנוּ	Lihyot 'am chofshi be'artzeinu,
אֶרֶץ צִיּוֹן וִירוּשָׁלַיִם	Eretz-tziyon (v)'Y(e)rushalayim.

HaTiqvah (literally "The Hope") is the national anthem of Israel. The words were written by Naphtali Herz Imber, a secular Galician Jew from Zolochiv (today in Lviv Oblast, Ukraine), who moved to Palestine in 1882. The music was written by Samuel Cohen, an immigrant from Moldavia, who based the melody on a musical theme in Smetana's "Moldau." The anthem's theme revolves around the nearly 2000-year-old hope of the Jewish people to be a free and sovereign people in *Eretz Israel,* a national dream that would eventually be realized with the founding of the modern nation of Israel. When the State of Israel was established in 1948, HaTiqvah was adopted by most Israelis as their unofficial national anthem. It was made the official national anthem by the Knesset in November, 2004.

Lyrics and comments courtesy of the Ministry of Foreign Affairs, State of Israel

Scripture

King James Version

BOOK OF DANIEL

Chapter 4 and Chapters 7-12

Chapter 4

1 Nebuchadnezzar the king, unto all people, nations, and languages, that dwell in all the earth; Peace be multiplied unto you. *2* I thought it good to shew the signs and wonders that the high God hath wrought toward me. *3* How great are his signs! and how mighty are his wonders! his kingdom is an everlasting kingdom, and his dominion is from generation to generation. *4* I Nebuchadnezzar was at rest in mine house, and flourishing in my palace: *5* I saw a dream which made me afraid, and the thoughts upon my bed and the visions of my head troubled me. *6* Therefore made I a decree to bring in all the wise men of Babylon before me, that they might make known unto me the interpretation of the dream. *7* Then came in the magicians, the astrologers, the Chaldeans, and the soothsayers: and I told the dream before them; but they did not make known unto me the interpretation thereof. *8* But at the last Daniel came in before me, whose name was Belteshazzar, according to the name of my god, and in whom is the spirit of the holy gods: and before him I told the dream, saying, *9* O Belteshazzar, master of the magicians, because I know that the spirit of the holy gods is in thee, and no secrct troubleth thee, tell me the visions of my dream that I have seen, and the interpretation thereof. *10* Thus were the visions of mine head in my bed; I saw, and behold a tree in the midst of the earth, and the height thereof was great. *11* The tree grew, and was strong, and the height thereof reached unto heaven, and the sight thereof to the end of all the earth: *12* The leaves thereof were fair, and the fruit thereof much, and in it was meat for all: the beasts of the field had shadow under it, and the fowls of the heaven dwelt in the boughs thereof, and all flesh was fed of it. *13* I saw in the visions of my head upon my bed, and, behold, a watcher and an holy one came down from heaven; *14* He cried aloud, and said thus, Hew down the tree, and cut off his branches, shake off his leaves, and scatter his fruit: let the beasts get away from under it, and the fowls from his branches: *15* Nevertheless leave the stump of his roots in the earth, even with a band of iron and brass, in the tender grass of the field; and let it be wet with the dew of heaven, and let his portion be with the beasts in the grass of the earth: *16* Let his heart be changed from man's, and let a beast's heart be given unto him; and let seven times pass over him. **17** This matter is by the decree of the watchers, and the demand by the word of the holy ones: to the intent that the living may know that the most High ruleth in the kingdom of men, and giveth it to whomsoever he will, and setteth up over it the basest of men. **18** This dream I king Nebuchadnezzar have seen. Now thou, O Belteshazzar, declare the interpretation thereof, forasmuch as all the wise men of my kingdom are not able to make known unto me the interpretation: but thou art able; for the spirit of the holy gods is in thee. **19** Then Daniel, whose name was Belteshazzar, was astonied for one hour, and his thoughts troubled him. The king spake, and said, Belteshazzar, let not the dream, or the interpretation thereof, trouble thee. Belteshazzar answered and said, My lord, the dream be to them that hate thee, and the interpretation thereof to thine enemies. **20** The tree that thou sawest, which grew, and was strong, whose height reached unto the heaven, and the sight thereof to all the earth; **21** Whose leaves were fair, and the fruit thereof much, and in it was meat for all; under which the beasts of the field dwelt, and upon whose branches the fowls of the heaven had their habitation: **22** It is thou, O king, that art grown and become strong: for thy greatness is grown, and reacheth unto heaven, and thy dominion to the end of the earth. **23** And whereas the king saw a watcher and an holy one coming down from heaven, and saying, Hew the tree down, and destroy it; yet leave the stump of the roots thereof in the earth, even with a band of iron and brass, in the tender grass of the field; and let it be wet with the dew of heaven, and let his portion be with the beasts of the field, till seven times pass over him; **24** This is the interpretation, O king, and this is the decree of the most High, which is come upon my lord the king: **25** That they shall drive thee from men, and thy dwelling shall be with the beasts of the field, and they shall make thee to eat grass as oxen, and they shall wet thee with the dew of heaven, and seven times shall pass over thee, till thou know that the most High ruleth in the kingdom of men, and giveth it to whomsoever he will. **26** And whereas they commanded to leave the stump of the tree roots; thy kingdom shall be sure unto thee, after that thou shalt have known that the heavens do rule. **27** Wherefore, O king, let my counsel be acceptable unto thee, and break off thy sins by righteousness, and thine iniquities by shewing mercy to the poor; if it may be a lengthening of thy tranquillity. **28** All this came upon the king Nebuchadnezzar. **29** At the end of twelve months he walked in the palace of the kingdom of Babylon. **30** The king spake, and said, Is not this great Babylon, that I have built for the house of the kingdom by the might of my power, and for the honour of my majesty? **31** While the word was in the king's mouth, there fell voice from heaven, saying, O king Nebuchadnezzar, to thee it is spoken; The kingdom is departed from thee.

Scripture: Book of Daniel, Chapter 4 and Chapters 7-12

32 And they shall drive thee from men, and thy dwelling shall be with the beasts of the field: they shall make thee to eat grass as oxen, and seven times shall pass over thee, until thou know that the most High ruleth in the kingdom of men, and giveth it to whomsoever he will. *33* The same hour was the thing fulfilled upon Nebuchadnezzar: and he was driven from men, and did eat grass as oxen, and his body was wet with the dew of heaven, till his hairs were grown like eagles' feathers, and his nails like birds' claws. *34* And at the end of the days I Nebuchadnezzar lifted up mine eyes unto heaven, and mine understanding returned unto me, and I blessed the most High, and I praised and honoured him that liveth for ever, whose dominion is an everlasting dominion, and his kingdom is from generation to generation: *35* And all the inhabitants of the earth are reputed as nothing: and he doeth according to his will in the army of heaven, and among the inhabitants of the earth: and none can stay his hand, or say unto him, What doest thou? *36* At the same time my reason returned unto me; and for the glory of my kingdom, mine honour and brightness returned unto me; and my counsellors and my lords sought unto me; and I was established in my kingdom, and excellent majesty was added unto me. *37* Now I Nebuchadnezzar praise and extol and honour the King of heaven, all whose works are truth, and his ways judgment: and those that walk in pride he is able to abase.

Chapter 7

1 In the first year of Belshazzar king of Babylon Daniel had a dream and visions of his head upon his bed: then he wrote the dream, and told the sum of the matters. *2* Daniel spake and said, I saw in my vision by night, and, behold, the four winds of the heaven strove upon the great sea. *3* And four great beasts came up from the sea, diverse one from another. *4* The first was like a lion, and had eagle's wings: I beheld till the wings thereof were plucked, and it was lifted up from the earth, and made stand upon the feet as a man, and a man's heart was given to it. *5* And behold another beast, a second, like to a bear, and it raised up itself on one side, and it had three ribs in the mouth of it between the teeth of it: and they said thus unto it, Arise, devour much flesh. *6* After this I beheld, and lo another, like a leopard, which had upon the back of it four wings of a fowl; the beast had also four heads; and dominion was given to it. *7* After this I saw in the night visions, and behold a fourth beast, dreadful and terrible, and strong exceedingly: and it had great iron teeth: it devoured and brake in pieces, and stamped the residue with the feet of it: and it was diverse from all the beasts that were before it; and it had ten horns. *8* I considered the horns, and, behold, there came up among them another little horn, before whom there were three of the first horns plucked up by the roots: and, behold, in this horn were eyes like the eyes of man, and a mouth speaking great things. *9* I beheld till the thrones were cast down, and the Ancient of days did sit, whose garment was white as snow, and the hair of his head like the pure wool: his throne was like the fiery flame, and his wheels as burning fire. *10* A fiery stream issued and came forth from before him: thousand thousands ministered unto him, and ten thousand times ten thousand stood before him: the judgment was set, and the books were opened. *11* I beheld then because of the voice of the great words which the horn spake: I beheld even till the beast was slain, and his body destroyed, and given to the burning flame. *12* As concerning the rest of the beasts, they had their dominion taken away: yet their lives were prolonged for a season and time. *13* I saw in the night visions, and, behold, one like the Son of man came with the clouds of heaven, and came to the Ancient of days, and they brought him near before him. *14* And there was given him dominion, and glory, and a kingdom, that all people, nations, and languages, should serve him: his dominion is an everlasting dominion, which shall not pass away, and his kingdom that which shall not be destroyed. *15* I Daniel was grieved in my spirit in the midst of my body, and the visions of my head troubled me. *16* I came near unto one of them that stood by, and asked him the truth of all this. So he told me, and made me know the interpretation of the things. *17* These great beasts, which are four, are four kings, which shall arise out of the earth. *18* But the saints of the most High shall take the kingdom, and possess the kingdom for ever, even for ever and ever. *19* Then I would know the truth of the fourth beast, which was diverse from all the others, exceeding dreadful, whose teeth were of iron, and his nails of brass; which devoured, brake in pieces, and stamped the residue with his feet; *20* And of the ten horns that were in his head, and of the other which came up, and before whom three fell; even of that horn that had eyes, and a mouth that spake very great things, whose look was more stout than his fellows. *21* I beheld, and the same horn made war with the saints, and prevailed against them; *22* Until the Ancient of days came, and judgment was given to the saints of the most High; and the time came that the saints possessed the kingdom. *23* Thus he said, The fourth beast shall be the fourth kingdom upon earth, which shall be diverse from all kingdoms, and shall devour the whole earth, and shall tread it down, and break it in pieces. *24* And the ten horns out of this kingdom are ten kings that shall arise: and another shall rise after them; and he shall be diverse from the first, and he shall subdue three kings. *25* And he shall speak great words against the most High, and shall wear out the saints of the most High, and think to change times and laws: and they shall be given into his hand until a time and times and the dividing of time. **26** But the judgment shall sit, and they shall take away his dominion, to consume and to destroy it unto the end. **27** And the kingdom and dominion, and the greatness of the kingdom under the whole heaven, shall be given to the people of the saints of the most High, whose kingdom is an everlasting kingdom, and all dominions shall serve and obey him. **28** Hitherto is the end of the matter. As for me Daniel, my cogitations much troubled me, and my countenance changed in me: but I kept the matter in my heart.

Chapter 8

1 In the third year of the reign of king Belshazzar a vision appeared unto me, even unto me Daniel, after that which appeared unto me at the first. **2** And I saw in a vision; and it came to pass, when I saw, that I was at Shushan in the palace, which is in the province of Elam; and I saw in a vision, and I was by the river of Ulai. **3** Then I lifted up mine eyes, and saw, and, behold, there stood before the river a ram which had two horns: and the two horns were high; but one was higher than the other, and the higher came up last. **4** I saw the ram pushing westward, and northward, and southward; so that no beasts might stand before him, neither was there any that could deliver out of his hand; but he did according to his will, and became great. **5** And as I was considering, behold, an he goat came from the west on the face of the whole earth, and touched not the ground: and the goat had a notable horn between his eyes. **6** And he came to the ram that had two horns, which I had there seen standing before the river, and ran unto him in the fury of his power. **7** And I saw him come close unto the ram, and he was moved with choler against him, and smote the ram, and brake his two horns: and there was no power in the ram to stand before him, but he cast him down to the ground, and stamped upon him: and there was none that could deliver the ram out of his hand. **8** Therefore the he goat waxed very great: and when he was strong, the great horn was broken; and for it came up four notable ones toward the four winds of heaven. **9** And out of one of them came forth a little horn, which waxed exceeding great, toward the south, and toward the east, and toward the pleasant land. **10** And it waxed great, even to the host of heaven; and it cast down some of the host and of the stars to the ground, and stamped upon them. **11** Yea, he magnified himself even to the prince of the host, and by him the daily sacrifice was taken away, and the place of his sanctuary was cast down. **2** And an host was given him against the daily sacrifice by reason of transgression, and it cast down the truth to the ground; and it practised, and prospered. **3** Then I heard one saint speaking, and another saint said unto that certain saint which spake, How long shall be the vision concerning the daily sacrifice, and the transgression of desolation, to give both the sanctuary and the host to be trodden under foot? *14* And he said unto me, Unto two thousand and three hundred days; then shall the sanctuary be [restored] cleansed. *15* And it came to pass, when I, even I Daniel, had seen the vision, and sought for the meaning, then, behold, there stood before me as the appearance of a man. *16* And I heard a man's voice between the banks of Ulai, which called, and said, Gabriel, make this man to understand the vision. *17* So he came near where I stood: and when he came, I was afraid, and fell upon my face: but he said unto me, Understand, O son of man: for at the time of the end shall be the vision. *18* Now as he was speaking with me, I was in a deep sleep on my face toward the ground: but he touched me, and set me upright. *19* And he said, Behold, I will make thee know what shall be in the last end of the indignation: for at the time appointed the end shall be. *20* The ram which thou sawest having two horns are the kings of Media and Persia. *21* And the rough goat is the king of Grecia: and the great horn that is between his eyes is the first king. *22* Now that being broken, whereas four stood up for it, four kingdoms shall stand up out of the nation, but not in his power. *23* And in the latter time of their kingdom, when the transgressors are come to the full, a king of fierce countenance, and understanding dark sentences, shall stand up. *24* And his power shall be mighty, but not by his own power: and he shall destroy wonderfully, and shall prosper, and practise, and shall destroy the mighty and the holy people. *25* And through his policy also he shall cause craft to prosper in his hand; and he shall magnify himself in his heart, and by peace shall destroy many: he shall also stand up against the Prince of princes; but he shall be broken without hand. *26* And the vision of the evening and the morning which was told is true: wherefore shut thou up the vision; for it shall be for many days. *27* And I Daniel fainted, and was sick certain days; afterward I rose up, and did the king's business; and I was astonished at the vision, but none understood it.

Chapter 9

1 In the first year of Darius the son of Ahasuerus, of the seed of the Medes, which was made king over the realm of the Chaldeans; *2* In the first year of his reign I Daniel understood by books the number of the years, whereof the word of the Lord came to Jeremiah the prophet, that he would accomplish seventy years in the desolations of Jerusalem. *3* And I set my face unto the Lord God, to seek by prayer and supplication,

Scripture: Book of Daniel, Chapter 4 and Chapters 7-12

with fasting, and sackcloth, and ashes: *4* And I prayed unto the Lord my God, and made my confession, and said, O Lord, the great and dreadful God, keeping the covenant and mercy to them that love him, and to them that keep his commandments; *5* We have sinned, and have committed iniquity, and have done wickedly, and have rebelled, even by departing from thy precepts and from thy judgments: *6* Neither have we hearkened unto thy servants the prophets, which spake in thy name to our kings, our princes, and our fathers, and to all the people of the land. *7* O Lord, righteousness belongeth unto thee, but unto us confusion of faces, as at this day; to the men of Judah, and to the inhabitants of Jerusalem, and unto all Israel, that are near, and that are far off, through all the countries whither thou hast driven them, because of their trespass that they have trespassed against thee. *8* O Lord, to us belongeth confusion of face, to our kings, to our princes, and to our fathers, because we have sinned against thee. *9* To the Lord our God belong mercies and forgivenesses, though we have rebelled against him; *10* Neither have we obeyed the voice of the Lord our God, to walk in his laws, which he set before us by his servants the prophets. *11* Yea, all Israel have transgressed thy law, even by departing, that they might not obey thy voice; therefore the curse is poured upon us, and the oath that is written in the law of Moses the servant of God, because we have sinned against him. *12* And he hath confirmed his words, which he spake against us, and against our judges that judged us, by bringing upon us a great evil: for under the whole heaven hath not been done as hath been done upon Jerusalem. *13* As it is written in the law of Moses, all this evil is come upon us: yet made we not our prayer before the Lord our God, that we might turn from our iniquities, and understand thy truth. *14* Therefore hath the Lord watched upon the evil, and brought it upon us: for the Lord our God is righteous in all his works which he doeth: for we obeyed not his voice. *15* And now, O Lord our God, that hast brought thy people forth out of the land of Egypt with a mighty hand, and hast gotten thee renown, as at this day; we have sinned, we have done wickedly. *16* O Lord, according to all thy righteousness, I beseech thee, let thine anger and thy fury be turned away from thy city Jerusalem, thy holy mountain: because for our sins, and for the iniquities of our fathers, Jerusalem and thy people are become a reproach to all that are about us. *17* Now therefore, O our God, hear the prayer of thy servant, and his supplications, and cause thy face to shine upon thy sanctuary that is desolate, for the Lord's sake. *18* O my God, incline thine ear, and hear; open thine eyes, and behold our desolations, and the city which is called by thy name: for we do not present our supplications before thee for our righteousnesses, but for thy great mercies. *19* O Lord, hear; Lord, forgive; O Lord, hearken and do; defer not, for thine own sake, O my God: for thy city and thy people are called by thy name.

20 And whiles I was speaking, and praying, and confessing my sin and the sin of my people Israel, and presenting my supplication before the Lord my God for the holy mountain of my God; *21* Yea, whiles I was speaking in prayer, even the man Gabriel, whom I had seen in the vision at the beginning, being caused to fly swiftly, touched me about the time of the evening oblation. *22* And he informed me, and talked with me, and said, O Daniel, I am now come forth to give thee skill and understanding. *23* At the beginning of thy supplications the commandment came forth, and I am come to shew thee; for thou art greatly beloved: therefore understand the matter, and consider the vision. *24* Seventy weeks are determined upon thy people and upon thy holy city, to finish the transgression, and to make an end of sins, and to make reconciliation for iniquity, and to bring in everlasting righteousness, and to seal up the vision and prophecy, and to anoint the most Holy. *25* Know therefore and understand, that from the going forth of the commandment to restore and to build Jerusalem unto the Messiah the Prince shall be seven weeks, and threescore and two weeks: the street shall be built again, and the wall, even in troublous times. *26* And after threescore and two weeks shall Messiah be cut off, but not for himself: and the people of the prince that shall come shall destroy the city and the sanctuary; and the end thereof shall be with a flood, and unto the end of the war desolations are determined. *27* And he shall confirm the covenant with many for one week: and in the midst of the week he shall cause the sacrifice and the oblation to cease, and for the overspreading of abominations he shall make it desolate, even until the consummation, and that determined shall be poured upon the desolate.

Chapter 10

1 In the third year of Cyrus king of Persia a thing was revealed unto Daniel, whose name was called Belteshazzar; and the thing was true, but the time appointed was long: and he understood the thing, and had understanding of the vision. *2* In those days I Daniel was mourning three full weeks. *3* I ate no pleasant bread, neither came flesh nor wine in my mouth, neither did I anoint myself at all, till three whole weeks were fulfilled. *4* And in the four and twentieth day of the first month, as I was by the side of the great river, which is Hiddekel; *5* Then I lifted up mine eyes, and looked, and behold a certain man clothed in linen, whose loins were girded with fine gold of Uphaz: *6* His body also was like the beryl, and his face as the appearance of lightning, and his eyes as lamps of fire, and his arms and his feet like in colour to polished brass, and the voice of his words like the voice of a multitude. *7* And

Scripture: Book of Daniel, Chapter 4 and Chapters 7-12

I Daniel alone saw the vision: for the men that were with me saw not the vision; but a great quaking fell upon them, so that they fled to hide themselves. *8* Therefore I was left alone, and saw this great vision, and there remained no strength in me: for my comeliness was turned in me into corruption, and I retained no strength. *9* Yet heard I the voice of his words: and when I heard the voice of his words, then was I in a deep sleep on my face, and my face toward the ground. *10* And, behold, an hand touched me, which set me upon my knees and upon the palms of my hands. *11* And he said unto me, O Daniel, a man greatly beloved, understand the words that I speak unto thee, and stand upright: for unto thee am I now sent. And when he had spoken this word unto me, I stood trembling. *12* Then said he unto me, Fear not, Daniel: for from the first day that thou didst set thine heart to understand, and to chasten thyself before thy God, thy words were heard, and I am come for thy words. *13* But the prince of the kingdom of Persia withstood me one and twenty days: but, lo, Michael, one of the chief princes, came to help me; and I remained there with the kings of Persia. *14* Now I am come to make thee understand what shall befall thy people in the latter days: for yet the vision is for many days. *15* And when he had spoken such words unto me, I set my face toward the ground, and I became dumb. *16* And, behold, one like the similitude of the sons of men touched my lips: then I opened my mouth, and spake, and said unto him that stood before me, O my lord, by the vision my sorrows are turned upon me, and I have retained no strength. *17* For how can the servant of this my lord talk with this my lord? for as for me, straightway there remained no strength in me, neither is there breath left in me *18* Then there came again and touched me one like the appearance of a man, and he strengthened me, *19* And said, O man greatly beloved, fear not: peace be unto thee, be strong, yea, be strong. And when he had spoken unto me, I was strengthened, and said, Let my lord speak; for thou hast strengthened me. *20* Then said he, Knowest thou wherefore I come unto thee? and now will I return to fight with the prince of Persia: and when I am gone forth, lo, the prince of Grecia shall come. *21* But I will shew thee that which is noted in the scripture of truth: and there is none that holdeth with me in these things, but Michael your prince.

Chapter 11

1 Also I in the first year of Darius the Mede, even I, stood to confirm and to strengthen him *2* And now will I shew thee the truth. Behold, there shall stand up yet three kings in Persia; and the fourth shall be far richer than they all: and by his strength through his riches he shall stir up all against the realm of Grecia. **3** And a mighty king shall stand up, that shall rule with great dominion, and do according to his will. **4** And when he shall stand up, his kingdom shall be broken, and shall be divided toward the four winds of heaven; and not to his posterity, nor according to his dominion which he ruled: for his kingdom shall be plucked up, even for others beside those. **5** And the king of the south shall be strong, and one of his princes; and he shall be strong above him, and have dominion; his dominion shall be a great dominion. **6** And in the end of years they shall join themselves together; for the king's daughter of the south shall come to the king of the north to make an agreement: but she shall not retain the power of the arm; neither shall he stand, nor his arm: but she shall be given up, and they that brought her, and he that begat her, and he that strengthened her in these times. **7** But out of a branch of her roots shall one stand up in his estate, which shall come with an army, and shall enter into the fortress of the king of the north, and shall deal against them, and shall prevail: **8** And shall also carry captives into Egypt their gods, with their princes, and with their precious vessels of silver and of gold; and he shall continue more years than the king of the north. **9** So the king of the south shall come into his kingdom, and shall return into his own land. **10** But his sons shall be stirred up, and shall assemble a multitude of great forces: and one shall certainly come, and overflow, and pass through: then shall he return, and be stirred up, even to his fortress. **11** And the king of the south shall be moved with choler, and shall come forth and fight with him, even with the king of the north: and he shall set forth a great multitude; but the multitude shall be given into his hand. **12** And when he hath taken away the multitude, his heart shall be lifted up; and he shall cast down many ten thousands: but he shall not be strengthened by it. **13** For the king of the north shall return, and shall set forth a multitude greater than the former, and shall certainly come after certain years with a great army and with much riches. **14** And in those times there shall many stand up against the king of the south: also the robbers of thy people shall exalt themselves to establish the vision; but they shall fall. **15** So the king of the north shall come, and cast up a mount, and take the most fenced cities: and the arms of the south shall not withstand, neither his chosen people, neither shall there be any strength to withstand. **16** But he that cometh against him shall do according to his own will, and none shall stand before him: and he shall stand in the glorious land, which by his hand shall be consumed. **17** He shall also set his face to enter with the strength of his whole kingdom, and upright ones with him; thus shall he do: and he shall give him the daughter of women, corrupting her: but she shall not stand on his side, neither be for him. **18** After this

Scripture: Book of Daniel, Chapter 4 and Chapters 7-12

shall he turn his face unto the isles, and shall take many: but a prince for his own behalf shall cause the reproach offered by him to cease; without his own reproach he shall cause it to turn upon him. *19* Then he shall turn his face toward the fort of his own land: but he shall stumble and fall, and not be found. *20* Then shall stand up in his estate a raiser of taxes in the glory of the kingdom: but within few days he shall be destroyed, neither in anger, nor in battle. *21* And in his estate shall stand up a vile person, to whom they shall not give the honour of the kingdom: but he shall come in peaceably, and obtain the kingdom by flatteries. *22* And with the arms of a flood shall they be overflown from before him, and shall be broken; yea, also the prince of the covenant. *23* And after the league made with him he shall work deceitfully: for he shall come up, and shall become strong with a small people. *24* He shall enter peaceably even upon the fattest places of the province; and he shall do that which his fathers have not done, nor his fathers' fathers; he shall scatter among them the prey, and spoil, and riches: yea, and he shall forecast his devices against the strong holds, even for a time. *25* And he shall stir up his power and his courage against the king of the south with a great army; and the king of the south shall be stirred up to battle with a very great and mighty army; but he shall not stand: for they shall forecast devices against him. *26* Yea, they that feed of the portion of his meat shall destroy him, and his army shall overflow: and many shall fall down slain. *27* And both these kings' hearts shall be to do mischief, and they shall speak lies at one table; but it shall not prosper: for yet the end shall be at the time appointed. *28* Then shall he return into his land with great riches; and his heart shall be against the holy covenant; and he shall do exploits, and return to his own land. *29* At the time appointed he shall return, and come toward the south; but it shall not be as the former, or as the latter. *30* For the ships of Chittim shall come against him: therefore he shall be grieved, and return, and have indignation against the holy covenant: so shall he do; he shall even return, and have intelligence with them that forsake the holy covenant. *31* And arms shall stand on his part, and they shall pollute the sanctuary of strength, and shall take away the daily sacrifice, and they shall place the abomination that maketh desolate. *32* And such as do wickedly against the covenant shall he corrupt by flatteries: but the people that do know their God shall be strong, and do exploits. *33* And they that understand among the people shall instruct many: yet they shall fall by the sword, and by flame, by captivity, and by spoil, many days. *34* Now when they shall fall, they shall be holpen with a little help: but many shall cleave to them with flatteries. *35* And some of them of understanding shall fall, to try them, and to purge, and to make them white, even to the time of the end: because it is yet for a time appointed.

36 And the king shall do according to his will; and he shall exalt himself, and magnify himself above every god, and shall speak marvellous things against the God of gods, and shall prosper till the indignation be accomplished: for that that is determined shall be done. *37* Neither shall he regard the God of his fathers, nor the desire of women, nor regard any god: for he shall magnify himself above all. *38* But in his estate shall he honour the God of forces: and a god whom his fathers knew not shall he honour with gold, and silver, and with precious stones, and pleasant things. *39* Thus shall he do in the most strong holds with a strange god, whom he shall acknowledge and increase with glory: and he shall cause them to rule over many, and shall divide the land for gain. *40* And at the time of the end shall the king of the south push at him: and the king of the north shall come against him like a whirlwind, with chariots, and with horsemen, and with many ships; and he shall enter into the countries, and shall overflow and pass over. *41* He shall enter also into the glorious land, and many countries shall be overthrown: but these shall escape out of his hand, even Edom, and Moab, and the chief of the children of Ammon. *42* He shall stretch forth his hand also upon the countries: and the land of Egypt shall not escape. *43* But he shall have power over the treasures of gold and of silver, and over all the precious things of Egypt: and the Libyans and the Ethiopians shall be at his steps. *44* But tidings out of the east and out of the north shall trouble him: therefore he shall go forth with great fury to destroy, and utterly to make away many. *45* And he shall plant the tabernacles of his palace between the seas in the glorious holy mountain; yet he shall come to his end, and none shall help him.

Chapter 12

1 And at that time shall Michael stand up, the great prince which standeth for the children of thy people: and there shall be a time of trouble, such as never was since there was a nation even to that same time: and at that time thy people shall be delivered, every one that shall be found written in the book. *2* And many of them that sleep in the dust of the earth shall awake, some to everlasting life, and some to shame and everlasting contempt. *3* And they that be wise shall shine as the brightness of the firmament; and they that turn many to righteousness as the stars for ever and ever. *4* But thou, O Daniel, shut up the words, and seal the book, even to the time of the end: many shall run to and fro, and knowledge shall be increased. *5* Then I Daniel looked, and, behold, there stood other two, the one on this side of the bank of the river, and the other on that side of the bank of the river. *6* And one said to the man clothed in linen,

Scripture: Book of Daniel, Chapter 4 and Chapters 7-12

which was upon the waters of the river, How long shall it be to the end of these wonders? *7* And I heard the man clothed in linen, which was upon the waters of the river, when he held up his right hand and his left hand unto heaven, and sware by him that liveth for ever that it shall be for a time, times, and an half; and when he shall have accomplished to scatter the power of the holy people, all these things shall be finished. *8* And I heard, but I understood not: then said I, O my Lord, what shall be the end of these things? *9* And he said, Go thy way, Daniel: for the words are closed up and sealed till the time of the end. *10* Many shall be purified, and made white, and tried; but the wicked shall do wickedly: and none of the wicked shall understand; but the wise shall understand. *11* And from the time that the daily sacrifice shall be taken away, and the abomination that maketh desolate set up, there shall be a thousand two hundred and ninety days. *12* Blessed is he that waiteth, and cometh to the thousand three hundred and five and thirty days. *13* But go thou thy way till the end be: for thou shalt rest, and stand in thy lot at the end of the days.

PLATE 1 - PROPHECY OVERVIEW (continued)

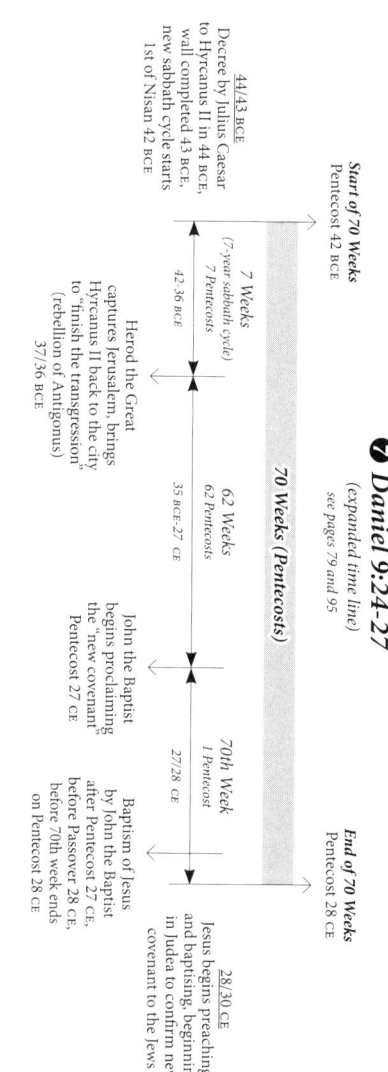

❼ Daniel 9:24-27
(expanded time line)
see pages 79 and 95

Start of 70 Weeks
Pentecost 42 BCE

44/43 BCE
Decree by Julius Caesar to Hyrcanus II in 44 BCE, wall completed 43 BCE, new sabbath cycle starts 1st of Nisan 42 BCE

7 Weeks
(7-year sabbath cycle)
7 Pentecosts
42-36 BCE

Herod the Great captures Jerusalem, brings Hyrcanus II back to the city, to "finish the transgression" (rebellion of Antigonus)
37/36 BCE

70 Weeks (Pentecosts)

62 Weeks
62 Pentecosts
35 BCE-27 CE

John the Baptist begins proclaiming the "new covenant"
Pentecost 27 CE

70th Week
1 Pentecost
27/28 CE

Baptism of Jesus by John the Baptist after Pentecost 27 CE, before Passover 28 CE, before 70th week ends on Pentecost 28 CE

28/30 CE
Jesus begins preaching and baptising, beginning in Judea to confirm new covenant to the Jews

End of 70 Weeks
Pentecost 28 CE

NOTE ON PLATE 1

The time lines shown on the "Prophecy Overview" chart on this page and the opposite page are not drawn to scale, but events on a particular time line are always shown in their correct chronological sequence in history when read left to right or *vice versa*, and all time lines, except where the need for clarity requires otherwise, are shown in the correct chronological relationship to one another.

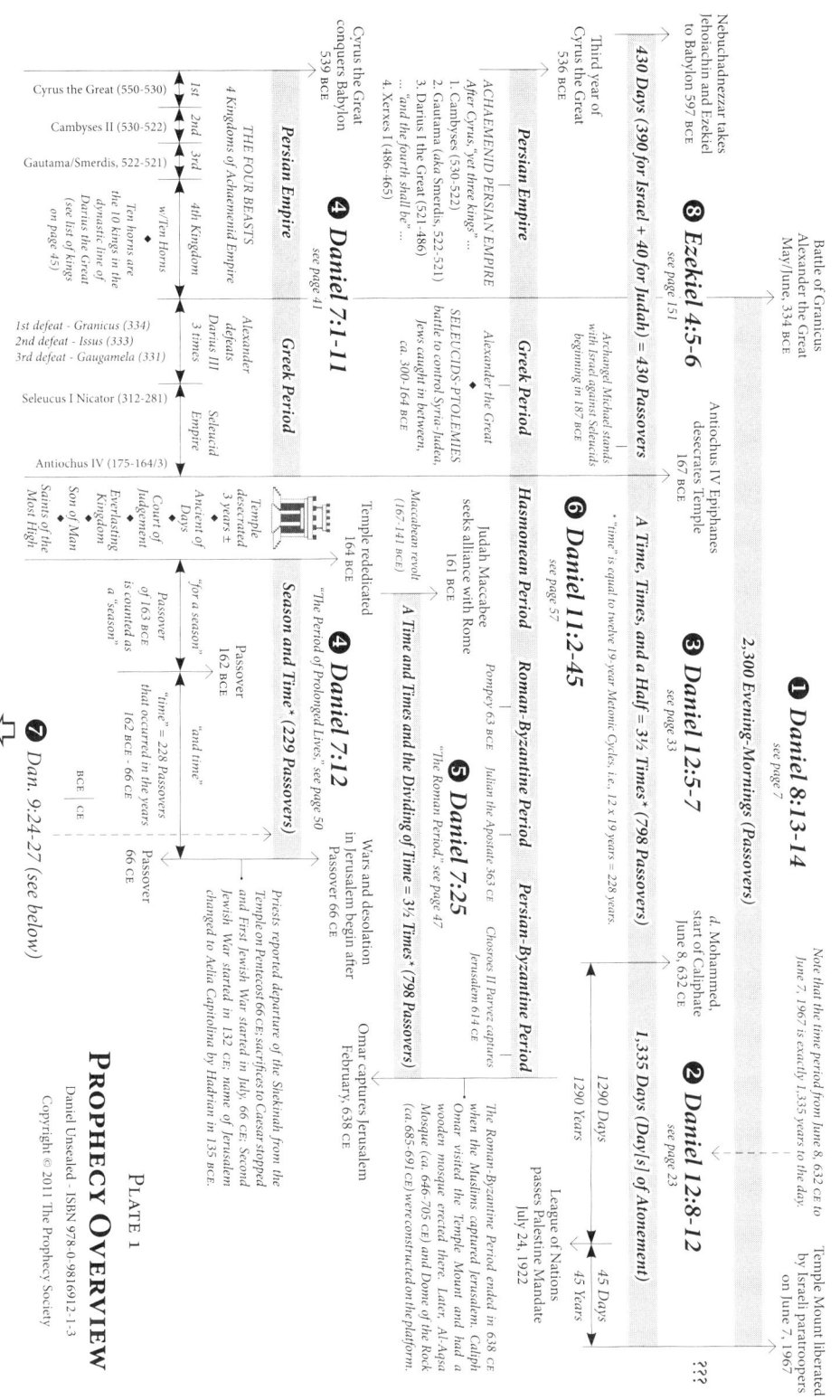

PLATE 1

PROPHECY OVERVIEW

Daniel Unsealed · ISBN 978-0-9816912-1-3
Copyright © 2011 The Prophecy Society

NOTE ON PLATE 2

The map shown on the opposite page gives the location of places associated with events mentioned in the Book of Daniel and/or associated with the interpretations of its prophecies that are set forth in this book. Not all places existed at the same time. Over the course of time, names changed, empires came and went. The time span shown ranges from approximately 750 BCE to 650 CE.

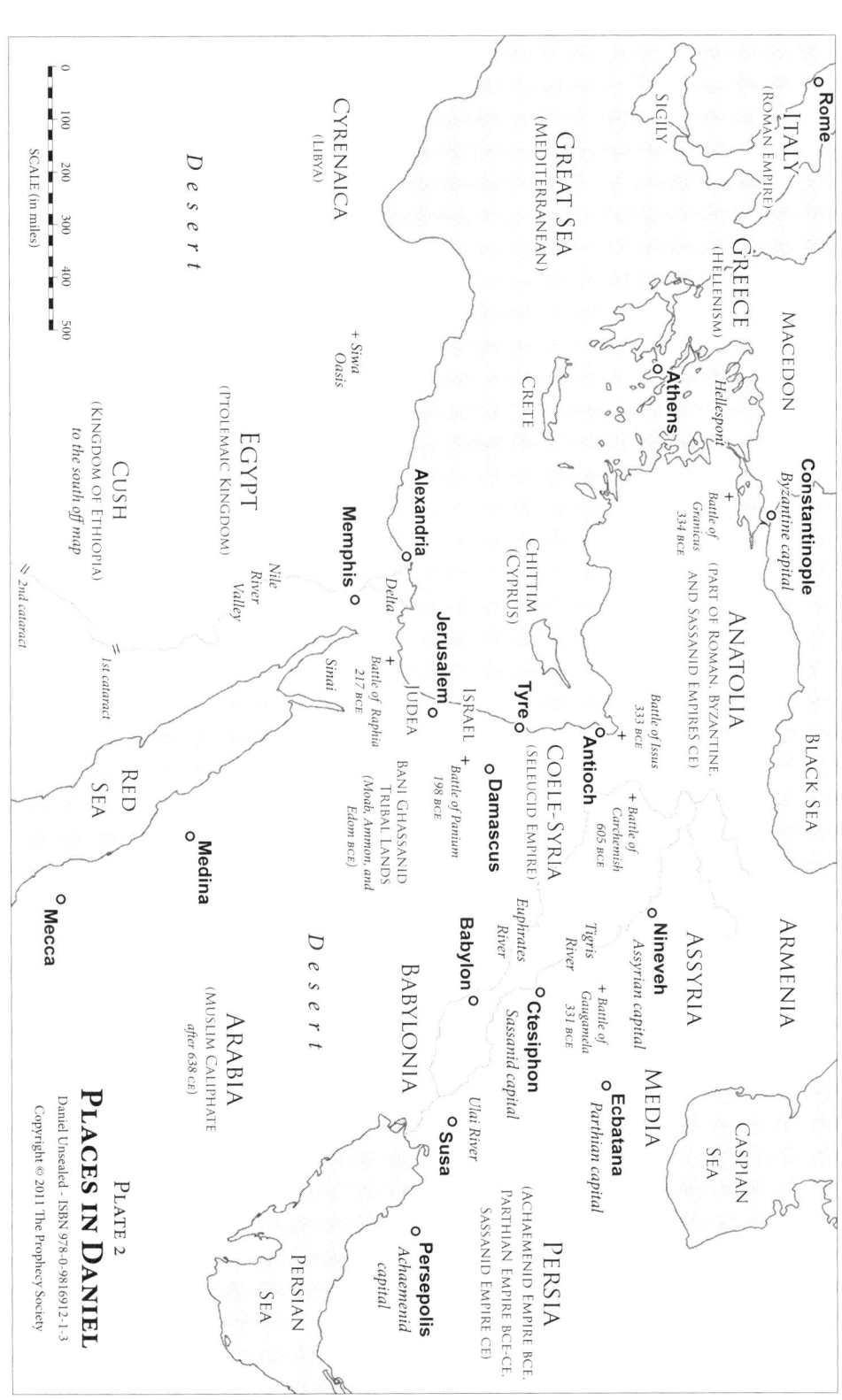

Prophecy Forum

This book is supported by a moderated internet forum available for your use on the Prophecy Society website. The forum allows readers to ask questions about and comment on the new interpretations of the chrono-specific predictive prophecies in the Book of Daniel and other chronological information presented in this book. Guidelines for using the forum are posted on the website. In addition, the forum has a section listing typographical and other production errors in this book discovered after publication, so that you can keep your copy as accurate and up-to-date as humanly possible.

Visit the forum at: www.prophecysociety.org